IBM® PC Assembly Language

MORE THAN THREE MILLION PEOPLE HAVE LEARNED TO
PROGRAM, USE AND ENJOY MICROCOMPUTERS WITH WILEY
PRESS GUIDES. LOOK FOR THESE TITLES AND OTHERS AT
YOUR LOCAL BOOK OR COMPUTER STORE.

The Wiley IBM Series
Laurence Press, Series Editor

CP/M for the IBM®: Using CP/M-86, Fernandez & Ashley
*Digital Communications Programming on the IBM PC, Schwaderer
DisplayWrite III, Williford
The Electronic Link: Using the IBM PC to Communicate, Magid &
Boeschen
Essential Framework, Ashley & Fernandez
File and Data-Base Management Programs for the IBM PC, Hecht
*IBM PC: Data File Programming, Brown & Finkel
IBM PC Pascal, Conlan
The IBM PC and Its Applications, Press
The IBM PC in Your Corporation, Walden
PC Assembly Language, Tabler
IBM PC DOS/2nd Edition:, Ashley & Fernandez
*PC Graphics: Charts, Graphs, Games and Art on the IBM PC,
Conklin
What If? A User's Guide to Spreadsheets on the IBM PC, Williams
Word Processing on IBM PCs, Hewes & Grout

*Book/Disk Pak Available

IBM®PC Assembly Language

Donna N. Tabler

A Wiley Press Book
John Wiley & Sons, Inc.
New York • Chichester • Brisbane • Toronto • Singapore

Publisher: Stephen Kippur
Editor: Theron Shreve
Managing Editor: Katherine Schowalter
Electronic Book Production Services: The Publisher's Network

Library of Congress Cataloging-in-Publication Data

Tabler, Donna N., 1934-
    IBM PC assembly language.

    (IBM PC series)
    Includes index.
    1. IBM Personal Computer—Programming.
2. Assembler language (Computer program language)
I. Title.   II. Series: Wiley IBM PC Series.
QA76.8.I2594T33   1985   005.265   85-12326
ISBN 0-471-82497-6

Printed in the United States of America
85 86 10 9 8 7 6 5 4 3 2 1

To my mother

Acknowledgments

Many thanks are due to Judi Fernandez for her continual encouragement and for her generous expenditure of time, knowledge, and experience in review and criticism of the text.

Contents

Preface

Is This Book For You?

Do you have an IBM PC or a compatible computer? Are you ready to move beyond BASIC programming? Have you heard that Assembler Language programs run faster and more efficiently? Or, maybe you simply want to include some Assembler Language subroutines in your BASIC programs. Have you looked at (or bought) the Macro Assembler and found the manual forbidding? Then this book is designed to help you.

The book doesn't try to teach you everything that's in the manual, but you will learn the most useful instructions and how to interpret the manual. You'll also learn some things that aren't in the manual: how to put instructions together to build routines for keyboard, CRT, and printer I/O for file handling and for data conversion; how to handle BASIC data formats in Assembler; how to include Assembler subroutines in BASIC programs.

You'll learn to take advantage of the Macro facility that gives Macro Assembler its name by developing a library of routines that can be used over and over again from program to program. When you complete this book, you'll be able to write Macro Assembler programs that are equivalent to many intermediate-level BASIC programs and will be ready to continue teaching yourself from the available manuals.

1

The Macro Assembler Language

This book is divided into two parts. The first part teaches you to use the IBM Personal Computer Macro Assembler by Microsoft to write programs. The second part provides information and sample routines to teach you to handle some specific situations that occur in many Macro Assembler programs.

The first part of the book begins with some general information about assemblers, microcomputers, and the process of programming in an assembler language. It gives you information about the IBM PC and its family that provides necessary background and terminology for programming in Macro Assembler language. Then, it teaches you the formats and instructions needed to write a simple program and takes you through the steps necessary to get the program running.

This section will improve your programming abilities by teaching you to use macros, to code more flexible operands, to use arithmetic and bit manipulation instructions, and to use the Macro Assembler manual to teach yourself more about the language.

You will find sets of review questions after every major chapter subdivision as well as at the end of each chapter. Answering these questions is an important part of the learning procedure. You may need to go back and reread a portion of the text in order to answer the questions. That's one reason the questions are there—to show you what you need to review.

You will also find suggestions for writing and running programs. Hands-on practice is probably the most important part of learning any computer language, so jump in and try it! Don't be discouraged by mistakes. Nobody's programs are perfrect the first time around, and few of them, the second time. Coding, assembling, running, finding and correcting mistakes, making improvements and refinements—that's the way you learn a language. And remember that my programs are not the only way to solve the problems presented; if your programs are different, and your programs work, so much the better!

1

Introduction

This chapter discusses which microcomputers can be programmed with IBM's Macro Assembler language (MASM). It also presents an overview of some concepts you should be familiar with before you begin to learn MASM, such as: how the MASM assembler converts the program you write to one that the microcomputer can understand, how the microcomputer is organized, and how it runs a program. These concepts are important to understanding assembler languages because the assembler-language program deals directly with the microcomputer and its operation. This chapter also includes a general comparison of MASM with some other languages.

The next chapter presents general information applicable to the IBM PC. In the third chapter, you will begin to look at and write programs.

Where Can You Use MASM?

The Macro Assembler language (MASM) by Microsoft was developed to program the IBM PC, PC/XT, and PC/AT. Throughout this book, IBM PC refers to this entire family of microcomputers. MASM is based on the assembler language for 8086 and 8088 microprocessors (the PC and PC/XT each uses an 8088 microprocessor). As Figure 1.1 indicates, an assembler is a program that translates assembler language into machine language, which can be understood by a microprocessor. The MASM assembler translates MASM programs into 8088 machine language.

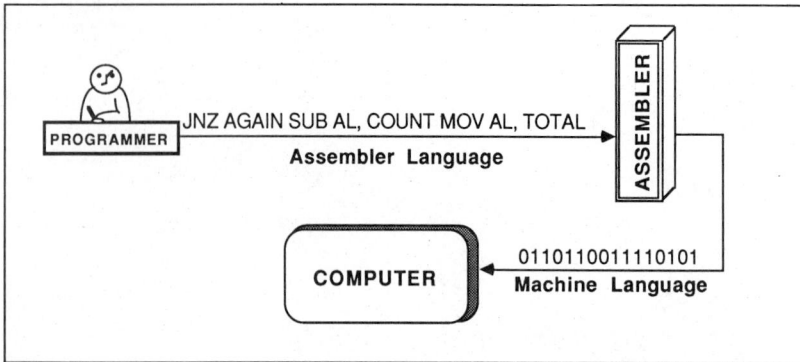

Figure 1.1 The Role of the Assembler

Theoretically, the resulting machine-language programs should run on any microcomputer with an 8088 microprocessor. However, some instructions may, in fact, refer to memory locations that have special functions on one type of computer or with a particular operating system. The programs, therefore, may not run correctly on other computers or with other operating systems. I/O (input and output) routines are especially liable to be incompatible with other microcomputers or with other operating systems. Unless otherwise indicated, the I/O routines you learn in this book run under version 1.1 of the IBM PC Disk Operating System (DOS) by Microsoft or subsequent versions.

Other assembler languages exist for programming 8086/8088 microprocessors. One of these, Microsoft's Small Assembler (ASM), is included when you purchase MASM. (We'll discuss the differences between MASM and ASM later in this chapter). All 8086/8088 assembler languages use the same set of instructions, which, in turn, are translated into the same machine-language instructions.

An assembler has other functions than translation, however. Most assemblers, for example, reserve and initialize data space and provide a listing of the program and its translation. MASM, like other assembler languages, directs the assembler to perform these functions using instructions known as **assembler directives** or **pseudo-ops**, which are not translated into machine language. The DB pseudo-op, for example, defines data space, while the PAGE pseudo-op controls the page size of the listing the assembler produces. MASM's pseudo-ops include all of ASM's and more. Other 8086/8088 assembler languages will have similar, but not identical, sets of pseudo-ops.

You can use the Macro Assembler Language taught in this book to write programs that will be converted to machine language by the MASM assembler. The machine-language programs will run on the IBM PC family using DOS 1.1 or later versions; they may or may not also run on other 8086/8088 microprocessors or with other operating systems. The basic concepts and the MASM instructions covered in this book will be useful, but not complete, guides to other 8086/8088 assembler languages.

Review Questions

1. MASM is intended for use on which computers? Which micro-processors? Which operating system?

2. What microprocessor does the IBM PC use?

3. From what type of language does an assembler translate?

4. Into what language does the MASM assembler translate programs?

5. True or False? A pseudo-op directs the assembler in its functions; it is not translated by the assembler.

6. True or False? All 8086/8088 assembler languages include the same instructions and pseudo-ops.

Answers

1. IBM PC and family; 8086/8088; DOS   **2.** 8088   **3.** Assembler language   **4.** 8088 machine language   **5.** True   **6.** False; they include the same instructions, but not necessarily the same pseudo-ops.

The Programming Process

Figure 1.2 illustrates the programming process. We will talk about each step, from writing the program to running it.

Where Does the Source Code Come From?

When you write a program, begin by deciding exactly what you want the program to do. Often, this means planning screen layouts and print diagrams on chart paper that has numbered rows and columns. Then, plan the program logic. The more time you spend planning in the beginning, the less time you will need to spend revising later.

Once you know what your program will do in detail, write the program in MASM Assembler language. The MASM language program is called the **source code**. Writing a program is often called **coding**, since it produces source code. Most assembler programmers write their programs first on

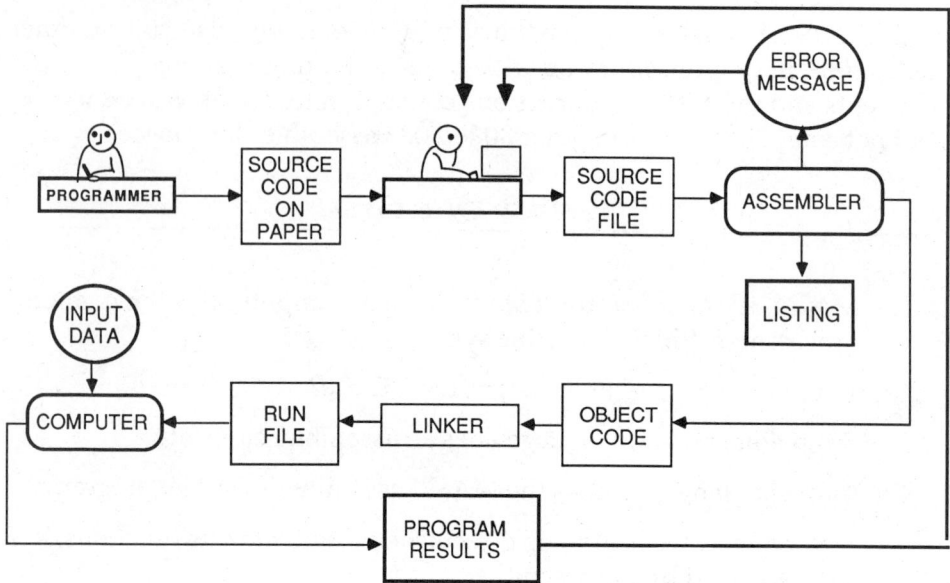

Figure 1.2   The Programming Process

paper, leaving plenty of room for changes. Next, the source code is entered into the computer, using either an editor such as EDLIN or a word processing program.

Notice the difference between MASM and BASIC. BASIC itself includes an editor. When you start to run BASIC you automatically are in the BASIC editor and can begin to enter your program. MASM, as well as most other computer languages, does not include its own editor. MASM programs must be entered using an independent editor or word processing program.

Where Does the Object Code Come From?

Once the source code is ready, it's time to call on the assembler. An assembler is a program. The source code is the input to the program. Machine language, known as **machine code** or **object code**, is the main output from the program. Usually, the assembler produces a listing and, sometimes, it also produces cross-reference files for the programmer's use in debugging the program. But, its real job is to produce the object code.

An assembler translates source-code instructions to object-code instructions on a one-to-one basis; that is, every 8086/8088 assembler-language instruction is translated into a 8086/8088 machine-language instruction. In addition, the assembler carries out the pseudo-op instructions by leaving room in the machine-language program for data areas and by putting initial values in the data areas. Other pseudo-op instructions may also affect the output from the assembler. For example, they may change the number of lines per page in the listing, or tell the assembler to copy source code from another file into your program's source code before translating it.

Figure 1.3 shows part of a listing from the assembly of a MASM program. The right-hand side of the page shows the source code, which includes comments written by the programmer. The left-hand side of the page shows the object code in hexadecimal. The object code is, in fact, in binary because it is the only form of data that a computer can understand. But, when printed or displayed on a CRT, the code is always shown in hexadecimal. (By the way, if you need to brush up on binary and hexadecimal, read Appendix A.)

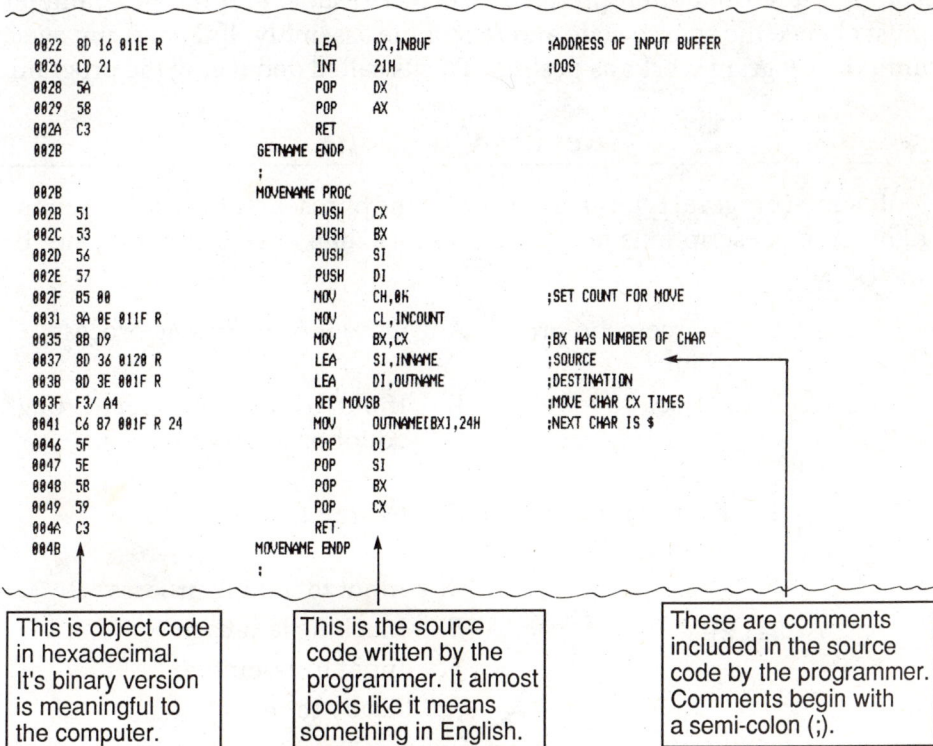

```
0022  8D 16 011E R        LEA    DX,INBUF        ;ADDRESS OF INPUT BUFFER
0026  CD 21               INT    21H             ;DOS
0028  5A                  POP    DX
0029  58                  POP    AX
002A  C3                  RET
002B              GETNAME ENDP
                          ;
002B              MOVENAME PROC
002B  51                  PUSH   CX
002C  53                  PUSH   BX
002D  56                  PUSH   SI
002E  57                  PUSH   DI
002F  B5 00               MOV    CH,0H           ;SET COUNT FOR MOVE
0031  8A 0E 011F R        MOV    CL,INCOUNT
0035  8B D9               MOV    BX,CX           ;BX HAS NUMBER OF CHAR
0037  8D 36 0120 R        LEA    SI,INNAME       ;SOURCE
003B  8D 3E 001F R        LEA    DI,OUTNAME      ;DESTINATION
003F  F3/ A4              REP MOVSB              ;MOVE CHAR CX TIMES
0041  C6 87 001F R 24     MOV    OUTNAME[BX],24H ;NEXT CHAR IS $
0046  5F                  POP    DI
0047  5E                  POP    SI
0048  5B                  POP    BX
0049  59                  POP    CX
004A  C3                  RET
004B              MOVENAME ENDP
                          ;
```

This is object code in hexadecimal. It's binary version is meaningful to the computer.

This is the source code written by the programmer. It almost looks like it means something in English.

These are comments included in the source code by the programmer. Comments begin with a semi-colon (;).

Figure 1.3 Part of an Assembler Listing

What's After Object Code?

The object-code program that results from assembly is a string of binary digits which includes both machine-language instructions and data storage areas. One more step, **linking**, is required to change the object-code program into an **executable** program, also in machine language. The linker program adds information that will be needed when your program runs, such as the program size and where to load the program in memory. The linker can also combine several object programs into one.

The individual object programs are often called **object modules**. The finished, executable program may be referred to as a **load module**, since it is ready to load into memory. The software that comes with some compilers includes libraries of object modules that must be combined via the linker with every object program generated by the compiler.

When you run a program, it is the executable version, the load module, this is run. That's why the disk file where the program's load module is stored is often called its **run file**. As you can see from Figure 1.2, usually the programming process is not finished when it is run for the first time. The first few runs often produce incorrect results, and the programmer must change the source code and repeat the assembly, link, and run cycle until the program works as desired. This is called debugging the program.

Review Questions

Match each program type on the left with the phrases that describe it on the right. Some descriptions may be used more than once; some may not be used at all.

_____ 1. Source code program   A. Output from linking process.

_____ 2. Object code program   B. Input by programmer through editor or word processor

_____ 3. Executable program   C. Output from assembler

D. Input to linking process

E. Machine language

F. Input to assembler

G. Ready to run

Answers

1. B, F   **2.** C, D, E   **3.** A, E, G

The Microcomputer

Before you learn how the microcomputer runs your program, you need to be aware of some of its parts. Figure 1.4 contains a generalized diagram of a microcomputer; refer to it as you read the following discussion.

The Microprocessor

The heart of any microcomputer is its microprocessor, which contains the Central Processing Unit (CPU). The CPU is the area where machine-language instructions are interpreted and carried out. The microprocessor also includes several, small memory areas called **registers**. The CPU can access the registers very quickly to store, manipulate, or retrieve data.

Flags   Most microprocessors have a register that contains the flags. Each flag is one bit, so it may have a value of zero or one. There are two types of flags: **status flags** and **control flags**. A status flag records information about the result of an instruction. Many microprocessors, for example, maintain a zero status flag. The zero flag is **set** (turned on, or given a value of 1) when an arithmetic result has a value of zero. The flag is **cleared** (turned off, or given a value of 0) when the result is not 0. Control flags are used to control the operation of the computer. For example, an interrupt flag may control whether or not a program can be interrupted by outside events, such as pressing a key on the keyboard. Such requests for service are handled if the flag is set and are ignored if the flag is cleared.

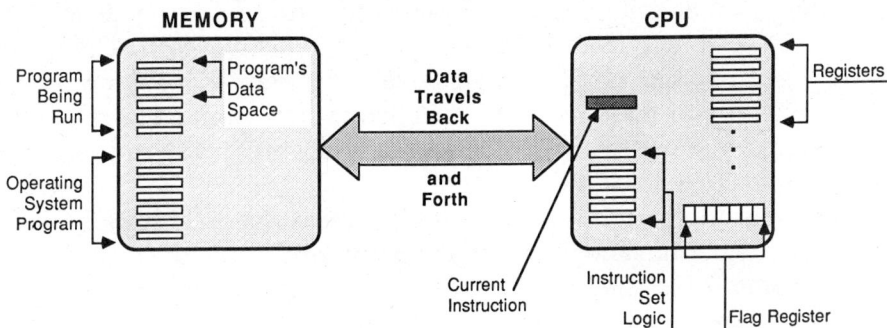

MEMORY

Program Being Run

Program's Data Space

Operating System Program

Data Travels Back and Forth

CPU

Registers

Current Instruction

Instruction Set Logic

Flag Register

Figure 1.4 Generalized Diagram of a Microcomputer

The Instruction Set

A microprocessor contains circuitry that enables the microprocessor to carry out a certain set of instructions. An 8088 microprocessor is designed to process about 90 instructions that make up the instruction set for both 8086 and 8088 microprocessors. Object and executable programs for any microcomputer with an 8086 or 8088 microprocessor must use these instructions and no others, since these are the only instructions the computer can actually carry out.

Some microcomputers have more than one microprocessor and can carry out more than one set of instructions. An IBM PC may have an 8087 microprocessor installed in addition to its basic 8088 microprocessor. The 8087 processes high-speed, high-precision arithmetic instructions that are not available on the 8088. MASM originally did not include the assembly-language equivalents of these instructions. The newest version of MASM does have 8087 instructions, but they will not be covered in this book.

Memory

Another important aspect of the microcomputer is its memory. It's probably easiest to visualize memory as a large number of storage cells, like a honeycomb. Each cell can contain one byte of information—that is, eight bits. Any ASCII character can be expressed in one byte, so you will sometimes see the number of bytes of memory in a computer referred to as the number of characters it can hold.

Each cell or byte of memory has a unique address, starting at 0H (addresses usually are written in hexadecimal). The maximum memory that can be addressed by the 8088 is 1,048,576 (1M or 1024K) bytes. That means that 1024K is effectively the maximum memory size for a microcomputer using an 8088 microprocessor. Memory addresses for an 8088-based microcomputer range from 0H to 0FFFFFH (0 to 1,048,575). The actual memory size of your computer, however, will vary depending on the number and size of memory chips installed in it. You must have at least 96K of memory to use the MASM assembler. However, you can assemble an ASM program with a 64K memory.

Sometimes memory is referred to as if it were a vertical stack of boxes with 0H at the bottom and the highest possible address at the top.

The memory installed in your computer is not all available for your programs. Some of it is reserved for system programs or other purposes over which you have no control. In the IBM PC, for example, the bottom 1024 bytes contain **interrupt vectors**, which are the addresses of programs that are executed when a special function needs to be handled by the operating system. Examples are many I/O functions, such as displaying a character on the screen. The top 16 bytes contain the system reset instructions that are executed when you turn on the computer. Additional memory is used when the operating system is loaded into other parts of memory, one of the first steps that occurs when the computer starts up.

Review Questions

1. Which part of the microcomputer determines what instructions the microcomputer can carry out?

2. In which part of the microprocessor are instructions interpreted and carried out?

3. What are the small, rapid-access memory areas in the microprocessor called?

4. What part of the microprocessor is used to record information about the results of an instruction?

5. True or False? A unique address is assigned to every bit of memory, starting with the address 0H.

6. True or False? The maximum memory size for a computer with an 8088 microprocessor is 1024K bytes.

7. How much memory is required to use the MASM assembler?

8. True or False? A flag is cleared when its value is zero.

Answers
1. The microprocessor   2. The CPU (central processing unit)   3. Registers   4. The status flags   5. False; a unique address is assigned to every byte of memory; a byte contains eight bits.   6. True   7. 96K bytes   8. True

How a Program is Run

To illustrate how a program is run in a microcomputer, let's look at a hypothetical computer, the TABLET, which uses an equally hypothetical microprocessor, the EZ3. The EZ3 contains three registers for program use and one flag, the zero status flag.

The EZ3 Instructions

Figure 1.5 shows the rather limited instruction set of the EZ3. Each instruction begins with a two-digit (hexadecimal) code that identifies the instruction. This is the **operation code** or **op-code** for the instruction. To make this discussion easier to read, a **mnemonic** has also been assigned for each operation code. A mnemonic is an easy-to-remember code that stands for an operation code in a discussion or in source code. MOV is the mnemonic for 11H, the move operation code. SUB is the mnemonic for 12H, the subtraction operation code. JNZ is the mnemonic for 13H, the jump-if-not-zero operation code, and END is the mnemonic for 14H, the operation code for the instruction that stops the program.

```
The EZ3 Instruction Set
```

Mnemonic	Instruction	Meaning
MOV	11rr11hh	Move value from hh11 to register rr
SUB	12rr11hh	Subtract value at hh11 from register rr
JNZ	1311hh	If zero flag cleared, next instruction is at hh11
END	14	End program; return to operating system

The Instruction Format		
Op Code	Operand 1	Operand 2
one byte	0, 1 or 2 bytes	0 or 2 bytes

```
Addresses in operands
are stored with low-
order byte first.  The
address 0120H is

    ┌─────────┐
    │ 20   01 │
    └─────────┘

as an operand.
```

Figure 1.5 The EZ3 Instruction Set

All the instructions except END also contain **operands**. If you think of the operation code as the verb of an instruction, the operands are the objects of the verb. They specify the data or locations that are to be used when the instruction is executed.

The MOV Instruction   The first operand for MOV is one byte that names a register into which a byte of data will be moved. Possible registers are 1, 2, and 3. The second operand is two bytes long; it names the memory address from which the data byte will come. The EZ3 machine language always puts addresses into "reverse notation". That is, the low-order byte is first, and the high-order last. An instruction to move a one-byte value from address 1289H to register 03H would be written in EZ3 machine language as 11038912H. For easier reading, object code usually is printed in groups of four hexidecimal digits with the H assumed, so the instruction would actually be printed or displayed as 1103 8912.

Take note of two points about MOV. Although it is described as a move instruction, in fact, it performs a copy. The source of the data is not changed, but keeps its original value. Most computer languages use "move" to mean "copy." Also notice that the direction of the move is **from** the second operand **to** the first operand. This is the usual direction of moves and other processes in most assembler languages.

The SUB Instruction   Look at the SUB instruction. It also names a register in the first operand and an address in the second. The one-byte value found at the address will be subtracted from the value found in the register. The result will be left in the register. The source operand is left unchanged. SUB will also set or clear the zero status flag to reflect the result of the subtraction. If the result is zero, the flag is set; otherwise, it is cleared.

The JNZ Instruction   JNZ has one operand, a two-byte address that points to the next instruction to be executed if the zero flag is cleared. If the zero flag is set, the next instruction executed will be the one following JNZ. The address in a jump instruction is sometimes called the **target** of the jump.

The END Instruction   END has no operands. When END is executed, it ends the program and returns control to the operating system. The OS will immediately display a prompt (A>) and wait for a command to be entered.

Loading the Program

When you tell the computer to run a program on the TABLET, the executable program is loaded into memory beginning at 0100H. (Addresses below 100H are used only by the operating system.) Figure 1.6 shows the contents of 0100H through 011FH with a program loaded. Each row in the figure displays 16 bytes arranged in groups of four hexadecimal digits, or two bytes per group. The leftmost column shows the beginning address for each row. On the right is the ASCII interpretation for each of the 16 bytes. If a byte contains an ASCII code that doesn't represent a printable character, it is shown as a dot. This is a standard way to display memory in a printout or on a screen.

Running the Program

The EZ3 CPU contains an area that holds a copy of the current instruction; we'll call that area CURRIN. It also includes a special-purpose register called the **instruction pointer** (IP) that usually contains the address of the instruction following the one being executed. When the computer is through with the instruction in CURRIN, it looks at IP to find the address of the next instruction. The program-loading procedure ends by setting IP to 0100H, so the next instruction executed is the first instruction of the program. Figure 1.7 shows the contents of IP, the zero status flag, and register 3 before and after each instruction is executed.

When the program begins, IP points to 0100H; we don't know the contents of register 3 or the value of the zero flag at this time. The CPU copies the byte at 0100H to CURRIN. The CPU identifies the copied value (11H) as an operation code for a four-byte instruction, so it also copies three operand bytes from 0101H, 01012H, and 0103H into CURRIN. IP is now changed to point to 0104H, the beginning of the next instruction. Then, the

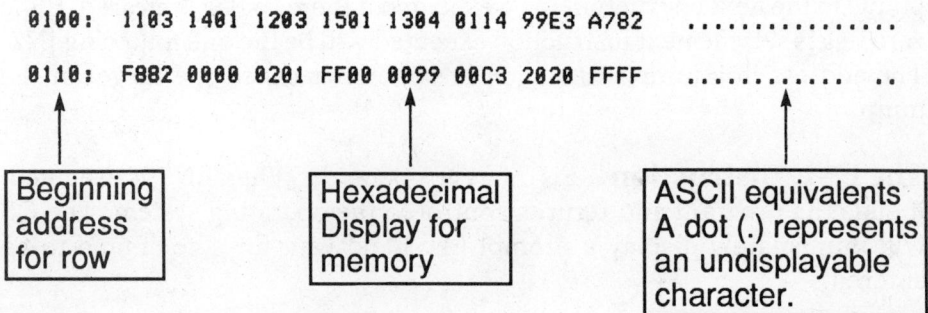

```
0100:   1103 1401 1203 1501 1304 0114 99E3 A782   ................

0110:   F882 0000 0201 FF00 0099 00C3 2020 FFFF   ............  ..
```

Beginning address for row	Hexadecimal Display for memory	ASCII equivalents A dot (.) represents an undisplayable character.

Figure 1.6 A Program in Memory

	Before				After		
Zero	Register			CURRIN	Zero	Register	
Flag	3	IP		Instruction	Flag	3	IP
?	?	0100		1103 1401	?	02	0104
?	02	0104		1203 1501	0	01	0108
0	01	0108		1304 01	0	01	0104
0	01	0104		1203 1501	1	00	0108
1	00	0108		1304 01	1	00	010B
1	00	010B		14	1	00	0025

END OF PROGRAM

Figure 1.7 The Program Runs

instruction in CURRIN is executed. The byte pointed to by the second operand (address 0114H) is copied to the register specified by the first operand (03H). Now, register 3 contains the value 2; we still don't know the value of the zero flag, since it is not affected by a MOV instruction.

MOV is finished. Now, IP provides the address of the next instruction, 0104H. When one instruction follows another sequentially in this way, we say that program control **falls through** to the next instruction. In this case, control falls through to another four-byte instruction, SUB. The SUB instruction is copied into CURRIN, and IP is changed to point to 0108H. Then, the value (01H) found at the address in the second operand (0115H) is subtracted from register 3, leaving 1 in the register. Since SUB's result is not zero, the zero flag is cleared.

Again, the instruction at the address in IP (0108H) is brought into CURRIN. This is a three-byte instruction, JNZ, so IP becomes 010BH. Execution of the instruction begins by checking the zero flag. The flag is clear, so the next instruction should be the one at 0104H, the address in JNZ's operand. This is specified by changing IP to 0104H. When a jump instruction changes the value in IP so that the next instruction executed is not the next in memory, we say that control is **transferred** to the target of the jump.

Since IP now points to 0104H, the SUB instruction at that address is executed again. This time, the result of the subtraction is zero, so the zero flag is set. The JNZ instruction is repeated. Again, IP is set to 010BH before the instruction is executed. Since the zero flag is set this time, IP is not changed by the JNZ instruction, and the instruction at 010BH is executed.

This is a one-byte instruction, so IP becomes 010CH. But, it doesn't really matter, because 14H is the END. The END instruction sets IP to 0025H, a location that contains an operating-system instruction. The program has ended, and the operating system is back in control of the TABLET.

The 8088, like the EZ3, uses machine-language instructions made up of operation codes and operands. Mnemonics have been assigned for the operation codes and are used in writing MASM programs. Addresses are written in reverse notation in the object code.

The 8088 also uses a special-purpose register called the instruction pointer (IP) to keep track of the next instruction to be executed. Like the EZ3, the 8088 begins execution by bringing the byte pointed to by IP into the CPU and interpreting that byte. Then, the CPU determines how many more bytes make up the complete instruction. IP is updated to point to the byte presumed to be the beginning of the next instruction. Then, the current instruction is executed. Control transfers are made by changing the address in IP.

On the other hand, 8088 programs are not always loaded at 0100H, and control is not returned to 0025H when the program ends. The process of transferring control from the operating system to your program and back again is more complex in the 8088, but you won't need to worry about it. It will be taken care of automatically when your programs are run. Also, 8088 operation codes and operands vary considerably in length. Again, you don't really need to worry about this since you do not program directly in machine language.

Review Questions

Match each word or phrase on the left with the most appropriate description from the column on the right. Not all the descriptions are used.

_____ 1. Operand

_____ 2. Operation code

_____ 3. Instruction pointer

_____ 4. Fall through

_____ 5. Mnemonic

A. Identifies the next instruction to be executed

B. Specifies data or location to be acted on

C. An easily remembered substitute for numeric code

D. Specifies action to be taken

E. Contains a copy of the instruction being executed

F. Pass control to the next instruction in sequence

Answers

1. B   **2.** D   **3.** A   **4.** F   **5.** C (E is not used)

MASM and Other Languages

Object code is the same no matter what language is used for the source code. However, object code is produced differently by assembler languages. Interpreted languages (the most common of which is BASIC), and compiled languages, (which include COBOL, C, many versions of PASCAL), and many others. We'll look at some of these differences and then discuss the major difference between MASM and ASM—the macro facility.

MASM vs. BASIC

The BASIC that comes with DOS is **interpreted** BASIC. BASIC, in fact, is the most commonly used interpreted language. An interpreted language translates one instruction at a time into object code, executing each one as soon as it is translated. Generally, each source-code instruction produces a sequence of several object-code instructions. Note that the interpreter does not produce an object-code program and, therefore, does not provide anything that can be used to create a run file.

When you issue the command BASIC or BASICA, the BASIC interpreter program is loaded into memory and run. Part of this program is an editor, used to enter or change your BASIC program. When you RUN your program, it is used as input data to the BASIC interpreter. The interpreter first reads, and then converts, an instruction to object code if it can. If the interpreter can't understand the instruction, or can't find all the information it needs for conversion, it tells you that there's an error and stops interpreting. If the instruction is converted to object code, it is carried out immediately. Control then returns to the interpreter, which begins to process the next instruction. When the interpreter reaches the end of your program, it stops interpreting, puts the BASIC prompt (OK) on the screen, and waits for an instruction. When you end the BASIC session by typing SYSTEM, control returns to the operating system.

You can see that this is very different from the way MASM programs are processed. For MASM, as well as other non-interpreted languages, the source code is checked completely for syntax errors and converted to object code before any object code is executed. By execution time, when the run file is loaded and processed, the assembler or compiler is out of the picture; it has already done its work.

Another major difference between BASIC and MASM is the way that data fields (called variables in BASIC) are handled. In BASIC, a variable name is simply used in a program. Integer, single-precision, double-precision, and string variables are identified by the names given to them. Each of the three types of numeric variables has a predefined size; a string variable's size depends on its current value. The BASIC interpreter takes care of storing variables in memory and keeping track of their addresses.

MASM, like most other computer languages, requires **data definitions**. Any name used to refer to a data field in an instruction must be defined in a special section of the program. Data definitions not only include the names and sizes of data fields, but also define their placement within the data storage area. The first field defined in the section starts at byte 0H of the data storage area. If the first field is 10 bytes long, the second field defined will start at byte 0AH of the area. The programmer determines the layout of the storage area by the way he or she codes the data definitions. A data definition can also assign an initial value to a field; this will be the value contained in the memory locations assigned to that field when the program is loaded.

Assembler vs. Compiler

A compiler shares some of the characteristics of an assembler and some of an interpreter. Many high-level languages are compiled. The compiler, like an assembler, translates an entire source-code program into object code, which can then be used with the linker to create a run file. The compiler does not execute the program. Its job is done when the translation is made.

Each compiler-language source-code instruction, like a BASIC instruction, is translated into several object-code instructions. Compiled languages usually require data definition. Often, the definitions limit what type of data can be used in the defined fields and how the fields can be used. A field described as the equivalent of a BASIC string variable, for example, cannot be used in arithmetic instructions in most compiler languages or in BASIC. Assembler languages are more flexible, but this flexibility places more responsibility on the programmer to validate data usage.

MASM vs. ASM

The major differences between the Small Assembler (ASM) and the Macro Assembler (MASM) as shown by their names, are the sizes of the assemblers and the macro capability of MASM. The differences are related; ASM assembler is smaller primarily because it does not include the code needed to handle macros. If you code a program that doesn't use any macros, you can assemble it either with ASM or MASM.

What's a Macro Anyway?   A macro is a predefined series of instructions that can be copied into a source-code program by using the macro's name in place of an operation code. The macro definition usually includes dummy names that are replaced when the macro is copied. You'll learn a lot more about macros, see many examples, and code your own macro definitions later in this book.

When the MASM assembler encounters a macro name used as an operation code, it copies the source code from the definition, replacing dummy names as appropriate. Then, the assembler treats the resulting source code as if it were coded there in the first place. In effect, this allows you to code frequently used routines once and use them over and over with different data fields. You'll really appreciate this facility when you see how many instructions are required by MASM to perform some simple-sounding functions, such as clearing the screen, positioning the cursor, or moving a string of characters from one place to another.

As you write more and more MASM programs, you will code more and more macros and use them from program to program. Some of your programs may eventually consist of long strings of macro calls. In a sense, this lets you have some of the advantages of a compiler language. The macro name corresponds to a compiler language's instruction. The assembler produces several object-code instructions for each macro call, just as the compiler produces several for each source-code instruction. The difference is that with MASM you can determine which macros will be useful, what details are needed in them, when to call a macro, and when to ignore it in favor of a one-time routine. With a compiler language, you must use instructions that call routines precoded by the compiler's designers. In a well-designed compiler language these may be very efficient, but sometimes you would prefer to code your own variations.

Review Questions

Choose the best answer for each of the following questions.

1. How does the MASM assembler know the length of a data field?

    A.   From the field's current value

    B.   From the field's data definition

    C.   From the data type implied by the field's name

    D.   None of the above

2.   Which of these program types is run by executing each instruction as soon as it is converted to object code?

   A.   Interpreted-language program

   B.   Assembler-language program

   C.   Machine-language program

   D.   Compiler-language program

3.   In which type of program does each source-code instruction usually produce only one object-code instruction?

   A.   Compiler-language program

   B.   Assembler-language program

   C.   Interpreted program

   D.   Both A and C

4.   What is a macro?

   A.   A subroutine executed from several places in a BASIC program

   B.   A predefined series of assembler-language instructions

   C.   A utility program that speeds up assembly

Answers

1. B   **2.** A   **3.** B   **4.** B

Key Points From Chapter 1

Chapter 1 has covered some general concepts that should help you understand the material in the rest of the book.

Some of the main points covered in the chapter are:

■   MASM is a language intended for writing programs on an IBM PC with at least 96K of memory and operating under DOS 1.1 or later.

- The MASM assembler translates MASM programs into 8088 machine language. The translated programs are used by the linker to produce executable programs.

- MASM includes both instructions that are translated into machine language and pseudo-ops that direct the assembler in its functions, such as defining data fields and producing the assembler listing.

- One of a microcomputer's major components is the microprocessor, which contains the CPU where machine-language instructions are interpreted and carried out.

- The microprocessor also contains the registers, used for high-speed manipulation of small amounts of data.

- The flag register contains a number of one-bit areas called flags. Status flags record information about the results of instructions, while control flags control the operation of the computer.

- The 8088 maintains a special-purpose register, the instruction pointer (IP), which always contains the address of the next instruction to be executed.

- An 8088-based microcomputer may have up to 1024K (1M) bytes of memory. Each byte has a unique address, ranging from 0H at the bottom of memory to 0FFFFFH at the top.

- When a program is run, its run file is loaded into memory and control is transferred to its first instruction.

- Each machine-language instruction begins with an operation code, which tells the CPU what action to perform. It also may include operands, which identify the data or locations to be acted on by the instruction.

- Control falls through from one instruction to the next unless it is specifically transferred to an out-of-sequence instruction.

- Data fields, which correspond to BASIC variables, must be named and defined in a specific area of a MASM program.

- MASM includes the capability to use macros, (predefined sequences of instructions) by coding the macro name as an operation code. The assembler will copy the predefined instructions into the source-code program wherever the macro name is coded.

- The macro capability is the major difference between the Macro Assembler (MASM) and the Small Assembler (ASM).

This chapter's most important feature is the definition of many terms that will be used throughout the book. The chapter review questions that follow will help you to make sure that you understand the most important of these terms.

Chapter Review Questions

Match each term on the left with the most applicable phrase from the list on the right. Not all of the phrases will be used.

___ 1.	ASM	A. Flag with value of 1
___ 2.	Assembler	B. Predefined series of instructions copied
___ 3.	Cleared flag	into the source code by the assembler
___ 4.	Control flag	C. Next instruction executed is the next one
___ 5.	CPU	in memory
___ 6.	Data definition	D. Language understood by the microprocessor
___ 7.	Data field	E. Program that translates assembler
___ 8.	Fall through	language to machine language
___ 9.	Flag	F. Machine language code
___ 10.	IP	G. Establishes name, size, initial value,and
___ 11.	Linker	location of field in data area
___ 12.	Machine language	H. Directs assembler functions
		I. Flag that controls computer
___ 13.	Macro	J. Identifies data or location to act on
___ 14.	MASM	K. One-bit area in special register
___ 15.	Object code	L. IBM's Small Assembler
___ 16.	Operand	M. IBM's Macro Assembler
___ 17.	Operation code	N. Next instruction to be executed not in sequence
___ 18.	Pseudo-op	O. Executable program; ready to load and run
___ 19.	Register	
___ 20.	Run file	P. Flag with value of 0
___ 21.	Set flag	Q. Address to which control is transferred
___ 22.	Status flag	R. Register which contains address of next instruction
___ 23.	Target	
___ 24.	Transfer control	S. Program used to enter source code into computer

T. Area where instructions are interpreted and carried out

U. Flag that records information about instruction result

V. A small fast-access memory area in the microprocessor

W. Equivalent to BASIC variable

X. Tells CPU what action to take

Y. Program that converts object code to program

Answers

1. L 2. E 3. P 4. I 5. T 6. G 7. W 8. C 9. K 10. R 11. Y 12. D 13. B 14. M 15. F 16. J 17. X 18. H 19. V 20. O 21 A 22. U 23. Q 24. N

2

Background for MASM

In Chapter 1 you learned some basic terms and concepts that apply to most or all microcomputers. This chapter presents information that is directly applicable to computers using the 8088 microprocessor. By the time you finish this chapter, you will know how the 8088's instructions use registers, the units in which the 8088 processes data, how it divides memory into segments and expresses addresses as segment numbers and offsets, and the names and uses of its 12 registers and four flags. This chapter will also introduce you to the use of interrupts for I/O in the IBM PC. Most of the things that you learn in this chapter will be used in every MASM program you write, even the beginning programs in Chapter 3.

The Register Set

The 8088 has 12 registers that are available for program use. Four of them are **general-purpose registers**, two are **index registers**, two are **pointer registers**, and four are **segment registers**. You'll learn about each type, and indeed each register, after you learn about their general use.

Register Use

Registers are used in several ways in 8088 (and therefore MASM) instructions. They can be named as operands. When a register is an operand, the register contents are the data to be acted on or changed. In this instruction:

MOV AX , 5

the first operand refers to the AX register; the instruction copies the value 5 into the register.

Some registers are also used to provide addresses indirectly in operands. A source-code operand may contain an address, one or two register names in brackets, or both. The object code will indicate both the address and the indirect registers. When the instruction is executed, the current contents of these registers are added to the **effective address**, or EA. The EA indicates the actual location of the data. In this instruction:

MOV 100[BX][S I] , AX

the contents of registers BX and SI are added to 100 to produce the EA and the contents of AX are moved to the location pointed to by EA. If the instruction is part of a loop, the loop may also change the contents of BX or SI (or both) so that the EA is different each time the instruction is repeated.

Some instructions use specific registers by implication. Many instructions that cause repetitions, for example, use register CX to control the number of repetitions. CX is not specified as an operand in the instruction, but nevertheless it is used and changed when the instruction is executed.

The Size of a Register

Each of the 8088's registers is 16 bits long. You know that a bit is a single binary digit and can contain a value of zero or one. You also know that a byte is a string of eight bits and can contain a value between 0H and 0FFH. The value in a byte can be interpreted in the following ways: an unsigned integer, a signed integer, part of a multibyte number, two BCD digits, or an ASCII character. (If you don't understand this, see Appendix A.)

The 8088 processes data in units of one or two bytes. A two-byte unit is a word. The size of a word is not standard as is the size of a byte. Different processors use different word sizes, but the 8088 uses a two-byte, or 16-bit, word that can contain values from 0H to 0FFFFH.

Review Questions

1.   How many registers does the 8088 provide for program use?

2.   Name the four types of registers provided by the 8088.

3.   Which of the following statements are true?

     A.   A register may not be named as an operand.

     B.   A register may be used to modify an operand address.

     C.   The use of a specific register may be implied by an instruction.

     D.   The effective address of an operand is computed when the instruction is assembled.

4.   What is the size of a register (in bits)?

5.   True or False? The 8088, and therefore MASM programs, handle data only in byte-size units.

6.   How long is an 8088 word (in bits)?

Answers

1. 12   **2.** General-purpose, pointer, index, and segment registers   **3.** B and C are true. Here's what's wrong with the others: A. A register **may** be named as an operand. D. The effective address is computed when the instruction is **executed**.   **4.** 16 bits.   **5.** False; the 8088, and therefore MASM programs, can handle data in byte- or word-size units.   **6.** 16 bits

The General-Purpose Registers

The general-purpose registers, AX, BX, CX, and DX, can each be used as a one-word register or as two one-byte registers. The high-order, or most significant, bytes of these registers are called AH, BH, CH, and DH, and the low-order, or least significant, bytes are called AL, BL, CL, and DL. In effect, then, the 8088 has eight one-byte or four one-word general-purpose registers. Figure 2.1 illustrates the general-purpose registers.

Many MASM instructions can refer either to a byte or a word. When a general-purpose register is an operand in one of these instructions, the register name determines the data unit. The instruction:

MOV 100[BX] , AX

moves one word of data from register AX to the EA (contents of BX + 100), while this instruction:

MOV 100[BX] , AH

moves one byte of data from register AH to the EA.

MASM assumes that words in memory are stored in reverse order, that is, with the low-order byte first. When a word is moved from memory to a register, the byte from the lower address, the EA, goes into the low-order byte register. The next byte, from EA+1, goes into the high-order byte register. When a word is moved in the other direction, the process is reversed. When the register is displayed, the high-order byte is first. If 1AH is moved from EA to AL and 37H is moved from EA+1 to AH, AX contains 371AH.

As shown in Figure 2.1, the AX register is referred to as the **accumulator**; BX, the **base register**; CX, the **count register**; and DX, the **data register**. To some extent these designations reflect specialized uses of the registers. These designations are not totally accurate, however; they are chosen partly to match the register names and partly to reflect the historical use of similar registers in the 8088's ancestors. In many microprocessors, for example, all arithmetic results are put into the A register,

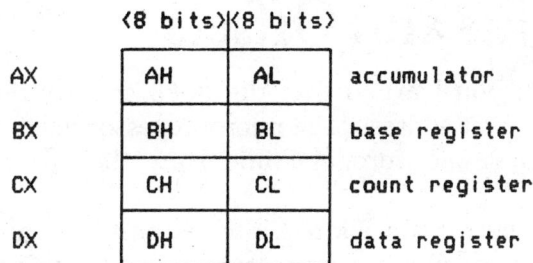

	⟨8 bits⟩	⟨8 bits⟩	
AX	AH	AL	accumulator
BX	BH	BL	base register
CX	CH	CL	count register
DX	DH	DL	data register

Figure 2.1 The General-Purpose Registers

which is, therefore, logically called the accumulator. In the 8088, any register except a segment register can be used for addition and subtraction, but AX is involved in all multiplication and division. BX is the only general-purpose register that can be used for indirect addressing; an address in BX is sometimes called a base address. With looping or repetitive instructions, CX holds the count of the remaining repetitions. As you learn various MASM instructions, you will learn about the specific ways in which they use the general-purpose registers.

Review Questions

1. How many one-word, general-purpose registers does the 8088 have?

2. How much data does BL hold? CX? DH?

3. Which register holds the count for repetitions?

4. True or false? All arithmetic is done in the accumulator?

5. Name the word-size register referred to as:

   A. Count
   B. Base
   C. Accumulator
   D. Data

Answers

1. 4   **2**. 1 byte or 8 bits; 1 word or 16 bits or 2 bytes; 1 byte or 8 bits   **3**. CX
4. False; addition and subtraction can be done in any of the general-purpose registers.   **5**. A. CX   B. BX   C. AX   D. DX

Segments and Offsets

In Chapter 1, you learned that the 8088 can address locations up to 0FFFFFH, a 20-bit address. The microprocessor itself, however, can only handle 16 bits, or one word, at a time. How, then, does it manage a 20-bit address?

The 8088 separates an address into two parts: a segment number and an offset. A segment number represents an address divisible by 16 (10H), sometimes called a segment boundary. (IBM documentation, including the MASM manual, refers to a segment boundary as a paragraph and to a segment number as a paragraph number or frame number.) An offset represents a number of bytes past a segment number. Figure 2.2 shows a similar situation in another context: a jogging track with a marker every 10 feet.

The runner in the figure is 35 feet from the beginning of the track. His position could also be described as being five feet past the third marker, 15 feet past the second marker, or 25 feet past the first marker. For convenience, let's use the notation "marker:distance" to describe the runner's position. But, let's make a rule that we never use this form with a distance of more than 20 feet. We'll call the position relative to the track's beginning the **actual position**.

The position of the runner in Figure 2.2, then, can be described as 3:5 or 2:15. We don't use negative distances, so we can't describe his position as a distance from marker 4. We don't use distances larger than 20 feet, so we also can't describe his position as a distance from marker 1. The runner's actual position is 35 feet. We can compute the actual position from the marker:distance form by multiplying the marker number by 10 and adding distance to the result. Each marker can be used to describe positions in a stretch of up to 20 feet. The marker stretches overlap; that is, marker 1 describes a stretch with actual positions from 10 to 30 feet; marker 2, a stretch from 20 to 40 feet; and so on. You can see that the area for one marker overlaps the next by 10 feet. Locations in this 10-foot overlap can be described by referring to either marker.

Segment and Offset Addresses

A segment boundary occurs at every 16 (10H) bytes in memory. The segment number is the boundary address divided by 16 (10H). The offset is the distance past the segment number. When we write an address in this form, we use a colon (:) to separate the two parts and we assume that both address parts are hexadecimal. The actual address is the sum of the segment number shifted one place to the left (that is, multiplied by 16) and the offset. Both the segment number and the offset are expressed as four hexadecimal digits, or 16 bits, and, thus, each can range from 0000H to

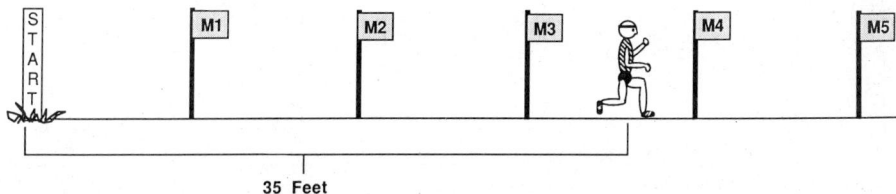

Figure 2.2 Marker:Distance

0FFFFH. 1234:0014, then, represents 12340H + 0014H, or address 12354H. The same address can be expressed using different segment numbers. 1235:0004H is another way to represent 12354H.

Since an offset can range from 0H to 0FFFFH, the same segment number can be used to refer to as many as 65,536 (64K) memory locations. Therefore, a segment boundary occurs every 16 bytes in memory and can be used to describe addresses stretching over 64K. This is another way of saying that segments can overlap, as shown in Figure 2.3.

Now you can see how the 8088 can handle a 20-bit address: it breaks it up into two 16-bit numbers, the first of which identifies a segment boundary and the second of which identifies a specific byte relative to that boundary.

The Segment Registers

How does this affect your MASM program? MASM operands usually specify only the one-word offset portion of an address; the segment number is taken from a segment register initialized when the program begins running. The four segment registers, CS, SS, DS, and ES, contain the segment numbers that mark the boundaries at which are loaded the code, stack, data, and extra segments respectively (see Figure 2.4). We refer to an address by its offset within one of these segments. SS:0008, for example, refers to byte 8 within the stack segment.

The Code Segment   The code segment contains all the instructions for your program. The first instruction starts at the boundary indicated by the number in the CS register. The next instruction follows that, and so on. When you code a control transfer instruction you usually specify the offset of the target instruction: the segment number comes from the CS register.

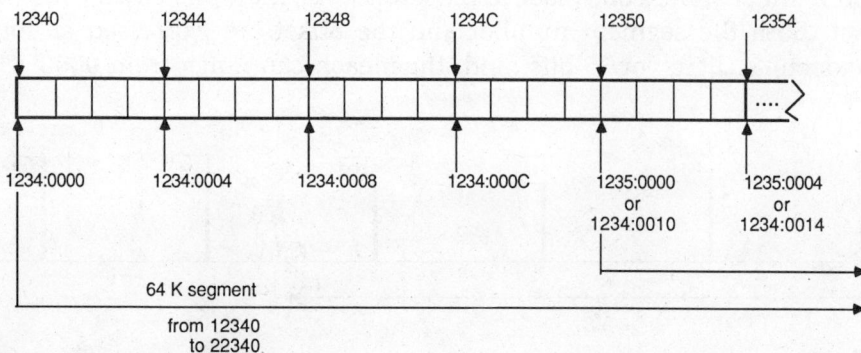

Figure 2.3 Segments in Memory

```
                                          Program in Memory

        < 1 6 b i t s >

CS    0  9  0  0  ───────────► 0900:0000 ──────► object code instructions
                               code segment

SS    0  A  0  0
                                                 end of instructions
DS    0  A  5  0

ES    0  A  5  0

                              ►0A00:0000 ──────► beginning of stack
                               stack segment
                                                 top of stack

                                                 bottom of stack

                              ►0A50:0000 ──────► data fields
                               data segment
                               extra segment

                                                 end of data
```

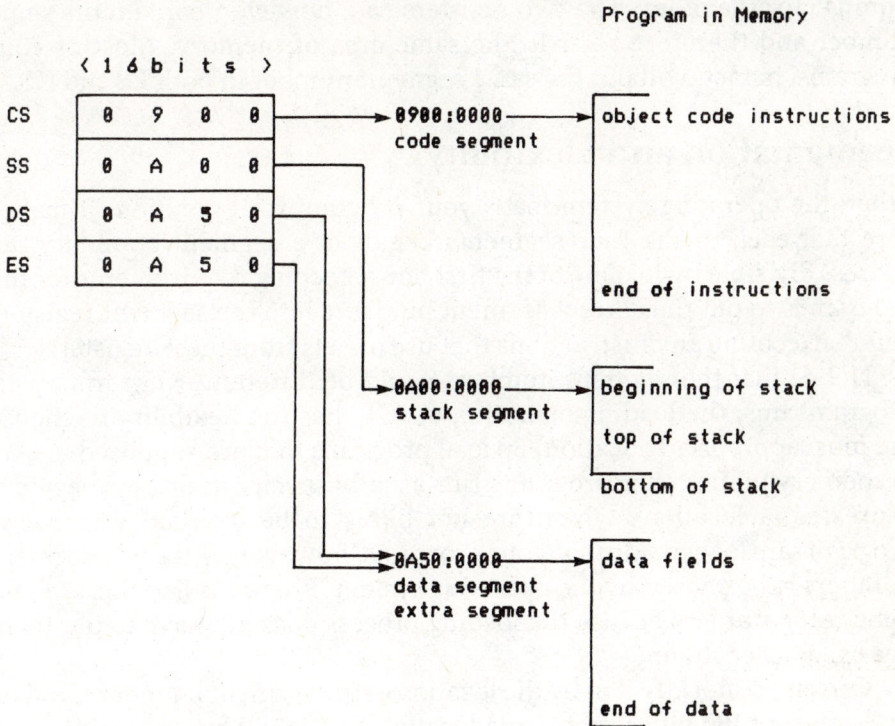

Figure 2.4 The Segment Registers

The Stack Segment   As you will see when you begin to write programs, you will often need to save the current contents of a register, use the register with new data, and then restore the original contents. A program can reserve a memory segment for saving register contents as well as other data; the reserved area is called the **stack**. The SS or stack segment register contains the segment number that marks the beginning of the stack.

The Data Segment   The data segment contains the program's data fields. When an operand refers to a data field it specifies the offset of the field. The segment number comes from the DS or data segment register. You will learn that it is sometimes possible to override this assignment by specifying a different segment register to be used with a particular operand.

The Extra Segment   The ES, or extra segment register can be used as an alternate data segment. As you will learn, some instructions take a segment number from the ES register for one of their operands and one from DS for the other. The two registers can, however, contain the same number and therefore refer to the same area of memory. Most of your programs, in fact, will put the same segment number in both ES and DS.

Segmentation and Flexibility

When the operating system loads your program for execution, it makes sure that each of the four segments begins at a segment boundary, an address divisible by 16. One of the first housekeeping requirements for the program is to put the correct segment numbers into the segment registers before executing any instructions that use offsets from these registers.

Notice that the segment numbers could be different every time your program runs; the loading operation usually has the flexibility to choose the most appropriate location. Special programs that are supposed to stay in memory while other programs run usually specify their own segment addresses at locations which are not likely to be overlaid when new programs are loaded. Most of your programs, however, will allow segment numbers to be chosen by the operating system. Programs like this are said to be **relocatable**, because the loading process does not have to put them in a specific location.

Offsets are not affected by the location of the segment boundary. A data area offset of 100 bytes refers to a location that is 100 bytes past the data segment boundary, regardless of where that boundary is. An operand's actual address is computed from the EA and the segment number when the instruction is executed.

Review Questions

1. What address is represented by 2314:0035? What is the segment number? What is the offset?

2. Name each of the following program segments:

    A. used to save register contents
    B. an alternate data area
    C. the program's main data area
    D. the instructions for your program

3. Name the segment register associated with each of the program segments from the previous question.

4. True or false? You must specify the address where each segment of your program is to be loaded.

Answers

1. 23175H (23140H + 0035H); 2314; 0035   **2.** A. stack segment B. extra segment C. data segment D. code segment   **3.** A. SS B. ES C. DS D. CS   **4.** False; you will usually allow the operating system to assign the addresses for program segments.

Pointer and Index Registers

The pointer and index registers are shown in Figure 2.5. These registers can be used in many of the same ways as the general-purpose registers, but the pointer and index registers are often used to contain offsets for fields in the stack or data area. An instruction that accesses the stack segment gets the segment number from SS and the offset from SP, (the stack pointer), or from BP, (the base pointer). Similarly, an instruction can access the data area using the segment number from DS combined with a data area offset from SI or DI, the source or destination indexes. You can override these assignments, specifying, for example, a combination such as ES:BP.

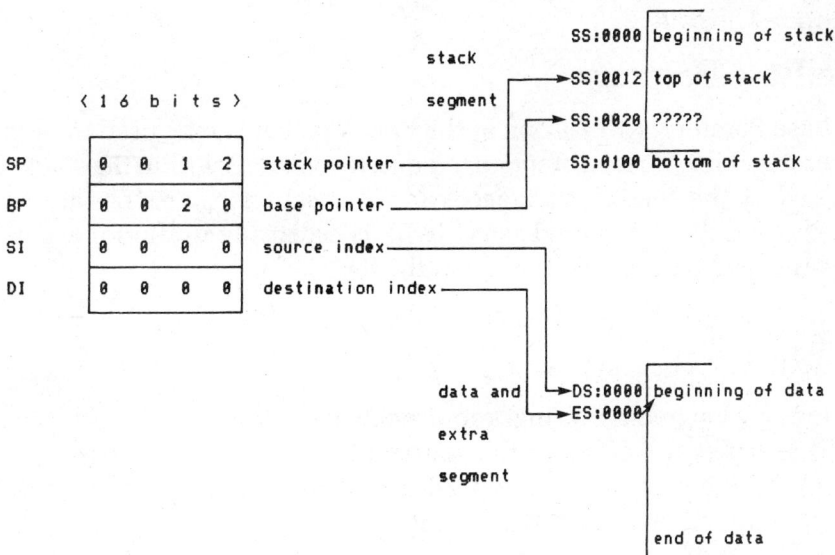

Figure 2.5 Pointer and Index Registers

The Stack and the Stack Pointer

The stack is often compared to a pile of dishes. The dish most recently placed on the pile is on the top and will be the next one removed from the pile. The pile grows and shrinks as dishes are added and removed. The height, or location, of the top varies with the number of dishes currently in the pile. The first dish was placed at the bottom of the pile and will be the last one removed.

The bottom of the stack is at the high-address end of the stack segment. When the program begins, SP contains this maximum offset. An instruction that places data on the stack reduces SP by two and copies one word to the new address indicated by SS:SP. We say the word is **pushed** on the stack. The reverse operation is called **popping** data. A word is copied from the address currently indicated by SS:SP, and SP is then increased by two. The formerly used offset will now be available for the next word placed on the stack.

Notice that stack operations always involve a word. The one-byte registers, AH, AL, BH, BL, and so on, cannot be saved on the stack as such; the entire one-word register must be pushed. Figure 2.6 illustrates this process with a 16-byte stack.

You can see that when a program uses a stack, and most of them do, it is important to maintain SP by the push and pop instructions. Though SP can be used as an operand in some instructions, you should never change its contents directly.

The Base Pointer

The Base Pointer, or BP, is one of the registers that can be used in indirect addressing. Like SP, it is intended to point to locations within the stack. It is not used by the special stack-accessing instructions, so it's not automatically increased or decreased as is SP. BP is especially useful for accessing items that are in the stack, but not at the top.

The Index Registers

Operations that involve strings require the use of the index registers SI and DI. SI specifies the offset of the source of the data, and DI specifies the offset of the destination. SI and DI are also used as operands in other instructions and in indirect addressing.

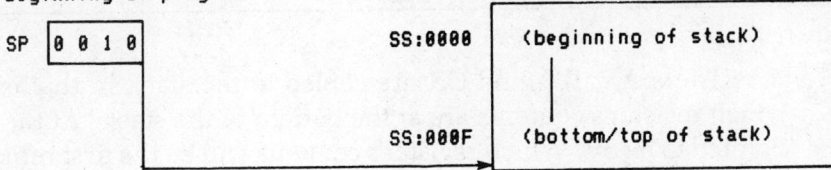

a) Beginning of program

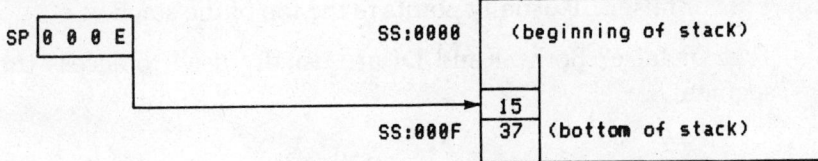

b) Push data

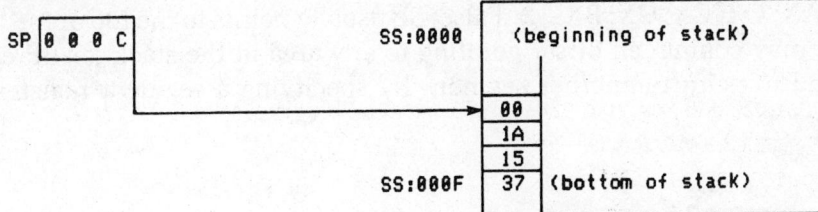

c) Push data

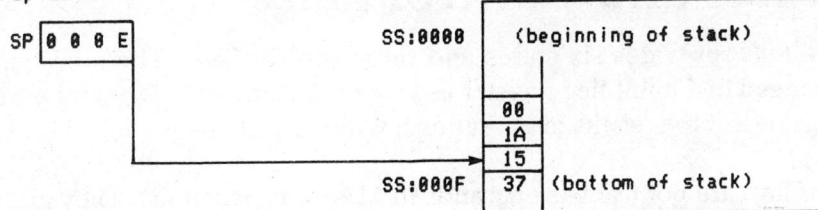

d) Pop data

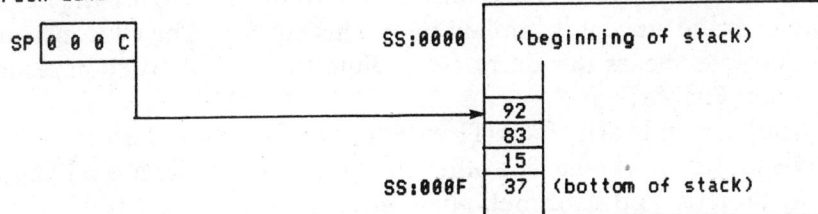

e) Push data

Figure 2.6 Using the Stack

Review Questions

1. If registers AX, BX, and CX are copied to the stack in that order, which register's contents are at the bottom of the stack? At the top? Pointed to by SP? Which register's contents will be the first removed from the stack? Then, to which register's contents will SP point?

2. True or false? BP usually points to the top of the stack.

3. True or false? Both SI and DI are usually used to access the data segment.

Answers

1. AX; CX; CX; CX; BX   **2.** False; SP usually points to the top of the stack. BP may contain an offset pointing to any area in the stack, or BP can be used to point to another segment by specifying a segment register.   **3.** True

Status and Control Flags

The 8088 provides six status and three control flags. The nine flags are arranged in a 16-bit flag register as shown in Figure 2.7. Remember: status flags reflect the results of operations, while control flags control the operations.

Flags are not used as operands in MASM instructions. They are, however, affected and tested by instructions. Special instructions are used to set and clear some flags. These instructions don't need to use the flag name as an operand since it is implied by the instruction. The CLC instruction, for example, clears the Carry flag, while the CLI instruction clears the Interrupt Enable flag.

The Trap and Parity flags (TF and PF) have specialized uses that will not be covered in this book. The other status flags generally are set or cleared by arithmetic and arithmetic-like instructions (comparison, shift and rotate, and logical). We'll discuss each of these status flags and, then, the other two control flags. As you follow this discussion, remember that a flag is set when its value is 1 and cleared when its value is 0.

				OF	DF	IF	TF	SF	ZF		AF		PF		CF

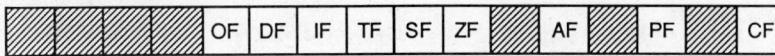

```
OF: Overflow           (Status)

DF: Direction          (Control)

IF: Interrupt Enable   (Control)

TF: Trap               (Control)

SF: Sign               (Status)

ZF: Zero               (Status)

AF: Auxiliary Carry    (Status)

PF: Parity             (Status)

CF: Carry              (Status)
```

UNMARKED BITS IN THE FLAG REGISTER ARE NOT USED

THEY ALWAYS CONTAIN ZERO

Figure 2.7 The Flag Register

The Carry Flag

The Carry flag (CF) is a status flag that reflects the size of an operation result. CF is set when the result field cannot hold the result, as when an add operation produces a carry or a subtraction ends with a borrow. Otherwise, CF is cleared. There are also specific instructions that set and clear CF.

CF not only reflects operation results, it is also used in some operations. If you are adding a two-byte number, for example, any possible carry from the first byte sum must be included when adding the second set of bytes. Special arithmetic instructions include CF's value in their operation.

CF can be tested by conditional jump instructions provided for that purpose. One instruction causes a transfer of control if the carry flag is set; another causes such a transfer only if CF is cleared.

The Auxiliary Carry Flag

AF, the Auxiliary Carry flag, is similar to CF, except it reflects the status from the low-order half-byte of an operation. AF is used by instructions that handle binary-coded decimal arithmetic since BCDs have one digit per half-byte. There are no special instructions that set, clear, or test AF.

The Zero Flag

The Zero flag, ZF, is a status flag that is set when the result of an operation is zero and, cleared when the result is not zero. Notice that this means ZF is 1 when the result is 0, but ZF is 0 when the result is nonzero. There are no special instructions to set and clear ZF, but there are conditional jump instructions that test its value.

The Sign Flag

The Sign flag, SF, is a status flag that is set when operations produce a negative result and is cleared when the result is positive. (Remember that 0 is a positive number). In other words, SF always reflects the high-order bit of the result of an operation; the flag is meaningful only if the operation involves signed numbers. There are conditional jump instructions that test SF, but no special instructions to set or clear it.

The Overflow Flag

The Overflow flag, OF, is a status flag that identifies a result that does not fit in a signed field. In general, if OF is set, it means that an operation result overflowed into the sign bit. Like SF, the value of OF is not significant after operations that do not involve signed numbers. There are jump instructions that test OF, but no special instructions to set or clear it.

The Interrupt Enable Flag

IF, the Interrupt Enable flag, is a control flag. It is set or cleared by special instructions. When IF is set, the 8088 recognizes signals from external devices such as the keyboard and the printer and handles requests for service from these devices. Such requests are called **external interrupts**; the operation of the currently running program must be interrupted to service the request. When IF is cleared, the 8088 ignores such requests. This book does not deal with external interrupts in any detail. The beginning programmer will do better to leave such matters to the operating system's preprogrammed routines.

The Direction Flag

The Direction flag, DF, is a control flag that determines the direction of string operations. When DF is cleared, a string operation starts with the lowest address and progresses to higher ones; in other words, the leftmost characters are processed first. If the entire string is not used, the characters on the far right are the ones that are left out. When DF is set, operations move in the opposite direction. The characters on the left are skipped if the full string is not handled. You will see an example of string operations in the program in the next chapter.

Saving the Flags

The flag register is usually not accessed as a whole. There are, however, two instructions that do handle the entire register. These instructions push and pop the flag register. There is no way to save or restore individual flags using the stack.

Review Questions

Match each flag name with applicable phrases from the list on the right. Some flags will match more than one phrase. Not all phrases are used. Some may be used more than once.

___ 1. CF
___ 2. AF
___ 3. ZF
___ 4. SF
___ 5. OF
___ 6. IF
___ 7. DF

A. used only in BCD arithmetic
B. set when result is zero
C. controls direction of string operation
D. cleared when subtraction doesn't result in borrow
E. set when signed result is too large
F. ends program if result is too large
G. set to allow interrupts
H. set when carry results from addition
I. set when result is negative

Answers

1. D, H   2. A, D, H   3. B   4. I   5. E   6. G   7. C (F is not used)

Using System I/O Routines

Input and output can be the most complicated part of assembly language programming. Each output device, such as a printer or CRT, is accessed through a particular location known as its port. A character to be output is written to the port and picked up from there by the output device. An input device, such as a keyboard, has a similar port where it places a byte of data to be read by the computer.

Printing a character may require several steps, such as checking a status address to see if the printer is ready to receive output, moving the character to be output into a register, and sending the contents of the register to the correct port. To print a string of characters, this process must be repeated for each one. Input from a keyboard requires similar procedures. Input and output to disk files can be extremely complicated.

Fortunately, the IBM PC operating systems have I/O routines already programmed that can be used by the assembler programmer. To use an I/O device, code an interrupt (INT) instruction that transfers control to one of these preprogrammed routines. Your program looks at one of the system's special purpose memory areas and there finds the address of the preprogrammed routine to which it transfers control. These I/O addresses in the reserved area are called **interrupt vectors**. They are also used to transfer control to the proper instructions when an external interrupt occurs.

BIOS and DOS

The IBM PC uses two operating system programs at once. One of these is BIOS, the Basic Input/Output System. BIOS is built into the computer and cannot change. The interrupt vectors are part of BIOS. Many of them transfer control to BIOS routines, which handle such basic operations as putting one character on the screen, checking to see if the printer is ready to receive data, and so on.

The second operating system is a program that is loaded, usually from disk, when the computer is turned on. We will assume that you are using some version of DOS for this purpose, but other operating systems are available. DOS does not replace BIOS, but supplements it. Some of the interrupt vectors point to locations that contain DOS I/O routines. These may be more complex than the BIOS routines, performing functions that would require several BIOS interrupts. One interrupt in DOS 2.0 (interrupt 21H) has 87 different functions. They include disk file handling and printer, CRT, and keyboard functions. Some of these are duplicates of functions available with non-DOS BIOS interrupts.

IBM recommends using the DOS functions rather than BIOS for your program's I/O. We will follow this recommendation when possible. However, there are some things that cannot be handled through DOS, but must use BIOS routines.

Review Questions

Which of the following are true?

1. Preprogrammed I/O routines are part of the 8088's instruction set.

2. An interrupt vector points to a preprogrammed routine.

3. DOS routines are available for disk I/O only.

4. IBM recommends using DOS rather than BIOS routines when possible.

Answers

2. and **4.** are true. Here's what's wrong with the others: **1.** The preprogrammed I/O routines are part of the operating system. **3.** DOS routines are available for disk, printer, CRT, and keyboard I/O.

Key Points From Chapter 2

Chapter 2 has presented information that will be used in every program you write. Some of the main points covered in the chapter are:

- ■ The 8088 has 12 16-bit registers.

- ■ Instructions use registers as operands, for indirect addressing, and by implication.

- ■ The effective address (EA) for an operand is computed when the instruction is executed by adding the current contents of the indirect registers to the original operand address.

- ■ The 8088 processes data in units of one byte (8 bits) or one word (16 bits).

- ■ The general-purpose registers are AX (accumulator), BX (base register), CX (count register), and DX (data register).

- ■ Each general-purpose register can also be treated as two 8-bit registers. The high-order byte registers are AH, BH, CH, and DH; the low-order byte registers are AL, BL, CL, and DL. Instructions can access each of the one-byte registers separately.

- ■ A 20-bit address can be represented as a segment number and an offset, using the form "segment:offset." To compute an address from this form, multiply the segment number by 10H and add the offset to it.

■ A program may contain four segments. The code segment contains the object-code instructions. The stack segment contains the stack, an area in which register contents can be saved. The data segment contains the data fields for the program. The extra segment is an alternate data area, but it usually coincides with the data segment.

■ The segment registers, CS, SS, DS, and ES, contain the segment numbers of the code, stack, data, and extra segments, respectively.

■ The pointer registers, SP (stack pointer) and BP (base pointer), point to locations within the stack segment unless otherwise specified.

■ The stack's highest address is the bottom of the stack. The top of the stack is the location to which the SP (stack-pointer register) currently points.

■ When a word is pushed on the stack, SP is decreased by two and the word is copied to the resulting stack offset. When a word is popped from the stack, the word pointed to by SP is copied to the destination, and SP is then increased by two.

■ The index registers, SI (source index) and DI (destination index), point to locations within the data segment, unless otherwise specified.

■ BX, BP, SI, and DI are the registers that can be used for indirect addressing.

■ The 8088 provides six status and three control flags placed in a 16-bit flag register.

■ The Carry, Auxiliary Carry, Sign, Zero, and Overflow flags reflect the results of an arithmetic or arithmetic-like operation. These include comparisons, shift and rotate instructions, and logical instructions.

■ The Carry flag (CF) reflects the size of an operation's result. CF is set when the result doesn't fit the field provided, as when a carry or borrow occurs and is cleared when the result does fit.

■ The Auxiliary Carry flag (AF) is similar to CF, but reflects the status at the half-byte position of an arithmetic operation. It is meaningful only in BCD arithmetic.

■ The Zero flag (ZF) is set when the result of an operation is 0 and is cleared when the result is not 0.

■ The Sign flag (SF) reflects the high-order bit of an operation's result. This is meaningful in signed arithmetic, where a set SF indicates a negative result, and a cleared SF, a positive result.

■ The Overflow flag (OF) is meaningful in signed arithmetic, where OF is set if the result will not fit in the result field and is cleared if the result does fit.

■ The Interrupt Enable flag (IF) is set to allow the processor to handle requests for service from external devices and is cleared when such interrupts should be ignored.

■ The Direction flag (DF) is set to indicate that string operations are to proceed from right to left and is cleared to indicate the reverse.

■ A program can use the interrupt vectors to transfer control to pre-programmed BIOS and DOS I/O routines.

The chapter review questions that follow will help you to make sure that you understand these points.

Chapter Review Questions

1. How many registers does the 8088 provide for program use? What size is each register (in bits)?

2. Name three ways an instruction may use a register.

3. True or false? The effective address for an operand is computed by the assembler.

4. How long (in bits) is an 8088 word?

5. Name the 16-bit general-purpose registers.

6. Name the high-order byte of the accumulator: The low-order byte of the count register: The one-word base register: The high-order byte of the data register:

7. What address is represented by 3017:000A? by 3015:002A? by 3010:017A?

8. What does the code segment contain? What register points to the code segment?

9. Name two segment registers that often point to the same area.

10. A stack segment begins at 1250:0000. Its last byte is at offset 0100H. SP contains 0052H.

    A.   Where is the top of the stack?

    B.   Where is the bottom of the stack?

    C.   What segment number is in SS?

11. The value 3445H is placed on the stack described in the preceding question.

    A.   Where will the first byte (34) go? (Give the offset within the stack segment.)

    B.   Where will the second byte (45) go?

    C.   What value will SP contain after this operation?

12. To which segment is BP assumed to point? SI? DI?

13. Which of the following are true?

    A.   ZF is cleared when an operation results in zero.

    B.   CF is set when a subtraction requires a borrow.

    C.   AF is set when an addition produces a carry from the half-byte position.

    D.   SF is set to indicate a zero result from signed arithmetic.

    E.   OF is cleared to indicate a positive result from signed arithmetic.

    F.   DF is cleared when string operations are to move from left to right.

    G.   IF is cleared to handle interruptions from external devices.

14. How does your program find the addresses of the operation systems I/O routines?

Answers

1. 12; 16 bits   **2.** as an operand; for indirect addressing; by implication   **3.** False; the EA is computed when the program is executed.   **4.** 16 bits   **5.** AX, BX, CX, DX   **6.** AH; CL; BX; DH   **7.** 3017AH; 3017AH; 3027AH   **8.** the program's object-code instructions; CS   **9.** DS, ES   **10.** A. 1250:0052 B. 1250:0100 C.1250   **11.** A. 0050H B. 0051H C. 0050H   **12.** SS ; DS; DS   **13.** B, C, and F are true. Here's what's wrong with the others: A. ZF is set when an operation results in zero. D. SF is set to indicate a negative result in signed arithmetic. E. OF is cleared to indicate that a signed arithmetic result is not too large. F. IF is cleared to cause external-device interrupts to be ignored. **14.** Through an interrupt vector.

3

Beginning to Program

This chapter presents a sample program in MASM. You'll examine the program in detail. First, though, you'll learn the format of MASM source-code lines. Then, you'll learn instructions to define segments and subroutines, to end a program, and to define data areas.

As you look at the sample program, you'll learn to move data in single bytes and strings, call and return from subroutines, save and restore register contents using the stack, and use interrupt routines for screen displays and keyboard input. You'll also learn to program loops with a definite number of repetitions. By the time you finish this chapter, you will know many commonly used MASM instructions, as well as the structure of MASM's programs and source-code lines, and you will be ready to write your first program.

Before you begin, you should know that this book is not going to teach you everything about each MASM instruction. It will explain instructions as they are used in the programs, sometimes indicating possible variations. Generally, it will prepare you to use the MASM manual to find out more about MASM and its instructions. Chapter 8 deals specifically with interpretation of the MASM manual.

A BASIC Program and a MASM Program

Figure 3.1 contains a BASIC program that prompts for a name and then prints a message that includes the name five times. Not a very complicated program, is it? Figure 3.12, at the end of this chapter, shows a MASM program that does the same thing. (Just glance at it now; don't try to figure it out.) You can see that the MASM program is a lot longer and seems more complex than the BASIC program.

```
10  INPUT "WHAT'S YOUR NAME";ANAME$
20  FOR N = 1 TO 5
30  PRINT "HELLO ";ANAME$
40  NEXT
50  END
```

Figure 3.1 NAMEX in BASIC

Computer Exercise

You can test the BASIC program: load BASIC and enter and run the program from Figure 3.1. If you wish, you can also use an editor or word processing program to type in the program in Figure 3.12 (NAMEX.ASM). You will be able to test the program after you learn to assemble, link, and run MASM programs.

Source-Code Line Format

Before we discuss the format of the whole program, let's look at the individual lines. Figure 3.2 shows part of the NAMEX program. Line numbers are provided for this discussion; they are not part of the program. Three dots represent missing code. Lines 1, 5, and 8, for example, each indicate one or more omitted lines.

The general format for a source-code line is:

```
name  operation_code  operands  ;comment
```

```
 1                        . . .
 2     INBUF            DB      255
 3     INCOUNT          DB      ?
 4     INNAME           DB      255 DUP(' ')
 5                        . . .
 6     ;
 7     PROG_CODE SEGMENT 'CODE'
 8              . . .
 9              PUSH    DS               ;SAVE DATA ON STACK
10              MOV     AX,0             ;     TO BE USED FOR RETURN TO
11              PUSH    AX               ;     SYSTEM WHEN PROGRAM ENDS
12              . . .
13     PRINTLOOP:
14              . . .
15              RET                      ;THEN RETURN TO OPERATING SYSTEM
16              . . .
 a
```

Figure 3.2 Source Code Line Format

The entries must be in the order shown and must be separated by at least one blank or tab. The line does not have to begin in column 1, but it cannot go past column 132. The assembler will ignore anything in columns past 132. In this instruction:

MOVER   MOV CL , INCOUNT   ; SET OUTPUT CONTROL

the name is MOVER, the operation code is MOV, CL and INCOUNT are the operands, and ;SET OUTPUT CONTROL is a comment. Let's look at each field in more detail.

The Name Field

Name is usually optional. It may contain up to 31 characters selected from uppercase letters, numeric digits, and the five special characters ? . @ __ and $. If you enter your program with lowercase letters, the assembler will convert them to uppercase. This means that **ENTRY**, **entry**, and **EnTry** are all the same name in a MASM program.

A name must start with a letter or special character, not a digit. A period that is included in a name must be the first character. Notice that a name *cannot* include a space, a hyphen, or an internal period. An underscore is frequently used to make compound names more readable (for example: PROG__CODE in line 7). Lines 2, 3, 4, 7, and 13 include the names INBUF, INCOUNT, INNAME, PROG__CODE, and PRINTLOOP, respectively.

Later in the chapter, we'll discuss how names are used by the assembler.

The Operation Code

The operation code, or opcode, is a mnemonic representing an 8088 operation code or an assembler-directing pseudo-op. Lines 2, 3, and 7 contain pseudo-op opcodes (DB and SEGMENT). 8088 mnemonic opcodes include PUSH in lines 9 and 11, MOV in line 10, and RET in line 15.

The Operands

The requirements for the operand field depend on the opcode. Some opcodes, such as RET in line 15, require no operands. Some, such as PUSH in lines 9 and 11, require one operand. Others, such as MOV in line 10, require two operands separated by a comma.

In the instruction set for our hypothetical machine TABLET, you saw registers and addresses used as operands. In MASM, there is a third type of operand called **immediate data**. Immediate data is a value coded directly in the instruction. These two instructions both use immediate data as the second operand:

```
MOV     AL,0
MOV     BH,'C'
```

The first instruction moves the value 0 to AL; the second moves 67, the ASCII code value for C, into BH. The maximum immediate data value is 0FFFFH, the maximum for one word of data.

Pseudo-ops, such as DB or SEGMENT, use the operand field to furnish additional or optional information used by the assembler in carrying out the instruction. The operands specified with DB in line 4, for example, tell the assembler to reserve 255 bytes initialized with blanks.

The Comment Field

The comment field is always optional. If included, it must begin with a semicolon (;). Comments, like remarks in a BASIC program, are used to document the programmer's intentions. Many comments have been included in NAMEX. In Figure 3.2, comments appear in lines 9, 10, and 11. Comments can be very helpful when you return to a program written some time ago or when someone else reads your program. If you have been programming in BASIC or any other language, you probably have already learned the value of good remarks or comments.

Source Code and Machine Code

As you know, the assembler translates source code to machine-code instructions that include operation codes and operands. Names are not directly translated into machine code. The assembler assigns a value to each name. In most cases, that value is the offset of the instruction that includes the name in its name field. (You'll learn an exception when you learn the EQU pseudo-op in Chapter 6.) When a name occurs as an operand, the assembler substitutes the assigned value for the name.

Comments are not translated into machine code at all. Neither are pseudo-ops, although they may affect the machine code. The DB instructions in lines 2 and 3 of Figure 3.2, for example, each reserve one byte in the machine code's data segment. The first of these bytes is initialized with the value 255 (0FFH), the highest value that will fit into one byte.

Review Questions

1. Name the four parts of a source-code line in the order in which they must appear.

2. True or False? The operand field for an 8088 instruction always contains two operands.

3. Which of these names are valid?

    A. NEW ITEM

    B. CUSTOMER_NAM

    C. 2ND_LINE

    D. LINE2

4. In this instruction

    MOV DI , 3

    What are the operands? What type of operand is the first one? What type is the second?

5. What character identifies the beginning of a comment or a comment line?

Answers

1. Name field, operation code, operand field, comment   2. False; the operand field may contain zero, one, or two operands. The number of operands required depends upon the instruction's opcode.   3. B, D. A is invalid because it includes a space; C, because it starts with a numeric digit.   4. DI and 3; register; immediate data   5. A semicolon (;)

The Framework of a Program

The beginning and end of each program segment are defined by pseudo-ops. The code segment is made up of one or more **procedures**, and the beginning and end of each procedure are also defined by pseudo-ops. Another pseudo-op identifies the end of the program. In Figure 3.3, these pseudo-ops are numbered for the discussion that follows.

```
     . . .
 1 PROG_STACK SEGMENT STACK 'STACK'
            DB    64 DUP ('STACK    ')
 2 PROG_STACK ENDS
   ;
 3 PROG_DATA SEGMENT 'DATA'
     . . .
 4 PROG_DATA   ENDS
   ;
 5 PROG_CODE        SEGMENT 'CODE'
 6 MAIN_PROG        PROC    FAR
        ASSUME CS:PROG_CODE,DS:PROG_DATA,SS:PROG_STACK,ES:PROG_DATA
        PUSH   DS                        ;SAVE DATA ON STACK
        MOV    AX,0                      ;     TO BE USED FOR RETURN TO
        PUSH   AX                        ;     SYSTEM WHEN PROGRAM ENDS
        MOV    AX,PROG_DATA              ;INITIALIZE DS
        MOV    DS,AX
        MOV    ES,AX                     ;     AND    ES
        . . .
        CALL   PROMPTER                  ;PROMPT FOR NAME
        . . .
        RET                              ;THEN RETURN TO OPERATING SYSTEM
 7 MAIN_PROG ENDP
     . . .
 8 PROMPTER PROC
     . . .
 9 PROMPTER ENDP
     . . .
10 PROG_CODE ENDS
            END   MAIN_PROG
```

Figure 3.3 Program Framework

Identifying Segments

Every program includes a code segment; most programs also include a stack segment and at least one data segment. The beginning and end of each segment must be identified by specific instructions.

The Beginning of a Segment   The SEGMENT pseudo-op (lines 1, 3, and 5) identifies the beginning of a segment. Its format is:

```
segname  SEGMENT  [combine-type]  [align-type]  ['class']
```

Brackets indicate an optional entry. Note that the segment name is required. In NAMEX, the stack, data, and code segments are named PROG__STACK, PROG__DATA, and PROG__CODE, respectively.

The three optional entries pass instructions to the linker to help determine where and how the segment is loaded when the program is run. Combine-type indicates how the segment is combined with segments from other programs already in the system at run time. A stack segment requires STACK for its combine-type (line 1). This segment will be combined with other stack segments, such as the one used by the operating system when the run file is loaded. The data and code segments in NAMEX have no combine-type; they will not be combined with segments from other programs.

Align-type indicates the type of boundary on which the segment should begin. If no align-type is given, the segment will be aligned on a paragraph boundary (an address divisible by 10H). In the programs in this book, all segments are aligned on paragraph boundaries, so align-type is never specified.

Class, enclosed in single quotes, identifies a segment type. When a run file is made up of several object modules, segments of the same class are grouped together by the linker. NAMEX includes segments of class STACK, DATA, and CODE. We will not use multiple-module programs in this book, so we use the class entry primarily for documentation. You may omit the class entry in your segment definitions if you prefer.

The End of a Segment   Each segment must end with a ENDS pseudo-op. The format is:

```
segname  ENDS
```

The segment name is required; it must match the name in the SEGMENT instruction that begins the segment. There are no operands for this instruction. Lines 2, 4, and 10 in Figure 3.3 contain ENDS instructions for NAMEX's stack, data, and code segments.

Identifying Procedures

A program's code segment is divided into blocks called procedures. Every program includes at least one procedure. Usually, we code programs with one main procedure and several secondary ones. Our main procedure is a **driver**, a routine that may do very little except to start the program, call subroutines, and end the program. This driver, then, can provide an outline of the program. Each of the other procedures is called as a subroutine and carries out a specific function. If the procedure's function is lengthy or complicated, such as "print a report," it may in turn call other procedures to carry out such subfunctions as "print a heading," "move data to a print line," or "convert a number to a printable format." The "print the report" procedure, then, may be considered a driver for the report-printing function. Dividing a program into short procedures that perform easily definable functions makes the program easier to code, debug, and modify. It also makes it easier to build a new program using procedures copied from existing programs.

Beginning a Procedure   Each procedure must begin with a PROC pseudo-op instruction, similar to those shown in lines 6 and 8 of Figure 3.3. The format of the instruction is:

```
procname   PROC  [type]
```

A name is required for every PROC. The procedure type may be NEAR or FAR; NEAR is the default if no type is specified (see line 8). NEAR defines a procedure that can be called only from within its own code segment. FAR defines a procedure that can be called from other code segments. The procedure containing the first instructions executed in a program must be FAR, as in line 6, since it will be called from another program's code segment. Usually, the other program is DOS. In most programs all procedures except the first one are NEAR.

Ending a Procedure   Each procedure ends with an ENDP instruction, as in lines 7 and 9 of Figure 3.3. The format of the instruction is:

```
procname   ENDP
```

The name must be the same as the one in the PROC pseudo-op that began the procedure.

Ending the Program

Each program ends with an END pseudo-op (line 11 of Figure 3.3). The format is:

END [expression]

where the optional expression gives the program's starting address, the location of the first instruction to be executed. This address is passed to the linker and becomes a permanent part of the run file. Usually, the name of the main procedure is the starting address in the END instruction.

What About Variations?

Most programs in this book include three segments defined as they are in NAMEX. Generally, the code segment is made up of several procedures; however, it is possible to define a procedure to include several code segments. When you are an experienced MASM programmer, you may want to refer to the MASM manual to code programs with complex segment definitions.

Procedures need not be subroutines called from other procedures. You can transfer control from one procedure to another with no intention of returning to the original (as with a BASIC GOTO instead of GOSUB). You can also use procedures to divide your source code into sequential blocks, letting control fall through from one procedure to the next. In our programs, however, we always use procedures as subroutines. In fact, we sometimes use the words interchangeably.

Review Questions

1. Match each opcode with its description. Not all the descriptions are used.

```
___ A.  SEGMENT        a.  Ends a procedure
___ B.  ENDS           b.  Ends a program
___ C.  PROC           c.  Begins a program
___ D.  ENDP           d.  Begins a segment
___ E.  END            e.  Ends a segment
                       f.  Begins a procedure
```

2. What is wrong with each of these instructions or combinations of instructions? How can each be corrected?

  A. STACK__SEG SEGMENT 'STACK'

  B. DATA__SEG SEG

  C. SEGMENT 'CODE'

  D. MY__DATA SEGMENT 'DATA'

      ...

     ENDS

  E. MAIN__PROC PROC FAR

     ...

     END MAIN__PROC

    MAIN__PROC ENDP

Answers

1. A. d B. e C. f D. a E. b, c is not used   2. A. A stack segment must indicate combine-type; insert STACK between SEGMENT and 'STACK' B. The pseudo-op should be SEGMENT, not SEG. C. A segment name is required; add a name such as MY__CODE before SEGMENT D. The segment name must be repeated on the ENDS instruction; add MY__DATA before ENDS E. END must be the last instruction in the program. Move it to the last line of the program.

Defining Data

Figure 3.4 shows another part of NAMEX with line numbers added. Lines 1, 2, 3, 4, and 5 illustrate the DB (Define Byte) instruction used to reserve and initialize a data field. Line 6 shows a data field name used as an operand.

Defining a Data Field

A data field is like a BASIC variable. In fact, it is often referred to as a variable in MASM as well. It is an area of memory reserved for data storage; the area's contents can be changed during program execution. Each data field must be defined before it is used. The definition tells the assembler how much memory to reserve and any initial data to put into the area. It may also assign a name to the beginning address of the data field.

```
            . . .
      PROG_STACK SEGMENT STACK 'STACK'
1                DB    64 DUP ('STACK    ')
      PROG_STACK ENDS
      ;
      PROG_DATA  SEGMENT 'DATA'
2     NAMEPROMPT DB    0AH,0DH,'WHAT IS YOUR NAME? ',24H
                 . . .
3     INBUF      DB    255
4     INCOUNT    DB    ?
5     INNAME     DB    255 DUP('  ')
      PROG_DATA  ENDS
                 . . .
6                MOV   CL,INCOUNT
                 . . .
```

Figure 3.4 Data Definitions

Several instructions can be used to define data fields. They are all pseudo-ops; they provide directions to the assembler, but they are not translated into 8088 instructions. DB is most commonly used. Its format is:

[variable-name] DB expression

The Data Field Name   A name is optional for a data field or variable definition. When one is provided, the assembler assigns it a value based on the address (segment number and offset) of the variable's first byte. Look at line 2 in Figure 3.4. The assembler will assign NAMEPROMPT a value of DS:0000 (offset 0 in the data segment).

Look at line 4. For the rest of the program, INCOUNT stands for the offset in the data segment of the field defined in line 4. In the actual assembly of NAMEX, that offset was 011FH, or 287. When the assembler translates line 6 into object code, it uses 011FH, INCOUNT's offset, as the second operand in the object instruction. When the instruction is executed at run time, the data to be moved comes from the address represented by DS:011F. Notice that the assembler uses the **value of** INCOUNT, which is its address. At run time, we are more often concerned with the **value in** INCOUNT, the data currently found at that address.

Initial Value   Compare lines 3 and 4 in Figure 3.4. Each reserves one byte. In line 4, the question mark means that no initial value is desired; INCOUNT'S initial value at run time is whatever happens to be there when the program is loaded. In line 3, the byte at INBUF is initialized with the value 255, the largest unsigned value that can be contained in one byte. The initial value could have been written in hexadecimal, as 0FFH, or in binary, as 11111111B. All three forms represent the same value and produce the same effect as far as the computer is concerned. It's up to you to decide which form you prefer to use in the source code.

Look at line 2. The DB instruction in this line reserves and initializes 22 bytes. The initial value begins with two single-byte numbers (0AH and 0DH), which are followed by a string of 19 ASCII characters and, then, by another single-byte number (24H). We intend to use the string that starts at NAMEPROMPT as a message displayed on the screen. 0AH and 0DH are cursor control characters: line feed (LF) and carriage return (CR), respectively. 24H is the ASCII representation for "$". The screen display routine we use in this program expects this character to mark the displayed string's end. For convenience, we may speak of NAMEPROMPT as a 22-byte field. As an operand, however, NAMEPROMPT refers only to the byte at offset 0000, a byte that initially contains 0AH.

Figure 3.5 shows a portion of the data segment with its initial values. Values are shown in hexadecimal; the actual values would be binary. Where appropriate, the ASCII interpretation of the values are also shown. No value is shown for INCOUNT. The definition does not include an initial value, so there is no way to tell what value would be there when the program begins.

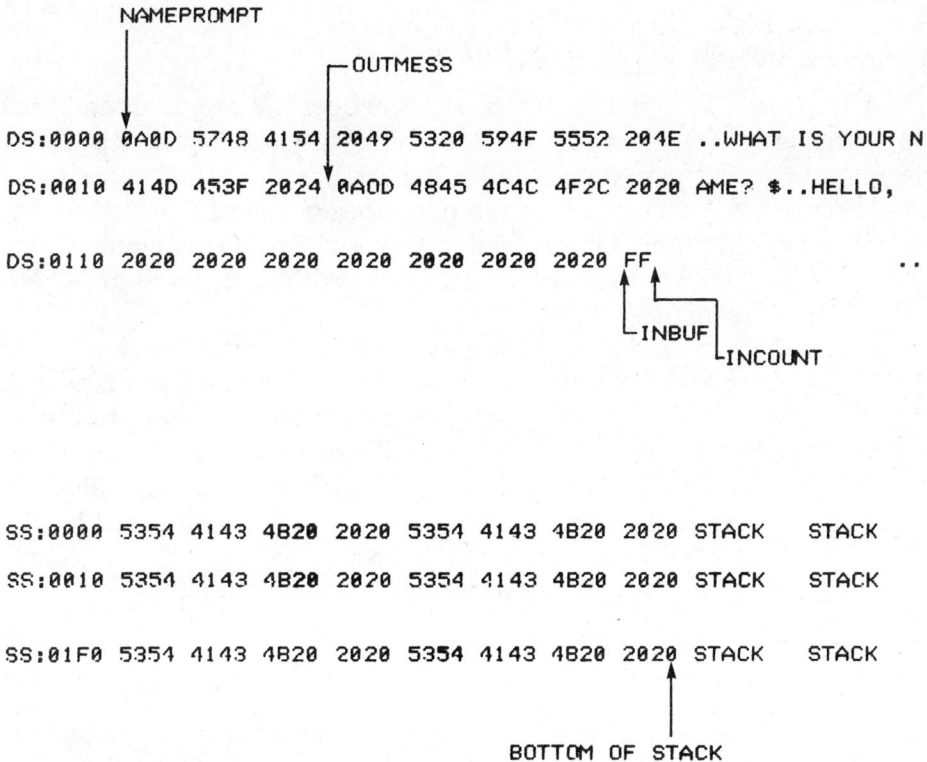

```
              NAMEPROMPT

                         ─OUTMESS

DS:0000 0A0D 5748 4154│2049 5320 594F 5552 204E  ..WHAT IS YOUR N
DS:0010 414D 453F 2024'0A0D 4845 4C4C 4F2C 2020  AME? $..HELLO,

DS:0110 2020 2020 2020 2020 2020 2020 2020 FF               ..
                                              └INBUF
                                                 └INCOUNT


SS:0000 5354 4143 4B20 2020 5354 4143 4B20 2020 STACK    STACK
SS:0010 5354 4143 4B20 2020 5354 4143 4B20 2020 STACK    STACK

SS:01F0 5354 4143 4B20 2020 5354 4143 4B20 2020 STACK    STACK

                         BOTTOM OF STACK
```

Figure 3.5 Initialized Data and Stack Segments

Note that line 2 in Figure 3.4 combines two methods of initializing multiple bytes. When ASCII characters are used in an initial value, they may be written as a string enclosed in either single or double quotes. Both ASCII characters and numeric values can also be written as a series of individual values separated by commas. The number of bytes reserved and initialized by one DB definition is limited only by the fact that the entire instruction must fit in a 132-character line. Line 2 could be written like this:

```
NAMEPROMPT DB 0AH,0DH,'WHAT ','IS ','YOUR ','NAME? ',24H
```

or like this:

```
NAMEPROMPT DB 10,13,'WHAT IS ','YOUR NAME? ','$'
```

or in many other ways. Initializing with numbers is not quite as flexible as with ASCII characters. To initialize a field with numbers from 1 to 10, you must separate the values:

```
ONE_TO_TEN DB 1,2,3,4,5,6,7,8,9,10
```

Duplication   In line 5, unlike line 2, 255 does not represent an initial value. Instead, it represents a number of duplications as indicated by DUP. The expression in parentheses following DUP is the initial value to be duplicated. A question mark in the parentheses means that no specific initial value is required. Line 5, then, reserves 255 bytes of memory, each byte initialized with a blank. When used as an address operand, INNAME refers to the first of these bytes.

Look at line 1. This instruction repeats an eight-byte initial value 64 times, reserving a total of 512 bytes. Notice that this area is a reserved area in the stack segment, not the data segment. It's not necessary to put an initial value in the stack, but later you will see that it can be useful for debugging. Figure 3.5 shows part of the initialized stack area also. It's difficult to predict exactly how much stack space a program needs, but 512 bytes is adequate for the programs in this book.

Duplications can be nested if necessary. This definition:

```
DATATABLE DB 100 DUP(20 DUP(' '),10 DUP(0))
```

reserves 3,000 bytes. The first 20 bytes are initialized with blanks and the next 10 with zeros. This 30-byte pattern is repeated a total of 100 times to reserve and intialize the entire 3,000 bytes.

Other Data Field Definitions

Other data-definition pseudo-ops reserve and initialize data in words(DW), doublewords(DD), quadruple words(DQ), or groups of ten bytes(DT). You will learn about the DW pseudo-op in Chapter 8 of this book.

Review Questions

1. Which statements are true?

   A. The DB pseudo-op can reserve more than one byte of storage.

   B. When a data field name is used as an operand, the assembler replaces the name with the initial value of the field.

   C. The instruction DB 100 DUP('X') reserves 100 bytes, initializing the first one with 'X'. No initial value is defined for the other 99 bytes.

   D. The instruction DB ? reserves one byte, but does not define an initial value for it.

2. Write an instruction to reserve seven bytes of uninitialized storage. Call the first byte SEVENTH.

3. Write an instruction to reserve a six-byte field initialized with the first six letters of the alphabet. Call the field BEGIN.

4. Write an instruction to reserve 150 bytes of storage initialized with spaces. Assign the name SPACES to the first byte.

5. Define a data field called EMESS containing the message "ERROR - TRY AGAIN " to be displayed on a CRT. Be sure that the message will be displayed at the beginning of a new line. (Don't forget the "$" to mark the end of the message.)

Answers

1. A and D. Here's what's wrong with the others: B. The assembler replaces the name with the data field's offset within the data segment. C. All 100 bytes are initialized with "X." **2.** SEVENTH DB 7 DUP(?) **3.** BEGIN DB 'ABCDEF' or BEGIN DB "ABCDEF" or BEGIN DB 'A','B','C','D','E','F'. You could have used several different combinations to code the initial string. **4.** SPACES DB 150 DUP(' ') **5.** EMESS 0AH,0DH,'ERROR - TRY AGAIN ',24H. You could have coded the numbers as decimals, or the end-of-text mark as '$'. You could have used double quotes instead of single. You could have broken the message string up in various ways.

Other Pseudo-Ops

You have learned pseudo-ops that define the beginning and ending of program segments and procedures and the end of the program, as well as ones that define data fields and constants. The NAMEX program also includes two other pseudo-ops, PAGE and ASSUME. Figure 3.6 illustrates how these instructions are used in NAMEX.

The PAGE Pseudo-Op

The PAGE pseudo-op sets the assembler listing's page length and width. Its format is:

PAGE [lines][,width]

Lines must be a number from 10 to 255; it indicates the number of lines per page for the printer on which the listing will be printed. The default value is 66. When the assembler produces the listing, it allows appropriate top and bottom margins within the lines-per-page indicated. In Line 1, we have allowed the lines-per-page for the NAMEX listing to default to 66.

Width indicates the number of characters per line. This may be a value between 60 and 132. The default value is 80. In Line 1, we have set the page width at 132 characters. The assembler listing includes both the generated object code and the source code for each instruction, so each line may be considerably longer than the corresponding source-code line. Setting the maximum page prints the listing without broken lines—if your printer can print a 132-character line. Note that the width is preceded by a comma even though the lines are not shown. If the comma was omitted, the assembler would give us a page with 132 lines and 80 columns.

```
1              PAGE     ,132
        ...
2              ASSUME   CS:PROG_CODE,DS:PROG_DATA,SS:PROG_STACK,ES:PROG_DATA
        ...
```

Figure 3.6 Other Pseudo-Ops

PAGE tells the assembler how to format pages; it does not send any command to the printer to set its width or change its type-face. Before printing the listing for NAMEX, we may need to set the printer to use compressed print. We may also need to use the DOS command MODE to set the printer width to 132 characters.

If you don't plan to print an assembler listing, you need not include PAGE in your source code, since PAGE affects only the assembler listing. PAGE has no effect on a listing of your source code file by a DOS command such as TYPE or PRINT, or by a word-processing or editor instruction.

The ASSUME Pseudo-Op

The ASSUME pseudo-op is required in every program. It must appear before the first instruction that will generate object code. In Figure 3.6, you can see that ASSUME (line 2) appears as the first instruction in the code segment; this is its usual position in our programs. In fact, it could be moved to precede the first PROC instruction.

ASSUME tells the assembler which segment's address will be in each segment register at run time. The assembler needs this information to generate addresses correctly. You might think that the assembler would assume that CS should contain the address of the program's only code segment along with DS, the data segment, and SS, the stack segment. But it cannot. I have not seen any fully satisfactory explanation of this require-ment, but it is a requirement. You must include an ASSUME statement in the code segment of every program you write.

The format of the pseudo-op is:

ASSUME seg-reg:seg-name[,seg-reg:seg-name...]

where seg-reg may be CS, DS, ES, or SS. In line 2 of Figure 3.6, we tell the assembler that CS will contain the segment address of PROG__CODE; both DS and ES, the segment address of PROG__DATA; and SS, the segment address of PROG__STACK. Note that ASSUME does not place these addresses into the registers; that will be done at run time. It simply tells the assembler to generate object code based on the assumption that these addresses will be in the registers.

Review Questions

1. Match words with phrases. More than one description may apply. Some descriptions may be used more than once; some may not be used.

    ___ A. PAGE   a. Required instruction
    ___ B. ASSUME   b. CS, DS, ES, or SS
    ___ C. Seg-reg   c. Optional instruction
    ___ D. Lines   d. 0 through 100
    ___ E. Width   e. 10 through 255
                            f. 60 through 132
                            g. default value 80
                            h. default value 66

2. Write an instruction to format a listing with 55 lines per page and 96 characters per line.

3. Write an instruction to format a listing using the default value for lines per page and 64 characters per line.

4. The stack, data, and code segments in a program are named MY__STACK, MY__DATA, and MY__CODE respectively. The extra segment will be the same as the data segment. Write the ASSUME instruction for the program.

Answers

1. A. c B. a C. b D. e, h E. f, g; d is not used   2. PAGE 55,96   3. PAGE ,64 (Did you include the comma?)
4. ASSUME SS:MY__STACK,CS:MY__CODE,DS:MY__DATA,ES:MY__DATA
    You could have named the registers in another order, such as
ASSUME CS:MY__CODE,SS:MY__STACK,ES:MY__DATA,DS:MY__DATA

The Main Procedure

Now let's look at the real action in NAMEX—those instructions that will be translated into 8088 object code and carried out when the program is executed. We'll go through each of the five procedures. I'll explain each new instruction as we come to it and show you how instructions go together to make up the routines that carry out the program's functions.

Figure 3.7 shows part of NAMEX with the instructions in the main procedure, or the program driver, numbered for this discussion. The first part, lines 1 through 3, saves information needed to get back to the calling program (usually DOS). The next part, lines 4 through 6, puts appropriate addresses in the data and segment registers. These six lines must be included at the beginning of every program. The next part of the driver, lines 7 through 13, calls subroutines to carry out program functions. The final instruction, in line 14, returns control to the calling program.

Saving the Return Parameters

Now let's go back and look at each part of this procedure. Two words must be pushed onto the stack at the start of the program. These words contain information, or **parameters**, passed by the calling program. Together they point to the address where instructions can be found to return to that program. The first word must be the current contents of the DS register; the second must be a value of zero. When the program ends, the two top words on the stack are expected to contain these values. How do you put them on the stack? By using two PUSH instructions (lines 1 and 3) and one MOV (line 2).

The PUSH Instruction   PUSH points the stack pointer (SP) to a new top-of-stack location and then copies a one-word value to that location. PUSH requires one operand. The format of the instruction is:

PUSH source

PUSH, like any other 8088 instruction, may be preceded by a name or followed by a comment. We won't show these optional fields in formats.

```
              . . .
1             PUSH      DS                    ;SAVE DATA ON STACK
2             MOV       AX,0                  ;      TO BE USED FOR RETURN TO
3             PUSH      AX                    ;      SYSTEM WHEN PROGRAM ENDS
4             MOV       AX,PROG_DATA          ;INITIALIZE DS
5             MOV       DS,AX
6             MOV       ES,AX                 ;      AND    ES
7             CALL      PROMPTER              ;PROMPT FOR NAME
8             CALL      GETNAME               ;GET NAME INPUT
9             CALL      MOVENAME              ;MOVE NAME TO OUTPUT LINE
10            MOV       CX,5                  ;LOAD COUNTER FOR PRINTLOOP
11  PRINTLOOP:
12            CALL      PRINTNAME             ;PRINT NAME MESSAGE
13            LOOP      PRINTLOOP             ;      AND REPEAT CX TIMES
14            RET                             ;THEN RETURN TO OPERATING SYSTEM
              . . .
```

Figure 3.7 The NAMEX Driver

Any 16-bit register (AX, BX, CX, DX, SI, DI, BP, SP, CS, DS, ES, or SS) can be the source of the data to be placed on the stack. An address operand can also be a source; but, in NAMEX, only register contents are PUSHed. (Immediate data cannot be a source for PUSH; that's why it takes two steps to put the zero on the stack.) Saving register values is the most common use of PUSH. Later in the program we will run across the POP instruction, which is the converse of PUSH.

The MOV Instruction   MOV is a two-operand instruction. Its format is:

```
MOV destination,source
```

Data is copied from the location named in the second operand to the location named in the first operand. The source may be any of the three types of operand that can be used in 8088 instructions: register, address, or immediate data. The destination may be a register or an address. A few restrictions apply: data cannot be moved directly from one memory address to another; immediate data cannot be moved to any segment register; and CS cannot be the destination of a move, though it may be the source. The MOV in line 2 copies immediate data to a register: we'll discuss other types of MOVs as we encounter them.

MOV handles either a single byte or a single word. When immediate data is moved to a register, the size of the move depends on the destination. In line 2, the destination is a one-word register, so even though the immediate data value (0) can fit in one byte (8 bits) it is extended to 16 bits by the assembler. A similar instruction could be used to move a one-byte value to a one-byte register, as in:

```
MOV AH,125
```

However, this instruction:

```
MOV AH,300
```

would cause an error; 300 is too large for one byte. The immediate data value can be expressed in decimal, hexadecimal, or binary, or as an ASCII character.

Each of these instructions generates the same object code:

```
MOV AH, 36
MOV AH, 24H
MOV AH, 00100100B
MOV AH, '$'
```

It's up to you to code the immediate value in the way that will best remind you of the instruction's purpose.

The Return Parameters   Now let's look at what lines 1 through 3 accomplish. Your program begins running as a FAR procedure. When a FAR procedure ends, two words are taken from the stack to find the next instruction address. The first is used as an offset, the second as a segment number. When your program is called from another program and loaded into the computer, a special area called the Program Segment Prefix is built by the system and kept in memory as well. This prefix contains a series of instructions that restores the conditions needed for the calling program to resume operation properly. The segment number of the prefix's address is put into DS. Putting DS and zero onto the stack allows your program to end by transferring control to the beginning of the Program Segment Prefix.

Why not just put DS on the stack and assume the zero? Because the instruction that ends a program is the same as that which ends any FAR procedure. When ending a procedure that's not a program, the offset will not always be zero. So, both a segment number and an offset are always taken from the stack when a FAR procedure ends.

Setting the Segment Registers

The next three lines (4, 5, and 6) load the data and extra segment registers with the segment portion of the data segment's address for the current execution of the program. It's not necessary to load the code or stack segment registers; these are set properly when the program is loaded. You must, however, load DS at the beginning of every program. You must also load ES if your program uses the extra segment. Usually, you will want ES and DS to contain the same segment number.

MOVing to Segment Registers   In line 4, a segment name is used as a source for MOV. When you do this, the segment number is the value that's moved. Thus, line 4 loads AX with the data segment's segment number. In line 5, the contents of AX are moved to DS, and in line 6, to ES. Why not save a line of code and just move PROG__DATA directly to DS? Because a segment name is considered immediate data. Remember that immediate data cannot be moved to a segment register. Don't worry about this step too much. Just include it in each program.

Outlining the Program

Lines 7 through 14 control the execution of NAMEX's functions. Each CALL instruction, like a BASIC GOSUB, transfers control to another procedure, which ends by returning control to the instruction following the CALL. Line 7 CALLs PROMPTER. When PROMPTER ends, it transfers control to line 8. Line 8 CALLs GETNAME. When GETNAME ends, it transfers control to line 9, and so on. Lines 10 through 13 initialize and carry out a loop that is repeated five times, so that PRINTNAME is CALLed five times. Then line 14 ends the program.

CALL and RET   As we have said, CALL is equivalent to BASIC's GOSUB. Its format is:

CALL target

where target identifies the address to which control is to be transferred. In its simplest form, as used throughout NAMEX, the target is the name of a NEAR procedure. The address of the next instruction is copied from IP to the stack. Then, IP is loaded with the target procedure's offset so that the next instruction executed is the first instruction of the target procedure. This is a direct CALL to a NEAR procedure. Indirect CALLs and CALLs to FAR procedures are advanced techniques that you will probably not use until you have much more MASM experience.

Look again at Figure 3.12 at the end of the chapter. Now, look at the four procedures called from the driver. Notice that each one ends with RET. This is equivalent to BASIC's subroutine RETURN. When RET is executed from a NEAR procedure, the top word from the stack is copied to IP. This should be the offset placed on the top of the stack by the CALL that started the procedure. Any other data placed on the stack during the procedure must be removed so that the return offset will be at the top when RET is executed. The segment number for the return address is found in CS; a NEAR procedure is always called from and returns to the current code segment.

RET from a FAR Procedure.   The RET that ends the program in line 14 is a little different from the RETs just discussed, although it looks the same.

This is a RETurn from a FAR procedure. As you know, it takes two words for the top of the stack, the words PUSHed in lines 1 and 3. Any other data PUSHed onto the stack during the course of the program must be removed before this FAR RETurn is executed. You can learn more about FAR RETurns as well as other RET options in the MASM manual. For practical purposes, however, just remember to use:

RET

to end the execution of every procedure, NEAR or FAR.

A Simple Loop

Lines 10 through 13 constitute a simple loop. The number of repetitions is controlled by the value in CX. MOV in line 10 and CALL in line 12 are similar to instructions already discussed. Lines 11 and 13 present new concepts that we will discuss in more detail below.

Names Used as Labels   You have already learned that both data definitions and other instructions may be assigned names. A name assigned to an instruction in the code segment is called a **label**. MAIN__PROG, PRINTLOOP, GETNAME, MOVENAME, PRINTNAME, and PROMPTER are labels in NAMEX. INBUF, INCOUNT, OUTMESS, and other data names are not labels, but variable names.

Every label has a type, either NEAR or FAR. You have learned how to specify the type of a label used as a procedure name. Other labels, such as PRINTLOOP in line 11, are identified as NEAR by a colon (:) following the label definition. If a label is not a procedure name and is not followed by a colon, it is a FAR label and can be accessed from external code segments. When a FAR label is used as an operand, the assembler must include in the object code information about the code segment to which it belongs. When a NEAR label is used as an operand, no such information is necessary; the segment boundary for the operand is assumed to be the one in CS at the time the instruction is executed. Note in line 13 that the colon is not included when the label is used as an operand. Most of the labels you use will be NEAR labels.

Notice that PRINTLOOP is defined on a line by itself. It could have been defined as a name of the instruction on line 12, like this:

PRINTLOOP: CALL PRINTNAME

We prefer to define labels on separate lines for two reasons: it is easier to change, add, or remove the instruction following the label, and it is easier to line up operation codes on the page for legibility. Data names, segment names, and procedure names cannot be handled in this way; they must be included in the pseudo-op definition of the variable, segment, or procedure.

Some programmers stress the use of informative names for labels. This can be overdone. Use good descriptive names for data fields, segments, and procedures, and possibly for labels in the program driver. If you need to code a label within a procedure, you may find it simpler to use some logical coding scheme such as GET1, GET2, GET3, ...GETN for labels in a procedure called GETNAME. Use comments rather than names to document the purpose of the instructions. Logically coded rather than descriptive labels are easier to locate when you are changing or debugging a program.

The LOOP Instruction   LOOP has the format:

```
LOOP target
```

where target specifies a label to which control may be transferred. When LOOP is executed, the value in CX is **decremented** (decreased by 1). Then, control transfers to the target if CX does not equal zero. If CX does equal zero, control falls through to the next instruction.

Note that CX is always used to control the number of repetitions of the loop. Also, the instructions within the loop are always executed at least once, and CX is decremented, before any test of CX is made. This means that CX must contain a value of 1 or more before the loop begins. If CX contains 0 or less when the loop begins, it will never reach 0 and an endless loop will result.

The instructions within the loop should not change the value of CX. If you need to code a loop that may end before the defined number of repetitions, you can use one of the variations of LOOP that you will learn in later chapters. An example would be a loop that allows you to enter 20 names, but ends if you enter "END" as one of the names.

The target for the LOOP instruction must be NEAR. Furthermore, it must be within a range of −128 to +127 bytes of the LOOP instruction in the object code. Many control-transfer instructions require a label within this range, a **short-label**, for their target. How can you tell if the desired target is within the required range? There's no simple way since MASM instructions vary considerably in length. If the target is within 20–25 instructions of LOOP, it will probably be a short-label. If it isn't a short-label, the assembler will let you know. You can avoid the problem by employing the following technique used in lines 11 through 13: put the detailed instructions in a separate procedure so that only the CALL instruction separates LOOP from its target.

Review Questions

1. The driver for a program called SAMPLE contains four general functions. Number the functions in the order in which they should occur in the driver.

    A.   Return control to the calling program.

    B.   Save DS and a value of 0 on the stack.

    C.   Call the procedures that carry out the program functions.

    D.   Initialize DS and ES with the segment number for the program's data section.

2. Here are the first six instructions in SAMPLE's driver. What changes, if any, must be made to these instructions? (Assume that segment and data names are correct).

```
MOV     AX , 0
PUSH    AX
PUSH    DS
MOV     AX , SAMPLE_DATA
MOV     AX , ES
MOV     AX , DS
```

3. Which MOV instructions are valid for moving immediate data to a register?

    A.   MOV BH,' # '

    B.   MOV CL,50

    C.   MOV DH,0100B

    D.   MOV AH,110H

    E.   MOV AX,0FFFFH

4.   Which instructions will affect the stack pointer?

  A. CALL NEW__PRO

  B. RET

  C. PUSH DX

  D. MOV AX,25H

  E. MOV SP,0200H

5.   What does this routine do?

```
        MOV     CX , 10
DO1 :
        CALL    DISPLAYER
        LOOP    DO1
```

6.   Match each instruction with the appropriate description. Some of the descriptions may not be used.

___	A. MOV X,Y	a.	Return control to the calling procedure.
___	B. MOV Y,X	b.	Copy the contents of DX to the top of the
___	C. CALL A1		stack.
___	D. LOOP A1	c.	Copy data from X to Y.
___	E. PUSH DX	d.	Copy the word at the top of the stack to
___	F. RET		DX.
		e.	Copy data from Y to X.
		f.	Save the instruction address on the stack and transfer control to A1.
		g.	Subtract 1 from CX; if CX is not zero, transfer control to A1.

7.   Identify the type of each label (NEAR or FAR).

_____   A. HI__TIME MOV AX,5

_____   B. LO__TIME: MOV BX,10

_____   C. EVERY__TIME:

_____   D. PRINTIT PROC

8.   True or False? A short-label is a NEAR label that occurs within -128 to $+127$ bytes of the instruction for which it is a target.

Answers

1. A. 4 B. 1 C. 3 D.   **2.** PUSH DS must be moved so that it is the first instruction, not the third one. The operands are in the wrong order in the fifth and sixth instructions; they should be changed to ES,AX and DS,AX, respectively.   **3.** A, B, C, and E. D is invalid becuase 110H is too large a value for AH, a one-byte register.   **4.** A, B, C, and E.   **5.** It causes the procedure DISPLAYER to be called 10 times.   **6.** A. e B. c C. f D. g E. b F. a; d is not used   **7.** A. FAR B. NEAR C. NEAR D. NEAR   **8.** True

Displaying a PROMPT

Figure 3.8 shows the instructions related to the PROMPTER procedure. This is the first procedure called by the driver. The purpose of PROMPTER is to display on the screen the message found in NAMEPROMPT. It uses DOS interrupt 21H to perform the screen display. We'll discuss the use of this interrupt, as well as other features of PROMPTER, in more detail.

PUSH and POP

PROMPTER uses DX and AX (in lines 5 and 6). When a called procedure affects a register's value, it is usually a good idea to save the original contents of the register first and restore them before leaving the procedure. That's because you have relatively few registers with which to work. The calling and called procedures must use the same registers; the calling procedure may have put data into these registers and be expecting to use that data after the called procedure finishes. Looking back at the NAMEX driver in Figure 3.7, you see that CX is being used to control a loop when PRINTNAME is called. What if PRINTNAME changed the value in CX? The loop would not work right if this happened. You may argue that registers AX and DX are not being used by the driver when PROMPTER is

```
                  . . .
1        NAMEPROMPT DB    0AH,0DH,'WHAT IS YOUR NAME? ',24H
                  . . .
2        PROMPTER PROC
3                 PUSH    AX
4                 PUSH    DX
5                 LEA     DX,NAMEPROMPT          ;ADDRESS OF PROMPT STRING
6                 MOV     AH,9H                  ;DISPLAY STRING FUNCTION
7                 INT     21H                    ;DOS
8                 POP     DX
9                 POP     AX
10                RET
11       PROMPTER ENDP
```

Figure 3.8 Displaying a Prompt

called, so why save them? On general principles. As your programs get more elaborate, you will call the same procedures from different places in your program. You will also want to copy procedures from one program to another. It's good practice to always preserve the registers.

One exception: sometimes you use a register to return a value from a procedure. Suppose, for example, that you call a procedure to read a record from a disk and use DX to indicate if the read was sucessful (set DX to 0 if ok, otherwise put an error code in DX). In this case you want to change DX so you don't save and restore its original value. Most of the time, though, you must preserve register values. Many runtime errors are eventually found to be caused by failure to preserve the registers.

In lines 3 and 4, PUSH is used to save the contents of AX and DX. Lines 8 and 9 use POP to restore the original values to DX and AX. POP is a one-operand instruction. Like PUSH, its operand may be a memory address, but more commonly it is a 16-bit register. The operand names the destination of the data to be taken from the top of the stack. After the data is moved, SP is changed so that it points to the next item in the stack. Note that our routine POPs the data in the reverse order of the way it is PUSHed. After lines 3 and 4, the top of the stack contains the original contents of DX. The POP in line 8 restores these contents and then points to the next item on the stack, which contains the original contents of AX. Think of PUSH and POP as left and right parentheses within a expression. You must pair PUSHes and POPs in a procedure, just as you do the parentheses. The innermost PUSH and POP are a pair, then, the next innermost, and so on, until the outermost pair is matched.

Displaying a String

In line 7, we call on interrupt 21H, a DOS interrupt with many functions. The actual transfer of control to the interrupt address is done with an INT instruction that simply specifies which interrupt to use. The format is:

```
INT inum
```

where inum is the interrupt number. Since the manuals that describe the interrupts use hexadecimal numbering, we usually write inum in hexadecimal; we could use decimal. The assembler would translate INT 33 the same as INT 21H. The interrupt routine uses certain information from the registers; that information must be loaded before the interrupt is called. To use an interrupt, you must know what information it expects, what information it will return, and which registers it uses. Registers that do not contain returned information are not changed by the interrupt routine. You can find detailed information about all the DOS 21H interrupt functions in the DOS manual. In this book we will describe several of these functions, as well as several useful BIOS interrupts.

Interrupt 21H requires a number in AH to tell it which function is desired; function 9 displays a string on the screen. Line 6 loads AH with the correct function number. Function 9 expects the string's starting address to be in DX. The end of the string must be indicated by "$" (24H). Note (in line 1) that the string being displayed by PROMPTER begins with a line feed and carriage return followed by the actual message seen on the screen.

The beginning address of the string is moved into DX in line 5, using LEA (Load Effective Address). The format of this instruction is:

```
LEA 16-reg, address
```

The first operand, the destination, may be any 16-bit non-segment register (AX, BX, CX, DX, SI, DI, SP, or BP). The source, the second operand, is any address operand. In line 9, the address operand is a simple offset represented by NAMEPROMPT. LEA's source can also be expressed in a more complex way using a base (BX or BP) or an index (SI or DI) register, or both, as well as expressions that the assembler can evaluate as offsets or displacements. In later programs, you will see these more complex addresses and learn how to code them. The effective address is computed when the instruction is executed and the offset is then loaded into the specified register. So, line 5 moves the address of NAMEPROMPT into DX.

·Function number and string address are the only parameters required for the string display function of interrupt 21H. No data is returned; the interrupt routine leaves all registers with their original values. The display begins at the current cursor position on the screen. The cursor is advanced so that it follows the last character displayed.

Review Questions

1. A procedure begins with these PUSH instructions:

    PUSH AX

    PUSH BX

    PUSH CX

    Write the series of instructions needed to restore the registers before the end of the procedure.

2.   A data segment includes this definition:

QUESTION DB 'WHAT IS THE DATE?$'

    A.   Write a routine to display QUESTION on the CRT.

    B.   How many characters (including spaces) will be displayed on the screen?

Answers

1. POP CX
  POP BX
  POP AX
2. A. LEA DX,QUESTION
      MOV AH,9H
      INT 21H
  (The order of the first two instructions could be reversed.)
  B. 17

Handling the Response

The other three procedures in NAMEX read the user's response to the prompt (GETNAME), move the answer to a location where it can be used as part of an output message (MOVENAME), and then print the output message on the CRT (PRINTNAME). We will discuss these routines briefly since you already know many of the instructions involved.

Getting Input from the Keyboard

Figure 3.9 shows GETNAME and some relevant data definitions. GET-NAME begins and ends with the usual PUSH and POP instructions to preserve the registers. Interrupt 21H is called again (line 9). This time, function 10 (0AH), the buffered keyboard input routine, is used.

Function 0AH of interrupt 21H waits for the user to type a string of characters from the keyboard. The characters are echoed on the screen as they are typed. (Pressing a key does not automatically produce a character on the screen unless the input function has been programmed to include an echo. Interrupt 21H has several input functions that do **not** produce an echo.) With function 0AH, the cursor moves on the screen as the characters are echoed.

```
                       . . .
 1       INBUF   DB        255
 2       INCOUNT DB        ?
 3       INNAME  DB        255 DUP(' ')
                       . . .
 4       GETNAME PROC
 5               PUSH    AX
 6               PUSH    DX
 7               MOV     AH,0AH          ;GET STRING FROM KEYBOARD/ECHO
 8               LEA     DX,INBUF        ;ADDRESS OF INPUT BUFFER
 9               INT     21H             ;DOS
10               POP     DX
11               POP     AX
12               RET
13       GETNAME ENDP
                       . . .
```

Figure 3.9 Getting Input from the Keyboard

The typed characters are saved in a buffer area within the calling program. Input ends when <Enter> is pressed. The usual editing keys, such as <Backspace> and <Del>, can be used. You can see that function 0AH resembles BASIC's INPUT.

Function 0AH requires an input buffer address in DX. In line 8, DX is loaded with INBUF's address. The first byte of the buffer must specify the maximum number of input characters, including <Enter>. The buffered input routine will place the count of characters actually received in the second byte of the buffer (INCOUNT). This count does not include <Enter>; at most, it can be one less than the maximum value in INBUF. The actual input character area begins in the third byte; we have named that area INNAME and given it a length of 255 bytes intialized to spaces. If the user types DONNA <Enter>, INCOUNT will be 5, but six characters will be saved in the input buffer. The last one will be 0DH, representing <Enter>.

We have allowed 255 characters to be input—or, more precisely, 254 and <Enter>. This is the maximum number of characters you can specify for any use of function 0AH, simply because 255 is the largest value that can be contained in the one-byte maximum-character field. Once 254 characters are in the input buffer, any key except <Enter> will produce a beep and be rejected. We have used this size for compatibility with the BASIC version of NAMEX; BASIC always allows up to 255 characters with string INPUT. Normally, 30 characters is a generous allowance for a name.

We could have defined our input buffer all at once, using only one data name, like this:

```
INBUF DB 255,0,255 DUP(' ')
```

Then we could have referred to the input count as INBUF + 1 and the actual input data as INBUF + 2 through INBUF + 256. Note that we allow 255 input characters for a 254 character name; we must include <Enter>, which is stored in the input buffer as 0DH.

Moving Input to Output

After the input string is read, it is moved to another area where it will be part of an output string. This move is accomplished by MOVENAME. Figure 3.10 shows MOVENAME and the data definitions relevant to its instructions.

The procedure begins and ends by saving and restoring four registers, in lines 7 through 10 and 18 through 21. Lines 11, 12, 14, 15, and 16 make up the routine that actually moves the data from the input buffer (INNAME) to the output area (OUTNAME). Why don't we just output the name from the input buffer? We could, but we want to make it part of a longer message for output. Lines 13 and 17 are used to move "$" to mark the end of the output string. Why don't we just put "$" permanently at the end of OUT-NAME? Because then we would always output the maximum characters for the name. The technique used in MOVENAME lets us end the output name at the same length as the input name. We'll look at each of lines 11 through 17 in detail so you can see how these routines work.

```
         . . .
1        OUTMESS   DB     0AH,0DH,'HELLO,
2        OUTNAME   DB     255 DUP('  ')
3        INBUF     DB     255
4        INCOUNT   DB     ?
5        INNAME    DB     255 DUP('  ')
         . . .
6        MOVENAME  PROC
7                  PUSH   CX
8                  PUSH   BX
9                  PUSH   SI
10                 PUSH   DI
11                 MOV    CH,0H            ;SET COUNT FOR MOVE
12                 MOV    CL,INCOUNT
13                 MOV    BX,CX            ;BX HAS NUMBER OF CHAR
14                 LEA    SI,INNAME        ;SOURCE
15                 LEA    DI,OUTNAME       ;DESTINATION
16                 REP MOVSB               ;MOVE CHAR CX TIMES
17                 MOV    OUTNAME[BX],24H   ;NEXT CHAR IS $
18                 POP    DI
19                 POP    SI
20                 POP    BX
21                 POP    CX
22                 RET
23       MOVENAME  ENDP
         . . .
```

Figure 3.10 Moving an Input String to Output

Lines 11 and 12 are used to move the input buffer's character count (INCOUNT) to CX, which will control the number of characters moved. Since INCOUNT is defined by DB, the assembler considers it to be a byte-sized field. A move between memory and a register, or between two registers, must use the same type of data (byte or word) in both operands. For this reason, we can move data from INCOUNT to CL, as in line 12, but not directly to CX. Later in the routine, however, we will need to have CX set to the value in INCOUNT. Line 11 clears the high-order byte of CX by moving zero into it. The total effect of lines 11 and 12 is the same as if we moved one word containing INCOUNT's value to CX. In line 13, we move data from one register to another; you will see later that we need to have INCOUNT's value in BX as well as in CX.

Lines 14 and 15 load the offsets for INNAME and OUTNAME into SI and DI respectively, where they are needed for line 16. Line 16 contains two instructions, REP and MOVSB. We'll consider MOVSB first. MOVSB (MOVe String Bytes) is the string move instruction that is most often used. Two things happen when MOVSB is executed. First, one byte of data is moved from the address pointed to by DI to the address pointed to by SI. In string operations such as MOVSB, DI always points to an address in the extra segment. That is why it is usually convenient to have the extra segment boundary be the same as the data segment boundary, so the same fields can be addressed in either segment. The address pointed to by SI, like most other data addresses, is assumed to be within the data segment. You will learn ways to override this assumption. However, DI in a string operation must always point to an offset in the extra segment; no override is allowed.

The second thing that happens when MOVSB is executed is that both SI and DI are changed. If the direction flag is cleared, both are incremented (increased by 1). If DF is set, both are decremented. We assume in NAMEX that DF is cleared, since that is its usual status when the system is turned on. (Later you will learn to set or clear DF so that you can be sure of its status every time your program is run.)

Well, then, one byte of data is moved from the address pointed to by SI to the address pointed to by DI, and SI and DI are then incremented. That's all that MOVSB does. Then the other part of line 16, REP, comes into operation. REP (REPeat) is a prefix that can be used only with string operations such as MOVSB. Like LOOP, REP decrements CX. Then, if CX is 0, control falls through to the next instruction. If CX is not 0, both MOVSB and REP are repeated. In effect, this means that when CX is initialized to n, n bytes will be moved from MOVSB's source to its destination, where SI and DI point to the initial addresses of the source and destination. If a 30-byte name was input by GETNAME, INNAME through INNAME + 29 will be moved to OUTNAME through OUTNAME + 29.

Notice that when this routine ends, CX contains 0. BX, however, still contains the original value from INCOUNT because we put it there in line 13. In line 17, a one-byte immediate value is moved to the EA which is computed at run time as the sum of OUTNAME's offset and the value in BX. If INCOUNT is 30, line 17 will move "$" to OUTNAME + 30, the byte following the last byte of the name. This is a one-byte move because OUTNAME is defined by DB; the size of an immediate-to-memory move is decided by the type (byte or word) of the destination.

Displaying Another Message

After the name has been input and moved to an output area, NAMEX calls the PRINTNAME procedure five times. Figure 3.11 shows PRINTNAME and its relevant data fields. The string display function of interrupt 21H is used again to display the message. You should be able to follow this entire procedure without any problems. Take special note of the following point: the output display begins with OUTMESS (see line 7), but does not end there. The display continues displaying each byte in the data segment until it reaches the "$" following the name in OUTNAME.

The Whole Program

We have gone over every part of NAMEX. Now, you should have no trouble following the whole program as shown in Figure 3.12. You might be curious about one thing: why aren't the procedures arranged in the order in which they are called? They could be; in fact, many programmers would arrange them that way. (This can be difficult to follow if a procedure is called from several places in the same program.) Other programmers place the most important procedures first, followed by subordinate procedures called from within the major ones. I have found when reading long pro-

```
               . . .
 1    OUTMESS   DB      0AH,0DH,'HELLO, '
 2    OUTNAME   DB      255 DUP(' ')
               . . .
 3    PRINTNAME PROC
 4              PUSH    AX
 5              PUSH    DX
 6              MOV     AH,9H            ;DISPLAY STRING FUNCTION
 7              LEA     DX,OUTMESS       ;ADDRESS OF STRING
 8              INT     21H              ;DOS
 9              POP     DX
10              POP     AX
11              RET
12    PRINTNAME ENDP
```

Figure 3.11 Displaying the Name Message

```
        PAGE      ,132
;
PROG_STACK        SEGMENT STACK 'STACK'
                  DB      64 DUP (('STACK   '))
PROG_STACK        ENDS
;
PROG_DATA         SEGMENT 'DATA'
NAMEPROMPT        DB      0AH,0DH,'WHAT IS YOUR NAME? ',24H
OUTMESS           DB      0AH,0DH,'HELLO, '
OUTNAME           DB      255 DUP(' ')
INBUF             DB      255
INCOUNT           DB      ?
INNAME            DB      255 DUP(' ')
PROG_DATA         ENDS
;
PROG_CODE SEGMENT 'CODE'
MAIN_PROG PROC    FAR
          ASSUME  CS:PROG_CODE,DS:PROG_DATA,SS:PROG_STACK,ES:PROG_DATA
          PUSH    DS                      ;SAVE DATA ON STACK
          MOV     AX,0                    ;    TO BE USED FOR RETURN TO
          PUSH    AX                      ;      SYSTEM WHEN PROGRAM ENDS
          MOV     AX,PROG_DATA            ;INITIALIZE DS
          MOV     DS,AX
          MOV     ES,AX                   ;      AND    ES
          CALL    PROMPTER                ;PROMPT FOR NAME
          CALL    GETNAME                 ;GET NAME INPUT
          CALL    MOVENAME                ;MOVE NAME TO OUTPUT LINE
          MOV     CX,5                    ;LOAD COUNTER FOR PRINTLOOP
PRINTLOOP:
          CALL    PRINTNAME               ;PRINT NAME MESSAGE
          LOOP    PRINTLOOP               ;       AND REPEAT CX TIMES
          RET                             ;THEN RETURN TO OPERATING SYSTEM
MAIN_PROG ENDP
;
GETNAME PROC
          PUSH    AX
          PUSH    DX
          MOV     AH,0AH                  ;GET STRING FROM KEYBOARD/ECHO
          LEA     DX,INBUF                ;ADDRESS OF INPUT BUFFER
          INT     21H                     ;DOS
          POP     DX
          POP     AX
          RET
GETNAME ENDP
MOVENAME PROC
          PUSH    CX
          PUSH    BX
          PUSH    SI
          PUSH    DI
          MOV     CH,0H                   ;SET COUNT FOR MOVE
          MOV     CL,INCOUNT
          MOV     BX,CX                   ;BX HAS NUMBER OF CHAR
          LEA     SI,INNAME               ;SOURCE
          LEA     DI,OUTNAME              ;DESTINATION
          REP MOVSB                       ;MOVE CHAR CX TIMES
          MOV     OUTNAME[BX],24H         ;NEXT CHAR IS $
          POP     DI
          POP     SI
          POP     BX
          POP     CX
          RET
MOVENAME ENDP
;
```

```
PRINTNAME PROC
          PUSH      AX
          PUSH      DX
          MOV       AH,9H                    ;DISPLAY STRING FUNCTION
          LEA       DX,OUTMESS               ;ADDRESS OF STRING
          INT       21H                      ;DOS
          POP       DX
          POP       AX
          RET
PRINTNAME ENDP
;
PROMPTER PROC
          PUSH      AX
          PUSH      DX
          LEA       DX,NAMEPROMPT            ;ADDRESS OF PROMPT STRING
          MOV       AH,9H                    ;DISPLAY STRING FUNCTION
          INT       21H                      ;DOS
          POP       DX
          POP       AX
          RET
PROMPTER ENDP
;
PROG_CODE ENDS
          END       MAIN_PROG
```

grams that it is easier to locate the procedures if they are simply arranged
alphabetically. So, I make a practice of arranging all my programs that
way. You may arrange your code segment any way you want as long as you
begin with the driver.

Review Questions

1. Which of the following apply to the operation of function 0AH of
    interrupt 21H?

    A. A string of characters typed at the keyboard are saved in a
        buffer area defined within the program.

    B. Characters are echoed on the screen as typed.

    C. The end of the input text is marked by typing "$".

    D. The screen cursor moves as characters are typed.

    E. The number of characters that can be input is determined
        by the size of the defined buffer area.

    F. The input routine puts the actual number of characters
        typed (not including the end-of-text character) into the sec-
        ond byte of the input buffer.

    G. The end-of-text character is not saved in the input buffer.

2.   Look at this program routine:

```
MOV CX , 10
LEA SI , FIRST
LEA DI , SECOND
REP MOVSB
```

A.   What does this routine do?

B.   Which is executed first, REP or MOVSB?

C.   What happens the first time that MOVSB is executed?

D.   What happens the first time that REP is executed?

Answers

1. A, B, D and F; Here's what's wrong with the others: C. The last character typed must be <Enter>. E. The maximum input size is specified in the first byte of the buffer area. G. The end-of-text character is included in the input buffer.   2. A. Moves FIRST through FIRST + 9 to SECOND through SECOND + 9. B. MOVSB C. One byte is moved from FIRST to SECOND; then, SI and DI are both increased by 1. D. CX is decreased to 9; then, MOVSB and REP are repeated.

Key Points From Chapter 3

In this chapter you have examined a sample program in detail. You have learned about the structure of a MASM program, how to code source code lines, how to define segments and procedures and end the program, and one way to define data fields. You have learned some of the most commonly used instructions and I/O routines. Some of the main points presented in this chapter were:

◼   The general format for a source code line allows up to four entries. The possible entries are name, operation code, operand field, and comments in that order. Entries must be separated by at least one blank or tab character. A line does not have to begin in column 1, but it cannot go past column 132.

◼   A name is from 1 to 31 characters long. It can contain uppercase letters, digits, and any of these five special characters: ? . @ − $. It cannot start with a digit. If a period is included, it must be the first character. Names are required for some pseudo-ops, such as SEG-MENT, ENDS, PROC, and ENDP. Otherwise, a name is optional for any instruction.

- The assembler assigns a name a value based on the offset of the instruction that defines the name. Operand references to the name are replaced by that offset.

- A variable-name is a data field name. A label is a name defined by an instruction in the code segment. A label may be coded as the only entry in a source-code line.

- Labels are of type NEAR or FAR. FAR labels may be referenced from external code segments. NEAR labels may be referenced only from the same code segment. A label used as a procedure name has a type defined by the PROC instruction. NEAR is the default. Other labels are identified as NEAR if they are followed by a colon when defined; otherwise they are FAR.

- Comments are identified by an initial semi-colon. They are always optional. A comment may be the only entry in a source-code line.

- Operation codes, or opcodes, are 8088 mnemonics or MASM pseudo-ops.

- The operand field requirements depend on the opcode. When more than one operand is required they are separated by commas.

- The SEGMENT pseudo-op defines the beginning of a segment. In its simplest form it consists of a segment name followed by SEGMENT. A stack segment definition must also include the combine-type STACK. If desired, a class name may be included in single quotes for each SEGMENT pseudo-op.

- The ENDS pseudo-op must end a segment. It consists of the segment name followed by ENDS.

- A procedure is a block of code. Usually, a code segment contains a main procedure, or driver, and several other procedures that function as subroutines called from the driver or from each other.

- The beginning of a procedure is defined by a PROC pseudo-op. A name is required, followed by PROC. If the procedure will be called from an external code segment, PROC must be followed by FAR. The first procedure executed in any program must be defined as FAR. All others are usually NEAR.

■ The ENDP pseudo-op must end a procedure. It consists of the procedure name followed by ENDP.

■ The END pseudo-op must be the last source-code instruction in the
program. It consists of END, optionally followed by the address of the
first instruction to be executed in the program. This is usually the
name of the main procedure.

■ Data fields can be defined using DB. A variable-name can be assigned
to a DB instruction. The initial value may be defined, or left undefined
by coding a question mark in the operand field. Multiple bytes can be
defined by initial values separated by commas or by a character
string. Multiple bytes can also be defined by including a duplication
factor in the operand, like this:

    n DUP ` ex ´

where n specifies the number of duplications of the initial values in
ex. Duplication factors can be nested.

■ The PAGE pseudo-op sets the assembler listing's page length and
width.

■ The ASSUME pseudo-op tells the assembler which segments'
addresses will be in the segment registers at run time.

■ To communicate properly with the calling program, each program
must begin by putting two words of data on the stack. The first word
contains the contents of DS, the second a value of 0. The program
must end with a RET instruction, which will use the two words at the
top of the stack to find the address to which control should be transferred. Any other data put on the stack during the program must be
removed before the program ends.

■ The second step in each program must be to put the data segment's
address into DS. Usually this address is also put into ES.

■ **PUSH r1** copies the contents of a 16-bit register (r1) to the top of the
stack. **POP r1** copies the word at the top of the stack to a 16-bit
register (r1). Both PUSH and POP use SP to find the current top of the
stack and adjust SP to point to the new top.

■ **CALL p1** transfers control to the beginning of procedure p1. **RET**
ends the execution of a procedure by transferring control to an
address found at the top of the stack. The return address is placed on

the top of the stack by CALL. Any data placed on the stack during execution of a procedure must be removed before RET so that the correct return address will be found by RET.

- **MOV x,y** copies data from y (source) to x (destination). The source may be a register, address, or immediate data operand. The destination may be a register or address operand. Data cannot be moved directly from one address to another, an immediate data value cannot be moved to any segment register, and CS cannot be the destination for any move.

- MOV can be used to move one byte or one word of data. When the source is immediate data, the destination determines the size of the move. In other cases, the source and destination must be the same size (byte or word).

- **LOOP short-label** is used to repeat a routine a preset number of times. The number of desired repetitions must be loaded into CX. When LOOP is executed, CX is decremented. If CX has become zero, control falls through to the next instruction. Otherwise, control is transferred to the location identified by short-label. Short-label must be a NEAR label within -128 to $+127$ bytes of the LOOP instruction.

- **LEA r1,x** loads the effective address computed from x into the 16-bit register r1. R1 cannot represent a segment register.

- **INT inum** calls the specified interrupt routine.

- Interrupt 21H calls a DOS routine for I/O. A function number must be loaded into AH before interrupt 21H is called.

- Function 9 of int 21H is used to display a character string on the screen. The beginning address of the string must be loaded into DX before the interrupt is called. The end of the string must be marked by "$" (24H). The string will be displayed starting at the current cursor position. The cursor will be moved by the display and will end in the position following the last character displayed. The end-of-text mark, $, is not part of the display.

- Function 0AH (10) of int 21H is used to get buffered keyboard input ended by <Enter>. The input is echoed on the screen and the cursor position is updated as the characters are echoed. DX must be loaded with the address of a buffer area before the interrupt is called. The first byte of the buffer must be initialized with the maximum input-string size. The number must include the end-of-text character

<Enter>. The second byte of the buffer will be set by the input routine to the actual number of characters input. This count will not include <Enter>. The characters entered will be stored in the buffer beginning at the third byte. <Enter> will be stored as 0DH.

■ **MOVSB** copies one byte from the address pointed to by SI to the address pointed to by DI. DI always points to an offset in the extra segment. After the move, both SI and DI are changed to point to the next byte to be moved. The direction of the change depends on the Direction Flag.

■ **REP** is a prefix used with MOVSB that is executed after MOVSB. REP causes CX to be decremented. If CX is still not zero MOVSB is repeated; when CX becomes zero control falls through to the next instruction.

Chapter Review Questions

1. Name the parts of this source code line:

    STARTLOOP : MOV AX , 0   ; I N I T I AL I ZE AX FOR TOTAL

    A.   STARTLOOP:

    B.   MOV

    C.   AX.0

    D.   ;INITIALIZE AX FOR TOTAL

2. Which of these names are valid?

    A.   MOV6TO7

    B.   BEGIN__LOOP

    C.   3MORE

    D.   CUSTOMER.NAME

3. Match the name being defined with the phrase from the right that best describes it. Phrases may be used more than once.

_____	A.	NOT_IF LEA DI,OUTNAME	a.	FAR label
			b.	NEAR label
_____	B.	OUTNAME DB 25 DUP(' ')	c.	variable-name
_____	C.	MAYBE: LEA SI, INNAME		
_____	D.	PRINT_ PROG PROC FAR		
_____	E.	DISPLAY PROC		

4.   Which of these are true?

    A.   A source-code line can contain a label as its only entry.

    B.   A source-code line can contain a comment as its only entry.

    C.   A source-code line can contain an operation code as its only entry.

    D.   Any source-code line that contains an operation code must contain two operands in the operand field.

5.   Write the simplest possible instructions to begin and end a data segment called THE_DATA.

6.   Write the simplest possible instructions to begin and end a stack segment called MORE_STACK.

7.   A code segment called CODE_SEG contains a main procedure called BEGINNING and one other procedure called PRINTIT. Write instructions in the proper order to define the beginning and ending of the segment, procedures, and program.

8.   Define data fields as described.

    A.   An uninitialized one-byte field named OUTCOUNT.

    B.   Twenty-five uninitialized bytes named MAJOR.

    C.   Three hundred bytes called SAVIT initialized with spaces.

    D.   Ten bytes named DIGITS initialized with the hexadecimal digits from 0AH to 0FH.

E. An output message named OUTMESS. The message should begin with line feed and carriage return and end with the correct end-of-text character. The message text is "WEL-COME TO THE TERMINAL".

9. Write an instruction to set the assembler listing's page length and width to 50 lines and 92 characters, respectively.

10. A program's segments are NEW_CODE, NEW_STACK, and NEW_DATA (for the code, stack, and data segments, respectively).

   A. Write the ASSUME instruction for the program, using NEW_DATA for the extra segment also.

   B. Write the first six instructions (not pseudo-ops) for NEW_CODE.

11. Match each of these instructions with the best description of its purpose. Some descriptions are not used.

   ___ A. MOV AX,0   a. Copies AX to the top of stack
   ___ B. MOV AX,   b. Copies zero to AX
           DFIELD   c. Copies offset of DFIELD to AX
   ___ C. LEA   d. Copies top of stack to AX
           AX,DFIELD   e. Copies AX to DFIELD
   ___ D. PUSH AX   f. Copies DFIELD to AX
   ___ E. POP AX

12. Match each type of control transfer with the most suitable instruction. Not all the instructions are used.

   ___ A. Transfer to a pro-   a. LOOP
           cedure   b. MOVSB
   ___ B. Go to address   c. CALL
           found at top of   d. REP
           stack   e. RET
   ___ C. Transfer to sys-   f. INT
           tem I/O routine
   ___ D. Repeat a series of
           instructions
   ___ E. Repeat a string
           operation

13.   A program displays the message "WHAT IS THE DATE?". Code the data description and instructions necessary to display this message on a new line on the screen.

14.   A program reads a date typed from the keyboard. The date has a maximum of eight characters. Code the necessary input fields and I/O routine (using buffered input).

15.   Code a routine to move an eight-byte field from INDATE to PRINT-DATE.

16.   Code a routine to call a procedure called BLANKER 24 times.

Answers

1. A. name B. operation code or opcode C. operands D.comment   **2.** A and B; C is invalid because it starts with a digit; D is invalid because it includes an internal period.   **3.** A. a B. c C. b D. a E. b   **4.** A, B, and C. D is false; an instruction may have zero, one, or two operands depending on the opcode.

5.   THE__DATA SEGMENT
          THE__DATA ENDS
6.   MORE__STACK   SEGMENT STACK
          MORE__STACK   ENDS
7.   CODE__SEG   SEGMENT
          BEGINNING   PROC FAR
          BEGINNING   ENDP
          PRINTIT   PROC
          PRINTIT   ENDP
          CODE__SEG   ENDS
                        END BEGINNING

    PRINTIT PROC

    PRINTIT ENDP

    CODE__SEG ENDS

        END BEGINNING

    Note that BEGINNING is optional in the END instruction.

8.   A. OUTCOUNT DB ?

    B. MAJOR DB 25 DUP(?)

    C. SAVIT DB 300 DUP(' ')

D. DIGITS DB 0AH,0BH,0CH,0DH,0EH,0FH or

DIGITS DB 10,11,12,13,14,15

E. OUTMESS DB 0AH,0DH,'WELCOME TO THE TERMI
NAL',24H

9.   PAGE 50,92

10.   A. ASSUME CS:NEW__CODE,SS:NEW__STACK,DS:
NEW__DATA,ES:NEW__DATA

B. PUSH DS

MOV AX,0

PUSH AX

MOV AX,NEW__DATA

MOV DS,AX

MOV ES,AX

11.   A. b B. f C. c D. a E. d; e is not used

12.   A. c B. e C. f D. a E. d; b is not used

13.   MESSAGE DB 0AH,0DH,"WHAT IS THE DATE?$"

MOV AH,9

MESSAGELEA

MESSAGEDX,MESSAGE

MESSAGEINT 21H

You could have coded the "$" as a separate entry; you probably used a
different name for the data field. The MOV and LEA instructions
could be in reverse order. You could have coded the function
number as 9H.

14.
```
INBUF      DB 8
INCOUNT    DB ?
INDATE     DB 8 DUP(?)
MOV        AH,0AH
LEA        DX,INBUF
INT        21H
```

Many variations are possible. You could, for example, have coded the buffer in one instruction, like this:

```
I NBUF DB 10 DUP` ? ´
```

and initialized the first byte as part of the routine, like this:

```
MOV I NBUF , 8
```

You could have coded the function number as 10.

```
15.   MOV        CX,8
      LEA        SI,INDATE
      LEA        DI,PRINTDATE
      REP        MOVSB
```

Not too many possible variations for this routine. You must use CX, SI, and DI as shown. The MOV and two LEA instructions could be in a different order; they must all precede REP MOVSB.

```
16.     MOV CX,24
        LOOPER:
        CALL BLANKER
        LOOP LOOPER
```

You probably used a different label where we used LOOPER. Did you remember the colon? You could have coded the label on the same line as the CALL instruction; but you must have loaded CX before the beginning of the loop.

Computer Exercise

Now it's your turn to try some programming. Write a program that will ask first for a name, then for an eight-character telephone number. Display the two fields (name and number) on one line. (HINT: Put the number in the first eight positions followed by several spaces; then the name followed by "$".) Repeat the entire process three times. Call the program PHONER. You'll assemble and run this program in the next chapter, and then modify it in later chapters, so save your source code. If you need some help, our version of PHONER is on the next page.

```
           PAGE      ,132                        ;THIS IS PHONE NUMBER
                                                  PROGRAM FOR CHAPTER 3
;
PROG_STACK         SEGMENT STACK 'STACK'
                   DB      64 DUP ('STACK   ')
PROG_STACK         ENDS
;
PROG_DATA          SEGMENT 'DATA'
NAMEPROMPT         DB      0AH,0DH,'NAME: ',24H
PHONEPROMPT        DB      0AH,0DH,'PHONE NUMBER: ',24H
OUTLINE            DB      0AH,0DH
OUTPHONE           DB      8 DUP(' ')
OUTSPACE           DB      3 DUP(' ')
OUTNAME            DB      31 DUP(' ')
INBUF              DB      31
INCOUNT            DB      ?
INDATA             DB      31 DUP(' ')
PROG_DATA          ENDS
;
PROG_CODE          SEGMENT 'CODE'
MAIN_PROG          PROC    FAR
                   ASSUME  CS:PROG_CODE,DS:PROG_DATA,SS:PROG_STACK,ES:PROG_DATA
                   PUSH    DS                    ;SAVE DATA ON STACK
                   MOV     AX,0                  ;      TO BE USED FOR RETURN TO
                   PUSH    AX                    ;      SYSTEM WHEN PROGRAM ENDS
                   MOV     AX,PROG_DATA          ;INITIALIZE DS
                   MOV     DS,AX
                   MOV     ES,AX                 ;      AND    ES
                   MOV     CX,3
MAINLOOP:
                   CALL    PROMPTNAME            ;PROMPT FOR NAME
                   CALL    GETNAME               ;GET NAME INPUT
                   CALL    MOVENAME              ;MOVE NAME TO OUTPUT LINE
                   CALL    PROMPTPHONE           ;PROMPT FOR PHONE
                   CALL    GETPHONE              ;GET PHONE INPUT
                   CALL    MOVEPHONE             ;MOVE PHONE TO OUTPUT LINE
                   CALL    PRINTLINE             ;DISPLAY LINE
                   LOOP    MAINLOOP              ;   AND REPEAT PROCESS
                   RET                           ;THEN RETURN TO OPERATING SYSTEM
MAIN_PROG          ENDP
;
GETNAME            PROC                          ;THIS PROCEDURE GETS NAME
                   PUSH    AX                    ;      INPUT FROM KEYBOARD
                   PUSH    DX
                   MOV     AH,0AH                ;GET STRING FROM KEYBOARD/ECHO
                   LEA     DX,INBUF              ;ADDRESS OF INPUT BUFFER
                   MOV     INBUF,31              ;MAX NAME IS 30 CHAR
                   INT     21H                   ;DOS
                   POP     DX
                   POP     AX
                   RET
GETNAME            ENDP
;
GETPHONE           PROC                          ;THIS PROCEDURE GETS
                   PUSH    AX                    ; PHONE NUMBER FROM KEYBOARD
                   PUSH    DX
                   MOV     AH,0AH                ;GET STRING FROM KEYBOARD/ECHO
                   LEA     DX,INBUF              ;ADDRESS OF INPUT BUFFER
                   MOV     INBUF,9               ;SET INPUT SIZE FOR PHONE
                   INT     21H                   ;DOS
                   POP     DX
                   POP     AX
                   RET
GETPHONE           ENDP
;
MOVENAME           PROC                          ;THIS PROCEDURE MOVES NAME
                   PUSH    CX                    ; TO OUTPUT AND ENDS
                   PUSH    BX                    ; OUTPUT STRING WITH $
                   PUSH    SI
                   PUSH    DI
```

```
                    MOV     CH,0H              ;SET COUNT FOR MOVE
                    MOV     CL,INCOUNT
                    MOV     BX,CX
                    LEA     SI,INDATA          ;SOURCE
                    LEA     DI,OUTNAME         ;DESTINATION
                    REP MOVSB                  ;MOVE CHAR CX TIMES
                    MOV     OUTNAME[BX],24H    ;NEXT CHAR IS $
                    POP     DI
                    POP     SI
                    POP     BX
                    POP     CX
                    RET
MOVENAME            ENDP
;
MOVEPHONE           PROC                       ;THIS PROCEDURE MOVES PHONE
                    PUSH    CX                 ; NUMBER TO OUTPUT LINE
                    PUSH    BX
                    PUSH    SI
                    PUSH    DI
                    MOV     CH,0H              ;SET COUNT FOR MOVE
                    MOV     CL,8               ;  PHONE ALWAYS 8 CHAR
                    LEA     SI,INDATA          ;SOURCE
                    LEA     DI,OUTPHONE        ;DESTINATION
                    REP MOVSB                  ;MOVE CHAR 8 TIMES
                    POP     DI
                    POP     SI
                    POP     BX
                    POP     CX
                    RET
MOVEPHONE           ENDP
;
PRINTLINE           PROC                       ;THIS PROCEDURE DISPLAYS
                    PUSH    AX                 ; THE OUTPUT LINE
                    PUSH    DX
                    MOV     AH,9H              ;DISPLAY STRING FUNCTION
                    LEA     DX,OUTLINE         ;ADDRESS OF STRING
                    INT     21H                ;DOS
                    POP     DX
                    POP     AX
                    RET
PRINTLINE           ENDP
;
PROMPTNAME          PROC                       ;THIS PROCEDURE PROMPTS THE
                    PUSH    AX                 ;  USER FOR A NAME
                    PUSH    DX
                    LEA     DX,NAMEPROMPT      ;ADDRESS OF PROMPT STRING
                    MOV     AH,9H              ;DISPLAY STRING FUNCTION
                    INT     21H                ;DOS
                    POP     DX
                    POP     AX
                    RET
PROMPTNAME          ENDP
;
PROMPTPHONE         PROC                       ;THIS PROCEDURE PROMPTS THE
                    PUSH    AX                 ;  USER FOR A PHONE NUMBER
                    PUSH    DX
                    LEA     DX,PHONEPROMPT     ;ADDRESS OF PROMPT STRING
                    MOV     AH,9H              ;DISPLAY STRING FUNCTION
                    INT     21H                ;DOS
                    POP     DX
                    POP     AX
                    RET
PROMPTPHONE         ENDP
;
PROG_CODE           ENDS
                    END     MAIN_PROG
```

4

Assemble, Link, and Run

Now that you have written a program, it's time to assemble, link, and run it. This chapter will teach you the simplest methods of performing these three steps. When you have finished the chapter, you will be able to assemble any MASM program, to link a simple single module program, and to run a program with or without the DEBUG utility.

Getting a Disk Ready

Before you begin to work on line with MASM, you should create a disk holding the programs you need. The disk that came with MASM has a great many files that you will not need to use the programs in this book. On the other hand, if you include some DOS programs on the disk, you won't need to swap disks all the time. On a single-sided drive, using DOS 2.0, I found the following procedure useful:

- format the disk as a system disk, which will include COM-MAND.COM and the hidden system files

- from the DOS disks, copy DEBUG.COM, EDLIN.COM, LINK.EXE, and MODE.COM

- from the MASM disk, copy MASM.EXE

The disk will be almost full at this point. I used EDLIN because it is small and convenient for making minor corrections to a source file after an assembly; my word processing program wouldn't fit on this disk. You may have some other small editor or word processor that you prefer to use. I include MODE because assembler listings are best printed at 132 characters per line, and you can't print them that way without using MODE. You may also need to send a character to the printer to change its setting. I have a very small program written in MASM that does just that, so it is also on my disk. I used the disk space that was left for PRINT.COM because I prefer PRINT to TYPE. When I converted to double-sided disk drives, I was able to combine all of this with my word-processing program. My MASM programs, source code, object code, run files, and listings, are all kept on a second disk. You can set up your disks any way that suits you; this is just a way that I have found convenient. If you are working with a fixed disk, of course, you will not need to worry about creating a working disk for MASM.

Assembling a Program

The Macro Assembler uses up to four files when assembling a program:

- the source code file
- the object code file
- the assembler listing file
- a cross-reference information file

The first file, the source code file, is required for any assembly. This file provides the input to the assembler. The other three files are output files created by the assembler; they are always optional. You may not want to produce an object-code file, for example, when you are using the assembler to find errors. Error messages from MASM are displayed on the screen as well as printed in the listing; you may not want to produce a listing until these errors have been corrected. The cross-reference information file is used as input to another program, CREF, to produce a cross-reference listing. This cross-reference listing lists every variable in the program and the line numbers where the variable occurs. The line numbers are those from the assembler listing, not the source code. We will not use CREF in this book, so we will never create a cross-reference file.

You must tell the assembler the filenames to be used. You don't need to specify the extensions. The source file is assumed to have an extension of

.ASM, the object file (.OBJ), the listing file (.LST), and the cross-reference file (.CRF). When you tell the assembler to assemble NAMEX, it will look for NAMEX.ASM to use for the source-code file.

The assembler assumes that the object- and source-code filenames will match (except for the extension). If you are assembling NAMEX.ASM, an object-code file named NAMEX.OBJ is produced unless you specify otherwise. If you don't want an object-code file, tell the assembler that the object code's filename is NUL or NUL.OBJ. Any file named NUL is nonexistent.

Running the Assembler

To start the assembler and tell it which files to use you must first be sure that the disk with MASM is in drive A, unless you have a fixed disk. Your program will probably be on another disk that can go in drive B. We make B the default drive so that MASM will look for its input and place its output on B. We also set a search path, PATH A: \ ;B: \ ;, so that the system will look on A and B to find commands and run files. That way we can use MASM on drive A and our programs on B without specifying drivenames.

The simplest way to start the assembler is to enter the command MASM (or ASM if you want to use the small assembler). The assembler will then ask for the filenames it needs; it shows you the default extensions or filenames for each file as it asks. To use the default name for an output file, just press < Enter >. The default names for the listing and cross-reference files are NUL.LST and NUL.CRF, respectively. A NUL file does not exist, so neither of these files will be produced unless you specify another name for one or both of them. To specify another name for an output file, type the name. You will be wise, however, not to specify any extension; let the system supply the default extensions. To send the listing directly to the printer, give it a filename of LPT1: or PRN:.

In Figure 4.1, we type the command MASM and the assembler responds with a two-line message. Then it asks for the source filename. We respond NAMEX, letting MASM add the default extension, .ASM. Next we are

```
B>MASM
The IBM Personal Computer MACRO Assembler
Version 1.00 (C)Copyright IBM Corp 1981

Source filename [.ASM]: NAMEX
Object filename [NAMEX.OBJ]:
Source listing  [NUL.LST]:
Cross reference [NUL.CRF]:

Warning Severe
Errors  Errors
0       0

B>
```

Figure 4.1 A Sample Assembly Session

asked for an object filename. The default, NAMEX.OBJ, is shown in brackets. Since we want the default, we just press <Enter>. We also choose the defaults shown for the listing and cross-reference files. MASM assembles the program, creating the object file, and displays a final message showing the count of warnings and severe errors found.

A Quicker Way

A quicker way to provide the necessary information is to type the file-names as part of the MASM command. Separate the names by commas. Don't use extensions. If you don't type a name, but still provide the separating comma that follows it, you will get an output file with the source-code name and default extension. Notice that for the listing and cross-reference file this is not the same as with the long form. There, if you omit a name, you get a NUL file. This command, for example, will assemble NAMEX.ASM with object file NAMEX.OBJ, listing file NAMEX.LST, and cross-reference file NAMEX.CRF:

MASM NAMEX , , ,

If you want to enter only one, two, or three filenames and let the rest be the long form defaults (NUL for listing and cross reference) put a semicolon after the last one you enter; then you don't need any more commas. If you forget the semicolon, the assembler will prompt you for any missing filenames. To assemble NAMEX.ASM producing (by default) object file NAMEX.OBJ and no listing or cross-reference, you can simply type:

MASM B : NAMEX ;

To assemble NAMEX.ASM with no object file or cross-reference file, but with a listing file called SAVE.LST, you can type:

MASM B : NAMEX , NUL , SAVE ;

To assemble NAMEX.ASM with object file NAMEX.OBJ and listing file NAMEX.LST but no cross-reference file, you can type:

MASM B : NAMEX , , ;

Note the difference between:

```
MASM B : NAMEX , , ,
```

which creates object, listing, and cross-reference files called NAMEX.OBJ, NAMEX.LST, and NAMEX.CRF, and:

```
MASM B : NAMEX ;
```

which creates only the object file. Remember that a file named NUL.ext is not created and that a file named LPT1: or PRN: will be sent directly to the printer.

Assembler Errors

As the assembler processes your program, it displays on the screen any syntax errors that it identifies. It displays the line where the error was found and a numeric error code. If you are using the Macro Assembler, an error message will also be displayed. If you are producing a listing, the error code and message will be included on the line following the error. If you are using the Small Assembler, only the numeric code will be displayed and listed, not the error message.

Appendix A of the MASM manual contains a complete list of error messages, error codes, and possible reasons for the errors. The reasons given are not always the real reasons for your errors, however. According to the manual the reason for a code 9 error, for example, is that "a symbol is used that has no definition." You may think you have provided a definition, but closer examination shows that you spelled a name differently in a data definition than when you used it in an operand. Or, an error in the data definition instruction itself may have caused the assembler to be unable to recognize the name when it is used later. Or, a typing error made the first character a semicolon, which caused the entire data definition to be interpreted as a comment. The error messages and reasons simply provide guidelines to the probable error causes. You must examine the actual program closely to track down all the problems.

Figure 4.2 shows a sample of errors displayed when an early version of NAMEX was assembled. Both errors shown had the same type of cause: INBUF and INCOUNT were not recognized because as operands, they were not spelled the same, as they were when the fields were defined. The

```
B>

B>MASM NAMES;
The IBM Personal Computer MACRO Assembler
Version 1.00 (C)Copyright IBM Corp 1981

  0022  8D 16 0000 U                    LEA      DX,INBUF              ;ADDRESS
OF INPUT BUFFER
  E r r o r   ---        9:Symbol not defined
  0031  8A 0E 0000 U                    MOV      CL,INCOUNT
  E r r o r   ---        9:Symbol not defined

Warning Severe
Errors  Errors
0       2

B>
```

Figure 4.2 An Assembly with Errors

sample was printed by turning on the simultaneous print option (Ctrl-P and Ctrl-PrtSc both turn on simultaneous print). For the first few assemblies of a program, when many error messages may appear, you will find it helpful to print the error messages in this way.

Use your text editor or word processing program to find and correct errors; then run the assembler again. Repeat the process until all the Syntax errors are out of the program. Then, you will be ready to go to the next step, linking the program. If you didn't get an assembler listing, however, you should assemble the program once more to get a listing to use in debugging.

Review Questions

1. What source code file will be assembled by this command:

    MASM MYPROG;

    How many output files will be produced? What will the name(s) of the output file(s) be?

2. Write the single command needed to assemble a source file called NEWPROG.ASM, producing an object code file called NEW-PROG.OBJ, a listing file called NEWPROG.LST, and no cross-reference file.

3. Write the single command needed to assemble a source file called XYZ.ASM, producing a listing on the printer but no other output.

Answers

1. MYPROG.ASM; 1 output file; MYPROG.OBJ (object)   2. MASM NEW-PROG,,,;   3. MASM XYZ,NUL,PRN: or MASM XYZ,NUL,LPT1:

Computer Exercise

Assemble NAMEX.ASM. When you assemble the program, produce an object file named NAMEX.OBJ and a printed listing. Save the listing; you will need it later in the chapter. Correct any errors; keep trying until you get no errors.

Linking a Program

As you know, the linker creates an executable file, called a run file, from one or more object modules. The object modules may have been produced by an assembler, a compiler, or both. The linker can be used to combine assembled subroutines with compiled object modules. When you buy a compiler, you often also receive an object-module library with routines produced either by the compiler or by an assembler. After you compile a program, use the linker to combine these library routines with your compiled object module. Even a one-module program, however, like NAMEX, must be linked, since the linker puts information needed to load and run the program into the run file.

The Simplest Link

To link your program, you must have available both LINK.COM and the object module produced by MASM. The simplest way to start the linker is by typing LINK. LINK will prompt you for four file names. The files are:

■ the input object-code file, with the default extension .OBJ. Several object files may be named and combined into one run file, but programs in this book contain only one object module.

■ the output run file, with extension .EXE. If you specify another extension, the linker ignores it and uses .EXE as the extension. The default run-filename is the object-code file's name. The run file is your program, ready to run.

■ the output list (or map) file, with default extension .MAP. The list file can be sent directly to a printer by using the name LPT1: or PRN:. If you don't specify a list file, none is created. The linker list file shows offsets of the segments within the run file. This can be useful for debugging programs that contain several object modules.

■   one or more input library files, with extension .LIB. If no library file is specified, none will be used. Library files are used with programs written in compiler languages. They are supplied with the compiler and contain routines used by the compiled programs. No libraries are needed with MASM programs.

Figure 4.3 shows a sample link session, linking NAMEX by this method and producing a run file but no listing.

A Faster Link

The necessary filenames can be included on the LINK command line. Commas and semicolons serve the same function as in the MASM command line. If a comma but no name is included for the list file, a list file will be produced with the same name as the object module and extension MAP. The command:

LINK NAMEX;

has the same effect as the longer version shown in Figure 4.3. It uses NAMEX.OBJ for input and produces NAMEX.EXE as output. No library files are used and no listing is produced. The command:

LINK NAMEX, NUL, LPT1:;

also uses NAMEX.OBJ for input and no libraries. It does not produce a run file, but it does print a map.

You will seldom see any errors in a simple link except from mistyped file names. Linker error messages and their meanings can be found in the MESSAGES section of the DOS manual.

```
B>
B>LINK

IBM Personal Computer Linker
Version 2.10 (C)Copyright IBM Corp 1981, 1982, 1983

Object Modules [.OBJ]: NAMEX
Run File [NAMEX.EXE]:
List File [NUL.MAP]:
Libraries [.LIB]:

B>
```

Figure 4.3 A Sample Link Session

Review Questions

1. What output files will be generated by this command?

   L I NK NEWPROG ;

2. Write a single command to link an object file called SUMMER.OBJ, creating a run file called SUMMER.EXE and a listing on the printer. No libraries are necessary.

Answers

1. A run file named NEWPROG.EXE   2. LINK SUMMER,,LPT1:;

Running the Program

Once the program is linked, you can run it by simply typing the filename as though it were a DOS command. Don't include the extension. To run NAMEX.EXE, just type:

NAMEX

Computer Exercise

Link the NAMEX.OBJ module you created in the preceding exercise and create a printed listing. Compare the map in the listing with the final page of the assembler listing. Observe that with a simple one-module program the linker listing does not really provide any new information.

Run the resulting program. If the program doesn't run correctly, go back over the source code and make sure there are no typing errors.

Running Under DEBUG

Often the first execution of a program doesn't provide any clues to what went wrong. It's quite common for the cursor to disappear and nothing else to happen. The only way out is to reboot the system. In such circumstances, as well as many other times, you will find it very helpful to run your program using the DEBUG utility provided with DOS.

You can find a description of DEBUG in the DOS manual. It is well worth your time to learn this or a similar utility and to explore a few assembler programs. Teaching you DEBUG is outside the scope of this book, but we will run through a sample session illustrating some commonly used commands and pointing out some items of interest. Keep your assembly listing of NAMEX at hand for reference.

To run NAMEX under DEBUG, enter the command:

DEBUG NAMEX.EXE.

Notice that you do need the file extension. DEBUG will load and will load NAMEX.EXE also. Then it will prompt you for a command. The DEBUG prompt is a dash (-).

Unassembly   The U command "unassembles" object code, translating it back into assembly language instructions. Each U unassembles about 15 instructions, displaying the address, object code, and assembler-language code for each instruction on the screen. When a program is first loaded, U will unassemble the first 15 instructions in the code segment. A second U will unassemble the next 15, and so on. If you don't want to start at the beginning and go on consecutively, you can name an instruction where unassembly should begin; just specify the offset. You must know the offset, however. You can't just give a number in the likely range. Disassembly must start at the beginning of an instruction, not somewhere in the middle of one. Our assembly listing tells us that the GETNAME procedure starts at 001E. U 001E would disassemble the first 15 instructions from GETNAME; another U (without an offset) would take up at the 16th instruction of GETNAME.

Figure 4.4 shows the CRT display for two U commands starting at the beginning of NAMEX's code segment. The far left of each line shows the segment number and offset for each instruction. If you DEBUG NAMEX, your segment numbers will probably be different, but the offsets should be the same.

Let's compare these first 30 instructions with the assembly listing. Notice that none of the pseudo-ops are included in the unassembly. Remember that these are not part of the object code. All the numbers in the DEBUG display are hexadecimal, shown with two digits for a one-byte field and four for a one-word field. All the variable names have been replaced by offsets, of course, since DEBUG would not find names in the object code. When DEBUG displays an address operand it always encloses it in brackets to distinguish it from an immediate data operand. You see several of these in Figure 4.4 and you will see more examples in other displays in this sample session. Look at offset 001D in Figure 4.4. There is

```
-U

0AAE:0000 1E          PUSH    DS
0AAE:0001 B80000      MOV     AX,0000
0AAE:0004 50          PUSH    AX
0AAE:0005 B8B50A      MOV     AX,0AB5
0AAE:0008 8ED8        MOV     DS,AX
0AAE:000A 8EC0        MOV     ES,AX
0AAE:000C E84900      CALL    0058
0AAE:000F E80C00      CALL    001E
0AAE:0012 E81600      CALL    002B
0AAE:0015 B90500      MOV     CX,0005
0AAE:0018 E83000      CALL    004B
0AAE:001B E2FB        LOOP    0018
0AAE:001D CB          RETF
0AAE:001E 50          PUSH    AX
0AAE:001F 52          PUSH    DX
-U

0AAE:0020 B40A        MOV     AH,0A
0AAE:0022 8D161E01    LEA     DX,[011E]
0AAE:0026 CD21        INT     21
0AAE:0028 5A          POP     DX
0AAE:0029 58          POP     AX
0AAE:002A C3          RET
0AAE:002B 51          PUSH    CX
0AAE:002C 53          PUSH    BX
0AAE:002D 56          PUSH    SI
0AAE:002E 57          PUSH    DI
0AAE:002F B500        MOV     CH,00
0AAE:0031 8A0E1F01    MOV     CL,[011F]
0AAE:0035 8BD9        MOV     BX,CX
0AAE:0037 8D362001    LEA     SI,[0120]
0AAE:003B 8D3E1F00    LEA     DI,[001F]
0AAE:003F F3          REPZ
0AAE:0040 A4          MOVSB
```

Figure 4.4 Unassembly

an instruction (RETF) that was not in NAMEX: NAMEX has RET. The instruction was assembled as a far return, so DEBUG unassembles it as RETF. You will see other examples where the output from DEBUG is slightly different from the input to MASM. If you have your assembly listing, this won't matter. The main reason for using U is to find the offsets of instructions so you can use them with other commands. When you can identify these offsets from the assembly listing, you don't need to unassemble the code.

Go   Let's execute the part of the program that sets up the return address and segment registers so that we can see where our segments will begin. The G command, used with a specified offset, executes the program up to (but not including) the instruction at that offset. Specifying an offset where execution should stop is called **setting a breakpoint**. Again, you must specify an offset that is the beginning of an instruction. Both the assembly listing and Figure 4.4 tell us that the location we are interested in is offset 000C, so we enter G 000C. Figure 4.5 shows the result.

When you enter a G command, the program runs from its current instruction to the specified breakpoint. In this example, it starts at the beginning and goes to 000C. Then, DEBUG displays the current contents of the registers, including IP, and the current status of the flags. It then shows the address, object code, and unassembled code for the next instruction to be executed—the one at the breakpoint. If the next instruction uses an address operand, the current value at that address is displayed on the right.

Look at the display in Figure 4.5. We can see the segment numbers in DS, ES, SS, and CS. The next instruction, in IP, is 000C, as we would expect. The value of AX is 0AB5, which Figure 4.4 tells us was placed there by the instruction at 0005. SP tells us that the top of the stack is at 01FC in the stack segment; we'll use that information a little later. Our program hasn't used the other registers yet, so their values are meaningless to us. The two-letter codes following IP indicate the status of OF, DF, IF, SF, ZF, AF, PF, and CF in that order. You can find the meanings of the codes in the DOS manual's DEBUG chapter under the Register command; we're not going to use the flags in this sample session.

Display   Before we continue executing NAMEX, let's look at the stack and data segments. You know that we start using the stack at the bottom, or end, and the assembly listing tells us that the end is offset 0200 of the segment. Let's look at the last 32 bytes, starting at 01E0. The command D, with an address, displays eight rows of 16 bytes each, with the beginning address for each row on the left and the ASCII translation on the right. Figure 4.6 shows the result of entering the command D SS:01E0. Remember that SP currently points to 01FC—that's the fourth byte from the right in the second row. We find two bytes, or one word, of zeros at that spot. Remember the zero pushed on the stack for the return address offset? Following that, at the bottom of the stack, we find 9E and 0A; this should be the return address segment number pushed from DS at the beginning of the program. Remember that words are written with the low-order byte first, so the actual return address being saved is 0A9E:0000.

Let's also look at the beginning of the data segment. Figure 4.7 shows the result of D DS:0000 and then another D without an address. The unaddressed D takes up where the last display left off: in this case, at DS:0080. The data segment does not contain much of interest at this point; we'll look back at it a little later in the program.

```
-G 000C


AX=0AB5  BX=0000  CX=0490  DX=0000  SP=01FC  BP=0000  SI=0000  DI=0000
DS=0AB5  ES=0AB5  SS=0AD7  CS=0AAE  IP=000C   NV UP DI PL NZ NA PO NC
0AAE:000C E84900         CALL      0058
```

Figure 4.5 Go

```
-D SS:01E0

0AD7:01E0  53 54 41 43 4B 20 20 20-53 54 41 43 4B 20 20 20   STACK    STACK
0AD7:01F0  53 54 41 43 4B 20 0C 00-AE 0A 98 07 00 00 9E 0A   STACK .........
0AD7:0200  C8 2A C5 74 03 E8 30 00-A0 74 46 0A C0 75 26 A0   H*Et.h0. tF.?u&
0AD7:0210  26 02 0A C0 B0 01 74 03-E8 2B 00 02 C1 A2 73 46   &..?0.t.h+..A"sF
0AD7:0220  04 03 3A 06 39 46 72 0D-32 C0 A2 73 46 A2 72 46   ..:.9Fr.2?"sF"rF
0AD7:0230  F6 D0 A2 74 46 5B 59 C3-C6 06 74 46 00 C3 FE 0F   vP"tF[YCF.tF.C~.
0AD7:0240  78 01 C3 FE 07 C3 B0 01-C3 E8 33 0A A0 DF 44 75   x.C~.C0.Ch3. _Du
0AD7:0250  01 C3 53 8D 1E B9 43 3A-07 73 02 8A 07 5B C3 E8   .CS..9C:.s...[Ch
```

Figure 4.6 Displaying the Stack

Register

Register   The Register Command, R, serves several purposes. When R is used alone, it simply repeats the display of current registers, flags, and next instruction. The beginning of Figure 4.8 shows the result using R in this way. Later, you will see R used to change a register's contents.

After recreating the current display, use G to continue to 0064, the instruction that returns from PROMPTER. Notice the name prompt displayed as PROMPTER is executed. Next, execute just one instruction, RET. To do this, use the Trace command.

Trace   The Trace command, T, executes the current instruction and then presents the current information and next instruction display. You can use T to execute a series of instructions; just include the number, as in T 3 or T 5. The end of Figure 4.8 shows the result of executing the single instruction RET with T. Executing RET returns the program to the main driver, where it is now waiting to carry out the next CALL.

WARNING: DO NOT USE T TO EXECUTE AN INT. A trace command will take you into the interrupt routine itself. Not only will you have no guide to what is happening, but the routine itself will often fail and go into an endless loop. I/O routines involve exact timing. The delays caused

```
-D DS:0000

0AB5:0000  0A 0D 57 48 41 54 20 49-53 20 59 4F 55 52 20 4E   ..WHAT IS YOUR N
0AB5:0010  41 4D 45 3F 20 24 0A 0D-48 45 4C 4C 4F 2C 20 20   AME? $..HELLO,
0AB5:0020  20 20 20 20 20 20 20 20-20 20 20 20 20 20 20 20
0AB5:0030  20 20 20 20 20 20 20 20-20 20 20 20 20 20 20 20
0AB5:0040  20 20 20 20 20 20 20 20-20 20 20 20 20 20 20 20
0AB5:0050  20 20 20 20 20 20 20 20-20 20 20 20 20 20 20 20
0AB5:0060  20 20 20 20 20 20 20 20-20 20 20 20 20 20 20 20
0AB5:0070  20 20 20 20 20 20 20 20-20 20 20 20 20 20 20 20
-D

0AB5:0080  20 20 20 20 20 20 20 20-20 20 20 20 20 20 20 20
0AB5:0090  20 20 20 20 20 20 20 20-20 20 20 20 20 20 20 20
0AB5:00A0  20 20 20 20 20 20 20 20-20 20 20 20 20 20 20 20
0AB5:00B0  20 20 20 20 20 20 20 20-20 20 20 20 20 20 20 20
0AB5:00C0  20 20 20 20 20 20 20 20-20 20 20 20 20 20 20 20
0AB5:00D0  20 20 20 20 20 20 20 20-20 20 20 20 20 20 20 20
0AB5:00E0  20 20 20 20 20 20 20 20-20 20 20 20 20 20 20 20
0AB5:00F0  20 20 20 20 20 20 20 20-20 20 20 20 20 20 20 20
```

Figure 4.7 Displaying the Data Segment

```
-R
AX=0AB5  BX=0000  CX=0490  DX=0000  SP=01FC  BP=0000  SI=0000  DI=0000
DS=0AB5  ES=0AB5  SS=0AD7  CS=0AAE  IP=000C  NV UP DI PL NZ NA PO NC
0AAE:000C E84900          CALL    0058
-G 0064


WHAT IS YOUR NAME?
AX=0AB5  BX=0000  CX=0490  DX=0000  SP=01FA  BP=0000  SI=0000  DI=0000
DS=0AB5  ES=0AB5  SS=0AD7  CS=0AAE  IP=0064  NV UP DI PL NZ NA PO NC
0AAE:0064 C3              RET
-T


AX=0AB5  BX=0000  CX=0490  DX=0000  SP=01FC  BP=0000  SI=0000  DI=0000
DS=0AB5  ES=0AB5  SS=0AD7  CS=0AAE  IP=000F  NV UP DI PL NZ NA PO NC
0AAE:000F E80C00          CALL    001E
```

Figure 4.8 Register and Trace

by stepping through with T can cause such routines to fail. When the next
instruction is INT, always choose a breakpoint address and use a G command to go there.

Continuing with the Program   At this point, use G 0015 to allow the
program to execute the GETNAME and MOVENAME procedures without
stopping. Notice the input (DONNA N. TABLER) in the beginning of
Figure 4.9 as the program reaches the place where the keyboard input
routine is executed. Next, as in the figure, display the beginning of the data
segment again; this time, you can see the output message moved into place.
Then, another R and T take us to the point where the printloop begins.
Here, try making a change: use the register command to make a change in
the count register so that the loop will repeat seven times instead of five.
The sequence of events is shown in Figure 4.10.

```
-G 0015

DONNA N. TABLER

AX=0AB5  BX=0000  CX=0490  DX=0000  SP=01FC  BP=0000  SI=0000  DI=0000
DS=0AB5  ES=0AB5  SS=0AD7  CS=0AAE  IP=0015  NV UP DI PL NZ NA PO NC
0AAE:0015 B90500          MOV     CX,0005
-D DS:0000

0AB5:0000  0A 0D 57 48 41 54 20 49-53 20 59 4F 55 52 20 4E   ..WHAT IS YOUR N
0AB5:0010  41 4D 45 3F 20 24 0A 0D-48 45 4C 4C 4F 2C 20 44   AME? $..HELLO, D
0AB5:0020  4F 4E 4E 41 20 4E 2E 20-54 41 42 4C 45 52 24 20   ONNA N. TABLER$
0AB5:0030  20 20 20 20 20 20 20 20-20 20 20 20 20 20 20 20
0AB5:0040  20 20 20 20 20 20 20 20-20 20 20 20 20 20 20 20
0AB5:0050  20 20 20 20 20 20 20 20-20 20 20 20 20 20 20 20
0AB5:0060  20 20 20 20 20 20 20 20-20 20 20 20 20 20 20 20
0AB5:0070  20 20 20 20 20 20 20 20-20 20 20 20 20 20 20 20
```

Figure 4.9 A Second Look at the Data

```
-R

AX=0AB5  BX=0000  CX=0490  DX=0000  SP=01FC  BP=0000  SI=0000  DI=0000
DS=0AB5  ES=0AB5  SS=0AD7  CS=0AAE  IP=0015   NV UP DI PL NZ NA PO NC
0AAE:0015 B90500        MOV     CX,0005
-T

AX=0AB5  BX=0000  CX=0005  DX=0000  SP=01FC  BP=0000  SI=0000  DI=0000
DS=0AB5  ES=0AB5  SS=0AD7  CS=0AAE  IP=0018   NV UP DI PL NZ NA PO NC
0AAE:0018 E83000        CALL    004B
-R CX

CX 0005
:0007

-R

AX=0AB5  BX=0000  CX=0007  DX=0000  SP=01FC  BP=0000  SI=0000  DI=0000
DS=0AB5  ES=0AB5  SS=0AD7  CS=0AAE  IP=0018   NV UP DI PL NZ NA PO NC
0AAE:0018 E83000        CALL    004B
-G


HELLO, DONNA N. TABLER

HELLO, DONNA N. TABLER

HELLO, DONNA N. TABLER

HELLO, DONNA N. TABLER

HELLO, DONNA N. TABLER

HELLO, DONNA N. TABLER

HELLO, DONNA N. TABLER
Program terminated normally
-Q
```

Figure 4.10 Changing a Register

First, we enter R CX. DEBUG displays the current contents of CX and gives us a special prompt, a colon (:). After the prompt, enter the new value. You can't change just AH or AL with this command; the new value must be a whole 16-bit value. Next, as shown in Figure 4.10, use R again to check that the change has been made. Finally, use G with no breakpoint address; this let the program continue until it ends. You can see that the message is displayed seven times, not five. After the program ends, we get out of DEBUG by using Q, for Quit.

Computer Exercise

Run NAMEX under DEBUG. First duplicate the session just discussed. Notice that while offsets are the same in your session, the numbers in the segment registers may be different because your program is probably loaded at different addresses. Explore some more with DEBUG. Try changing the contents of some data fields. For example, change INBUF to 20 and see what happens when you enter more than 19 characters.

Key Points From Chapter 4

In this chapter you have learned to assemble, link, and run a MASM program. Key points covered in this chapter include:

■   The simplest way to assemble a MASM program is to type:

MASM

and let the assembler prompt you for the names of the source-code, object-code, listing, and cross-reference files. The extensions for these names should default to ASM, OBJ, LST, and CRF, respectively.

■   The quickest way to assemble a MASM program is to type the desired filenames on the MASM command line. To assemble a program from source code file PROG.ASM type:

MASM PROG ;

which will produce an object file PROG.OBJ, but no listing or cross reference. Or else, type:

MASM PROG , , LPT1 : ;

to produce both the object file and a printed listing.

■   The easiest way to link a MASM program is to type:

LINK

and let the linker prompt you for the desired filenames.

■ The quickest way to link an object program called PROG.OBJ is to type:

LINK PROG;

which will produce a run file name PROG.EXE and no listing.

■ To run a program, type the run file name without the extension. To run PROG.EXE, type:

PROG

■ Use DEBUG to trace your program's execution and find out what is happening during a run.

Chapter Review Questions

1. What command would you use to assemble NEWPROG with an object file but no listing or cross-reference file?

2. What command would you use to link NEWPROG without producing a list file?

3. What command would you use to assemble SAMPLER with a printed listing, but no object file?

4. You have assembled and linked NEWPROG, producing a run file named NEWPROG.EXE. What command would you use to run NEWPROG?

Answers

1. MASM NEWPROG; 2. LINK NEWPROG; 3. MASM SAMPLER,,LPT1:; 4. NEWPROG

Computer Exercise

Assemble, link, and run PHONER, the program you wrote at the end of Chapter 3. Run PHONER under DEBUG, looking at the changes in the stack and data areas as the program runs. Try some changes, such as repeating the main part of the program five times instead of three. Explore. Enjoy. You can't hurt the computer; at worst, you may have to turn it off and restart it.

5

Defining and Using Macros

Now that you know something about writing, assembling, and running a MASM program, you are ready to learn to use macros in your programs. You will find several advantages to using macros: you can write programs faster, you can be sure that similar situations are handled uniformly, and you can reduce both assembler and run time errors. In this chapter you will learn to define macros and their parameters, to call macros, to pass values to them, and to build a macro library to use in your programs. Some of the most useful macros handle I/O interrupts. So far you have learned only two interrupt functions; in this chapter you will learn several that will serve as examples of macros.

Defining Macros

Most MASM programs include many repeated sequences of instructions. Every time a message is displayed on the screen, for example, the address of the message must be moved to DX, AH must be set to function 9, and then interrupt 21H must be called. A program that interacts with a user repeats these instructions many times. We can code this function in a general way like this:

```
LEA DX , MESSAGE
MOV AH , 9
I NT 21H
```

To make this general series of instructions into a macro, we must begin and end the definition with special pseudo-ops.

Beginning and Ending the Macro Definition

Every macro definition begins with a MACRO pseudo-op. The format is:

```
name MACRO [dummy l i s t]
```

Name is required. The macro name is used to call the macro in the rest of the program. We'll name our sample macro DISPLAY.

Dummylist is a list of the macro's parameters (separated by commas). The list is optional; not all macros have parameters. You will see examples of macros with and without parameters in this chapter. The parameters from the dummylist are used within the macro definition; they are called **dummy parameters**. When the macro is called, the dummy parameters are replaced by names or values specified by the calling instruction.

DISPLAY needs one dummy parameter, MESSAGE, to identify the beginning offset of the message being displayed. The MACRO pseudo-op for DISPLAY, then, will be:

```
D I SPLAY MACRO MESSAGE
```

The **macro body** contains the series of instructions that will be copied into the program (with appropriate replacement values) when the macro is called. We have already defined three instructions (LEA, MOV, and INT 21H) that will be the body of the macro DISPLAY.

Each macro definition must end with an ENDM pseudo-op. This pseudo-op cannot have a name or operand. It's just the operation code, ENDM. The definition of DISPLAY, then, could look like this:

```
DISPLAY    MACRO    MESSAGE
           LEA      DX,MESSAGE
           MOV      AH,9
           INT      21H
           ENDM
```

Later in this chapter, we'll discuss how macros are called and used. Now, though, let's review what you have learned by coding another simple macro definition, this one without parameters.

Clearing the Screen

A program that uses screen displays often needs to clear the screen. In BASIC, you do this with the CLS command; in MASM, you must use a function of interrupt 10H. This is a BIOS interrupt that has 15 different functions, all of them concerned with video I/O. We will discuss several of these functions in this book. You will find the information needed to use all of them in Chapter 12 along with a discussion of some other useful BIOS interrupts.

We will use function 6, upward scroll, to clear the screen. (We could just as well use function 7, downward scroll.) The scrolling action takes place within a window. The window's upper left and lower right positions must be defined before the function is called. The number of lines to be scrolled must also be defined. If n lines are scrolled, the top n lines of the window disappear. The remaining lines in the window move up n lines, and n blank lines appear at the bottom of the window. Usually, the scrolling action takes place too rapidly for your eyes to follow; the new screen just appears. To scroll the entire window, scroll 0 lines. To clear the entire screen, define a window that starts at row 0, column 0 and ends at row 24, column 79 and scroll the entire window.

You must also specify an attribute value for the blank lines scrolled in. Each character on the screen has an attribute. The attribute assigned for the line will be attached to any character later written on that line.

Attribute values for black and white display are:

    7 - white on black, normal intensity (normal display)

  112 - black on white, normal intensity (reverse video)

    0 - black on black, normal intensity (no display)

  119 - white on white, normal intensity (no display)

Add 8 to any value to produce high intensity. Add 128 to produce blinking characters. An attribute of 248, then, will produce high-intensity reverse video with blinking characters. When clearing the screen, you usually assign blank lines an attribute value of 7. (See the IBM Technical Reference Manual for color-display attribute values.)

The registers used for this function, and their appropriate settings when clearing the screen, are:

AH - function number - 6

AL - number of lines - 0

CH - upper left row - 0

CL - upper left column - 0

DH - lower right row - 24

DL - lower right column - 79

BH - attribute value - 7

Let's name the macro CLS, since we are duplicating the CLS command from BASIC. The macro definition will be:

```
CLS     MACRO
        MOV             AH , 6
        MOV             AL , 0
        MOV             CH , 0
        MOV             CL , 0
        MOV             DH , 24
        MOV             DL , 79
        MOV             BH , 7
        INT             10H
        ENDM
```

This macro uses no dummy parameters; all the parameters are fixed.

```
The MOVE Macro
        MOVE    MACRO   TO,FROM,CHAR
                LEA     SI,FROM
                LEA     DI,TO
                MOV     CX,CHAR
                REP MOVSB
                ENDM
```

Figure 5.1 The MOVE Macro

One More Sample

Figure 5.1 shows a definition for a macro named MOVE that handles string moves. It has three dummy parameters: the locations between which data is to be moved and the number of characters to be moved. To be consistent with the general pattern of MASM instructions, we have coded the parameters using the destination as the first parameter and the source as the second. The number of characters is the third parameter.

Review Questions

1. For each of these statements, specify whether it is true of the MACRO pseudo-op, the ENDM pseudo-op, both, or neither.

    _____ A.   Required in every macro definition
    _____ B.   Requires a name
    _____ C.   Name is optional
    _____ D.   Name is not permitted
    _____ E.   Requires parameter list in operand field
    _____ F.   Parameter list is optional
    _____ G.   No parameter list is permitted

2. Function 2 of Interrupt 10H sets the cursor position. DH must contain the row, and DL the column, for the position. BH must contain the number of the page for which the cursor position is set. We will always use the first page, page 0, in this book. Look at this definition of a macro intended to duplicate BASIC's LOCATE function:

```
LOCATE    MACRO   ROW,COL
          MOV     AH,2
          MOV     DH,ROW
          MOV     DL,COL
          MOV     BH,0
          INT     10H
```

A.   What is the name of this macro?

B.   How many lines are in the body of the macro?

C.   How many dummy parameters are used in this macro?

D.   What are the dummy parameters?

E.   What is missing from this macro definition?

3.   Function 1 of interrupt 10H can be used to turn the cursor on by setting both CH and CL to 7, or to turn it off by setting CH to 39 and CL to 7. (These values assume that you have a Color Graphics Adaptor. For the Monochrome Adaptor, use 31 as the value in CH and CL to turn the cursor on; use 63 and 31, respectively, to turn it off.)

A.   Code a definition for macro CURSORON to turn the cursor on.

B.   Code a definition for macro CURSOROFF to turn the cursor off.

Answers

1. A. Both B. MACRO C. Neither D. ENDM E. Neither F. MACRO G. ENDM   2. A. LOCATE B. 5 C. 2 D. ROW and COL E. There should be an ENDM pseudo-op at the end of the macro definition.
3. A. CURSORON MACRO

```
         MOV   AH,1
         MOV   CH,7
         MOV   CL,7
         INT   10H
         ENDM
```

  B. CURSOROFF MACRO

```
         MOV   AH,1
         MOV   CH,39
         MOV   CL,7
         INT   10H
         ENDM
```

Using Macros

Defining a macro is like providing a new operation code for MASM. To call (use) the macro, code its name as the opcode of an instruction. In the operand field, code a list of **actual parameters** corresponding to MACRO's list of dummy parameters.

To use DISPLAY to display NAMEPROMPT, MESSAGE must be replaced by NAMEPROMPT. To display ERROR__MESSAGE, MESSAGE must be replaced by ERROR__MESSAGE. To display ENDMESS, MESSAGE must be replaced by ENDMESS. To display these three messages, one after another, you could code this series of instructions:

```
D I SPLAY NAMEPROMPT
D I SPLAY ERROR__MESSAGE
D I SPLAY ENDMESS
```

The CLS macro has no parameters; calling it is simply a matter of coding CLS as an operation code. The MOVE macro, on the other hand, requires three actual parameters in every call. You could call it with:

```
MOVE OUTMESSAGE , I NMESSAGE , 20
```

or:

```
MOVE PR I NTMESS , ERRMESS , COUNT
```

Expanding the Macro

Remember that the MASM assembler makes two passes through the program. One of its jobs on the first pass is to **expand** each macro call. Expanding a macro means copying each line of the macro body into the source program and replacing dummy parameters by actual parameters. Replacement values are assigned on the basis of position. That means that the dummy parameter list in the MACRO instruction is compared to the actual parameter list in the operand field of the macro call. The first actual parameter replaces the first dummy parameter and so on. On the second pass, the macro expansion is translated into machine code.

When a program that uses DISPLAY is assembled, each DISPLAY instruction is replaced by the macro body with appropriate substitutions for parameters. DISPLAY NAMEPROMPT, for example, is replaced by:

```
LEA    DX,NAMEPROMPT
MOV    AH,9
INT    21H
```

These three instructions are translated into object code by the assembler; DISPLAY NAMEPROMPT is not translated. If you unassemble your program under DEBUG, you never see a DISPLAY instruction. Instead, you see a series of three instructions:

```
LEA    DX,[....]
MOV    AH,09
INT    21
```

wherever you coded DISPLAY in your program.

Looking at Macro Expansions

Figure 5.2 shows part of an assembler listing that includes several calls to the MOVE macro. Notice the segment offsets that are printed on the left for each assembled instruction. Look at the procedure named MESSAGES, starting at offset 0010H in the code segment. The MOVE macro is first called to move 20 characters from INPUT__MESSAGE to OUT-PUT__MESSAGE. (Notice that no offset or object code is generated for the MOVE instruction; the instruction is not part of the object code.) The next four lines contain the actual source code translated by the assembler. The "+" between the object code and the source code indicates that the line is generated by a macro call.

Compare those lines (offsets 0010H through 001BH) with those generated by the second call to MOVE (offsets 001DH through 0028H). Notice that all the source and count parameters have been replaced by different names or immediate values.

```
0010                                    MESSAGES PROC
                                            MOVE      OUTPUT_MESSAGE,INPUT_MESSAGE,30
0010  B9 001E                      +        MOV       CX,30
0013  8D 36 0040 R                 +        LEA       SI,INPUT_MESSAGE
0017  8D 3E 0000 R                 +        LEA       DI,OUTPUT_MESSAGE
001B  F3/ A4                       +        REP MOVSB
                                            MOVE      OUTPUT_MESSAGE,ERROR_MESSAGE,15
001D  B9 000F                      +        MOV       CX,15
0020  8D 36 0080 R                 +        LEA       SI,ERROR_MESSAGE
0024  8D 3E 0000 R                 +        LEA       DI,OUTPUT_MESSAGE
0028  F3/ A4                       +        REP MOVSB
                                            MOVE      OUTPUT_MESSAGE,INPUT_MESSAGE,COUNT
002A  8B 0E 00C0 R                 +        MOV       CX,COUNT
002E  8D 36 0040 R                 +        LEA       SI,INPUT_MESSAGE
0032  8D 3E 0000 R                 +        LEA       DI,OUTPUT_MESSAGE
0036  F3/ A4                       +        REP MOVSB
```

Figure 5.2 Macro Expansions

```
                                            MOVE      OUTPUT_MESSAGE,ERROR_MESSAGE
0038  B9 0000                      +        MOV       CX,
003B  8D 36 0080 R                 +        LEA       SI,ERROR_MESSAGE
003F  8D 3E 0000 R                 +        LEA       DI,OUTPUT_MESSAGE
0043  F3/ A4                       +        REP MOVSB
                                            MOVE      OUTPUT_MESSAGE,,COUNT
0045  8B 0E 00C0 R                 +        MOV       CX,COUNT
0049  8D B6 0000                   +        LEA       SI,
E r r o r    ---        56:No immediate mode
004D  8D 3E 0000 R                 +        LEA       DI,OUTPUT_MESSAGE
0051  F3/ A4                       +        REP MOVSB
```

Figure 5.3 Missing Parameters

Look at the third call to MOVE (following offset 0028H). This time the "number of characters" parameter names a data field instead of an immediate value. When the parameter is used (offset 002AH), it still produces a legitimate instruction since MOV can move data from an address to a register as well as from an immediate value.

Omitting Parameters

What happens if you leave out an actual parameter in the call? Figure 5.3 shows two expansions of the MOVE macro. In the first one, the third parameter has been omitted. In the second, following offset 0043H, the source-field parameter has been skipped. In both cases, the appropriate dummy parameter has been replaced by a nul (00) immediate value. The instruction generated at offset 0038H is a valid instruction, since MOV can use an immediate value in the second operand. But, it will cause invalid results and possibly an endless loop at execution time. The instruction generated at offset 0049H causes an assembler error, since you can't use an immediate value with LEA.

Review Questions

1. Which statements are true?

    A. To call a macro, code the macro name as an operation code.

    B. Actual parameters are those in the body of the macro definition.

    C. All macro calls require a parameter list.

    D. If an actual parameter is omitted in a macro call, a null value will be supplied in the macro expansion.

2. Using macros defined in this chapter and the preceding set of questions, code instructions to:

    A. Turn the cursor on.

    B. Turn the cursor off.

    C. Move the cursor to position 0,0.

    D. Move the cursor to the lower left corner of the screen (row 24, column 79).

Answers

1. A and D are true. Here's what's wrong with the others: B. Actual parameters are those found in the macro call. D. A parameter list is required in a macro call only if the macro definition includes parameters.   **2.** A. CURSORON B. CURSOROFF C. LOCATE 0,0 D. LOCATE 24,79

Improving Macros

Let's write a more flexible macro to display messages, one that can display a message a number of times. We'll call this new macro MULTDISP. Part of its definition could go like this:

```
MULTDISP    MACRO    MESSAGE , COUNT
            . . .
            MOV      CX , COUNT
REPEAT :
            LEA      DX , MESSAGE
            MOV      AH , 9
            INT      21H
            LOOP     REPEAT
            . . .
            ENDM
```

If MULTDISP is called first using OUTMESS and 5 as replacement values, the first expansion of the macro includes:

```
          . . .
          MOV      CX , 5
REPEAT :
          LEA      DX , OUTMESS
          MOV      AH , 9
          INT      21H
          LOOP     REPEAT
```

A second expansion, using ERRMESS and 3 as replacement values, produce these lines:

```
          . . .
          MOV      CX , 3
REPEAT :
          LEA      DX , ERRMESS
          MOV      AH , 9
          INT      21H
          LOOP     REPEAT
```

The label REPEAT now occurs twice in the program. This causes an assembler error. Each label in the code segment must be unique. How can you manage that and still be able to use labels within macros? By using the LOCAL pseudo-op.

The LOCAL Pseudo-op

The LOCAL pseudo-op lists all the labels used within a macro. Each time the macro is expanded, the assembler creates a unique symbol for each label listed and substitutes that symbol for the label used in the macro definition. The format of the pseudo-op is:

```
LOCAL dummylist
```

where dummylist is a list of labels separated by commas. LOCAL must be the first instruction after MACRO; not even comments can come between MACRO and LOCAL.

When we add LOCAL to MULTDISP, it looks like this:

```
MULTDISP   MACRO    MESSAGE , COUNT
           LOCAL    REPEAT
           . . .
           MOV      CX , COUNT
REPEAT :
           LEA      DX , MESSAGE
           MOV      AH , 9
           INT      21H
           LOOP     REPEAT
           . . .
           ENDM
```

When the macro is expanded, the assembler replaces REPEAT by a unique symbol made up of two question marks (??) followed by a four-digit hexadecimal number. If a program's macro expansions include several local labels, the first one used will be replaced by ??0000, the second by ??0001, and so on. Suppose that MULTDISP is the first macro expanded in a program (or at least the first one that includes a local label). The expansion includes these lines:

```
           . . .
??0000 :
           . . .
           LOOP     ??0000
           . . . .
```

If MULTDISP is also the second expanded macro, the second expansion will include these lines:

```
           . . .
??0001 :
           . . .
           LOOP     ??0001
           . . .
```

Caution: Don't try to use this capability to define data fields within a macro. Remember that data fields are expected to be in a data segment, while macros generally are used within a code segment. Data for macros is generally either passed by parameters or by placing values in registers. If a macro must use a data field that cannot be a parameter, define the field in the data segment of each program that calls the macro.

Nesting Macros

Macros can be nested. This means that a macro definition can call another previously defined macro. We could have defined MULTDISP like this:

```
MULTDISP     MACRO     MESSAGE , COUNT
             LOCAL     REPEAT
             MOV       CX , COUNT
REPEAT :
             DISPLAY MESSAGE
             LOOP      REPEAT
             ENDM
```

as long as the definition of DISPLAY occurred in the source code before MULTDISP.

Preserving Register Values

You have learned that it is wise to preserve the original values of registers when using subroutines (except when a changed register value is specifically expected as a result of the subroutine). The same principle applies to the use of registers in macros. When you code a macro definition, you don't know what the situation will be when the macro is called. The MULTDISP macro, for example, could be called on as part of a routine that is using AX, CX, or DX for its own purposes. It's good practice, then, to preserve the original values of registers in a macro as well as in a subroutine. Our full MULTDISP macro should look like this:

```
MULTDISP     MACRO     MESSAGE , COUNT
             LOCAL     REPEAT
             PUSH      AX
             PUSH      CX
             PUSH      DX
             MOV       CX , COUNT
REPEAT :
             LEA       DX , MESSAGE
             MOV       AH , 9
             INT       21H
             LOOP      REPEAT
             POP       DX
             POP       CX
             POP       AX
             ENDM
```

```
Sample Macros

CLS     MACRO                   MOVE    MACRO    TO,FROM,CHAR
        PUSH    AX                      PUSH     SI
        PUSH    BX                      PUSH     DI
        PUSH    CX                      PUSH     CX
        PUSH    DX                      LEA      SI,FROM
        MOV     AH,6                    LEA      DI,TO
        MOV     AL,0                    MOV      CX,CHAR
        MOV     CH,0                    REP  MOVSB
        MOV     CL,0                    POP      CX
        MOV     DH,24                   POP      DI
        MOV     DL,79                   POP      SI
        MOV     BH,7                    ENDM
        INT     10H             ;
        POP     DX              STARTER MACRO
        POP     CX                      PUSH     DS
        POP     BX                      MOV      AX,0
        POP     AX                      PUSH     AX
        ENDM                            MOV      AX,PROG_DATA
;                                       MOV      DS,AX
DISPLAY MACRO   MESSAGE                 MOV      ES,AX
        PUSH    AX                      ENDM
        PUSH    DX
        LEA     DX,MESSAGE
        MOV     AH,9
        INT     21H
        POP     DX
        POP     AX
        ENDM
;
LOCATE  MACRO   ROW,COL
        PUSH    AX
        PUSH    BX
        PUSH    DX
        MOV     AH,2
        MOV     DH,ROW
        MOV     DL,COL
        MOV     BH,0
        INT     10H
        POP     DX
        POP     BX
        POP     AX
        ENDM
```

Figure 5.4 Sample Macros

Similar PUSH and POP instructions should be added to the other sample macros from this chapter. Figure 5.4 shows complete definitions for all these macros.

Learning More About Macros

You have learned enough to code many simple and useful macros. Four other pseudo-ops are used in macros: EXITM, IRP, IRPC, and REPT. One of them, PURGE, deletes a macro definition when it is no longer needed in a program (to save program space). Additionally, there are four symbols used for special purposes within macros (& %, !, :). As you become an experienced MASM programmer you may want to learn about these from the MASM manual so you can write more complex macros.

Review Questions

1. Here is part of the definition of CMAC:

```
CMAC          MACRO
                . . .
ALABEL :

              . . .
              LOOP    ALABEL
              . . .
              ENDM
```

   A.   Code an instruction that will ensure that no duplicate labels are generated by calling CMAC.

   B.   Where should the instruction go?

2. Revise the definitions of CURSORON and CURSOROFF to preserve register values.

3. Define a macro called CENTER that will clear the screen and display a message at position 12,30. The message will vary each time the macro is called. (Using already defined macros you should be able to code this macro in five lines.)

Answers

1. A. LOCAL ALABEL   B. Immediately following MACRO

2.
```
     CURSORON   MACRO
                PUSH        AX
                PUSH        CX
                MOV         AH , 1
                MOV         CH , 7
                MOV         CL , 7
                INT         10h
                POP         CX
                POP         AX
                ENDM
     CURSOROFF  MACRO
```

```
                    PUSH        AX
                    PUSH        CX
                    MOV         AH,1
                    MOV         CH,39
                    MOV         CL,7
                    INT         10H
                    POP         CX
                    POP         AX
                    ENDM
3.
        CENTER      MACRO       MESSAGE
                    CLS
                    LOCATE      12,30
                    DISPLAY     MESSAGE
                    ENDM
```

Placing the Definition

A macro definition must precede the first use of the macro. Usually, we put all the macro definitions at the beginning of the program, but this is not required as long as each definition comes before the first use of the macro.

You will probably want to use the same macro definitions in many programs. Macros such as CLS and MOVE, for example, may be useful in every program you write. You can use your editor or word processing program to create a file containing commonly used macro definitions; such a file is called a **macro library**. A macro library (or any other file) can be copied into a program by using the INCLUDE psuedo-op.

The INCLUDE Pseudo-Op

The format of the INCLUDE pseudo-op is simply:

```
    INCLUDE filename
```

The filename should include any necessary drive or path designations as well as the full filename. Valid INCLUDE statements might be:

```
INCLUDE B:MYLIB.LIB
INCLUDE A:VIDMAC01.ASM
INCLUDE DEFINES.LIB
```

When the assembler encounters INCLUDE, it looks for the specified file and copies it into the program being assembled. The copied source code is assembled as if it were part of the original program. The assembler listing shows a "C" in column 30 of each line copied from an INCLUDE file.

INCLUDE can occur at any point in a program. You can use INCLUDE at the beginning to copy a file of macro definitions. You might INCLUDE a file with a list of data definitions within the data segment. You might build a library file with commonly used PROCs and INCLUDE it within a code segment. Each INCLUDE causes the specified file to be copied into the program at the place where the INCLUDE occurs; then, the copied lines are treated as part of the original source code. The only restriction is that the INCLUDE file cannot itself contain an INCLUDE pseudo-op.

Multiple Macro Libraries

You can use several macro libraries in the same program. You might build one library containing only macros involving video routines, another with string-handling macros, and a third with printer routines. You could then INCLUDE one, two, or all of these libraries in a program, depending on which sets of macros would be useful in that program. A program can have a combination of macro definitions from one or more libraries as well as macros coded directly in the source code.

What happens if you include two macro libraries that happen to contain macros with the same name? No error message is generated and the most recent definition is used to expand macro calls. Look at this sequence of instructions (numbers are provided for reference):

```
1   AMAC      MACRO
                . . .            ;macro definition 1
              ENDM
                . . .
2             AMAC
                . . .
3             AMAC
                . . .
4   AMAC      MACRO
                . . .            ;macro definition 2
              ENDM
                . . .
5             AMAC
                . . .
```

The first two calls to AMAC (2 and 3) use the first macro definition (1). Then, the new definition (4) replaces the original one, and the next call (5) is expanded according to the new definition.

NAMEX with

```
        PAGE    ,132
;
        INCLUDE FIRSTLIB.LIB
;
PROG_STACK SEGMENT STACK 'STACK'
        DB      64 DUP ('STACK   ')
PROG_STACK ENDS
;
PROG_DATA  SEGMENT 'DATA'
NAMEPROMPT DB   0AH,0DH,'WHAT IS YOUR NAME? ',24H
OUTMESS DB      0AH,0DH,'HELLO, '
OUTNAME DB      255 DUP(' ')
INBUF   DB      255
INCOUNT DB      ?
INNAME  DB      255 DUP(' ')
ENDMESS DB      'END OF PROGRAM',24H
PROG_DATA  ENDS
;
PROG_CODE SEGMENT 'CODE'
MAIN_PROG PROC  FAR
        ASSUME  CS:PROG_CODE,DS:PROG_DATA,SS:PROG_STACK,ES:PROG_DATA
        STARTER
        CALL    PROMPTER                ;PROMPT FOR NAME
        CALL    GETNAME                 ;GET NAME INPUT
        CALL    MOVENAME                ;MOVE NAME TO OUTPUT LINE
        MOV     CX,5                    ;LOAD COUNTER FOR PRINTLOOP
PRINTLOOP:
        DISPLAY OUTMESS                 ;PRINT NAME MESSAGE
        LOOP    PRINTLOOP               ;     AND REPEAT CX TIMES
        CALL    FINAL
        RET                             ;THEN RETURN TO OPERATING SYSTEM
MAIN_PROG ENDP
;
FINAL   PROC
        LOCATE  24,0
        CURSOROFF
        DISPLAY ENDMESS
        RET
FINAL   ENDP
;
GETNAME PROC
        PUSH    AX
        PUSH    DX
        MOV     AH,0AH                  ;GET STRING FROM KEYBOARD/ECHO
        LEA     DX,INBUF                ;ADDRESS OF INPUT BUFFER
        INT     21H                     ;DOS
        POP     DX
        POP     AX
        RET
GETNAME ENDP
;
MOVENAME PROC
        PUSH    BX
        MOV     BH,0H                   ;SET COUNT FOR MOVE
        MOV     BL,INCOUNT
        MOVE    OUTNAME,INNAME,BX
        MOV     OUTNAME[BX],24H         ;NEXT CHAR IS $
        POP     BX
        RET
```

```
MOVENAME ENDP
;
PROMPTER PROC
         CLS
         CURSORON
         LOCATE  10,0
         DISPLAY NAMEPROMPT
         RET
PROMPTER ENDP
;
PROG_CODE ENDS
          END    MAIN_PROG
```

Figure 5.5 NAMEX with Macros

It's not a good idea to use different definitions for the same macro; your program will be easier to read and follow if each macro has one and only one definition. If your program uses several macro libraries or includes both macro libraries and separately coded macro definitions, be sure that you don't unintentionally use the same macro name for two different definitions. On the other hand, if you have the same macro definition in two (or more) libraries, you don't need to worry about errors arising from the inclusion of both libraries in the same program.

Computer Exercise

Enter the macro definitions from Figure 5.4 and the review questions as FIRSTLIB.LIB. Your library should include at least CLS, CURSORON, CURSOROFF, STARTER, LOCATE, DISPLAY, and MOVE. Then, enter NAME2.ASM, the program shown in Figure 5.5.

Now assemble NAME2, printing the assembly listing. Notice the copied lines (marked by "C") and the lines generated by the macro expansions (marked by " + "). Link and run NAME2. You can use the macros from FIRSTLIB.LIB as the basis of your own macro library.

Macros and Subroutines

Both macros and subroutines are used to reduce the number of lines coded by a programmer, thus reducing the possibility of errors. Even though a macro is coded only once, however, each of its lines is included in the program each time the macro is called. No program space is saved by using a macro. Subroutine lines, on the other hand, are included in the program only once, no matter how many times the subroutine is called. A long or frequently called routine may be better coded as a subroutine than as a macro.

The use of parameters makes a macro much more flexible than a subroutine. If you are going to use the same general routine with different data items, you will probably want to code it as a macro.

In many cases, the choice of coding a routine as a macro or a subroutine depends on the programmer's preference. Most programmers seem to prefer to use macros for routines that are used in many programs or that will be used in only one program, but with different data items. In turn, they often prefer to use subroutines for those routines used within a single program and to which data can easily be passed through registers or data fields.

Key Points From Chapter 5

- A macro definition must begin with a MACRO pseudo-op. The pseudo-op must include a name. The operand field may contain a list of dummy parameters, separated by commas.

- A macro definition must end with an ENDM pseudo-op. This pseudo-op has no name or operands; it consists solely of the operation code ENDM.

- The macro body contains the instructions to be copied into the program at the points where the macro is called.

- If the macro body includes one or more labels, the second statement in the definition must be a LOCAL pseudo-op that lists (in the operand field) all such labels, separated by commas.

- To call a macro, code its name as an operation code. The operand field must contain a list of actual parameters corresponding to the dummy parameters in the definition's MACRO pseudo-op.

■ On the first pass through the source code, the assembler expands any macros called. It replaces each calling instruction by the instructions copied from the appropriate macro body, with actual parameters replacing the dummy parameters in the body. Labels defined as local are also replaced by unique labels.

■ A macro definition must precede the first use of the macro in the source program.

■ A macro definition may include a call to a previously defined macro.

■ A source-code library that contains macro definitions (or any other source code) can be copied into a program during assembly by coding an INCLUDE pseudo-op which specifies the file to be copied.

Chapter Review Questions

1. Match each pseudo-op with the description that best fits it. Not all descriptions are used.

   _____ A.   MACRO   a.   Causes assembler to generate
   _____ B.   ENDM   unique labels
   _____ C.   LOCAL   b.   Causes macro expansion
   _____ D.   INCLUDE   c.   Begins a macro definition
                               d.   Ends a macro definition
                               e.   Causes assembler to copy a
                                    source code file

2. Which statements are true?

   A.   Every macro definition must end with an ENDM pseudo-op.

   B.   Every macro definition must include at least one dummy parameter.

   C.   The assembler matches actual parameters to dummy parameters by position in the parameter list.

   D.   The LOCAL pseudo-op tells the assembler that a macro definition is to be used in one program only.

3. Look at this macro definition:

```
SWAPBYTE    MACRO    ONE , TWO
            PUSH     AX
            MOV      AH , ONE
            MOV      AL , TWO
            MOV      ONE , AL
            MOV      TWO , AH
            POP      AX
            ENDM
```

A. What is the name of this macro?

B. Code an instruction that will call on this macro to swap two one-byte fields named HIGH and LOW.

Answers

1. A. c B. d C. a D. e; b is not used.   2.   A and C. B is false because a macro may have any number of parameters, or no parameters. D is false because the LOCAL pseudo-op identifies labels within a macro that must be replaced by unique symbols when the macro is expanded. 3. A. SWAP-BYTE B. SWAPBYTE HIGH,LOW or SWAPBYTE LOW,HIGH

Computer Exercise

Revise the PHONER program so that it clears the screen, turns on the cursor, and begins prompting somewhere near the middle of the screen. End the program by displaying the message "GOODBYE" on the bottom line of the screen and turn off the cursor. Use macros from your library as much as possible. Assemble, link, and run your revised program. If you have problems, look at our version of the program which follows.

```
        PAGE    ,132                    ;THIS IS THE SECOND
;                                       ;  VERSION OF THE PHONE
        INCLUDE FIRSTLIB.LIB            ;   NUMBER PROGRAM
;
GETDATA MACRO INBUF,COUNT
        PUSH  . AX
        PUSH    DX
        MOV     AH,0AH                  ;GET STRING FROM KEYBOARD/ECHO
        LEA     DX,INBUF                ;ADDRESS OF INPUT BUFFER
        MOV     INBUF,COUNT             ;SET INPUT SIZE FOR NAME
        INT     21H                     ;DOS
        POP     DX
        POP  ·  AX
        ENDM
;
```

```
PROG_STACK SEGMENT STACK 'STACK'
        DB        64 DUP ('STACK    ')
PROG_STACK ENDS
;
PROG_DATA  SEGMENT 'DATA'
NAMEPROMPT DB    0AH,0DH,'NAME: ',24H
PHONEPROMPT DB   0AH,0DH,'PHONE NUMBER: ',24H
ENDMESSAGE  DB   'GOODBYE',24H
OUTLINE DB       0AH,0DH
OUTPHONE DB      8 DUP(' ')
OUTSPACE DB      3 DUP(' ')
OUTNAME  DB      31 DUP(' ')
INBUF    DB      31
INCOUNT DB       ?
INDATA  DB       31 DUP(' ')
PROG_DATA  ENDS
;
PROG_CODE SEGMENT 'CODE'
MAIN_PROG PROC   FAR
        ASSUME   CS:PROG_CODE,DS:PROG_DATA,SS:PROG_STACK,ES:PROG_DATA
        STARTER
        CLS
        CURSORON
        LOCATE   10,0
        MOV      CX,3
MAINLOOP:
        CALL     GETNAME                ;PROMPT, INPUT, AND MOVE NAME
        CALL     GETPHONE               ;PROMPT AND INPUT PHONE
        DISPLAY OUTLINE                 ;DISPLAY LINE
        LOOP     MAINLOOP               ;   AND REPEAT PROCESS
        CALL     FINAL
        RET                             ;THEN RETURN TO OPERATING SYSTEM
MAIN_PROG ENDP
;
FINAL   PROC
        LOCATE   23,10
        DISPLAY ENDMESSAGE
        CURSOROFF
        RET
FINAL   ENDP
;
GETNAME PROC
        PUSH     BX
        DISPLAY NAMEPROMPT              ;PROMPT FOR NAME
        GETDATA INBUF,31                ;GET NAME IN BUFFER
        MOV      BH,0H                  ;SET UP NAME COUNT
        MOV      BL,INCOUNT
        MOVE     OUTNAME,INDATA,BX      ;MOVE NAME TO PRINT
        MOV      OUTNAME[BX],24H        ;NEXT CHAR IS $
        POP      BX
        RET
GETNAME ENDP
;
GETPHONE PROC
        DISPLAY PHONEPROMPT             ;PROMPT FOR PHONE
        GETDATA INBUF,9                 ;GET PHONE IN BUFFER
        MOVE     OUTPHONE,INDATA,8      ;MOVE PHONE TO PRINT
        RET
GETPHONE ENDP
;
PROG_CODE ENDS
        END      MAIN_PROG
```

6

Coding Operands

You have used the three operand types (registers, addresses, and immediate data) in their simplest forms. This chapter shows you how to code address operands with displacements and modifying registers. You will also learn to replace constants, such as those used in immediate operands, with symbolic names, which are more legible and easier to change. Furthermore, you will learn to use special operators to designate and change a variable field's attributes.

So far you don't have very many instructions in which to use these operands; most of the examples in this chapter involve MOV. You'll expand your instruction set in the next few chapters. If you learn a wide range of possible operands now, you will be able to make full use of new instructions as you encounter them.

Address Operands

Remember that an address operand specifies the location in which data will be found or placed during an operation. So far in this book, we have written address operands using the variable names (names of fields defined in the data segment, such as NAMEPROMPT) and variable names modified by the contents of a register (OUTNAME[BX]). The assembler replaces source-code variables by their offsets. The contents of modifying registers are added to the offset at run time to calculate the effective address. In most cases, the EA is assumed to be an offset within the data segment. We will discuss exceptions to this rule later in this chapter.

Using Registers to Modify Addresses

An address can be modified by a base register (BX or BP), an index register (SI or DI), or a combination of one base and one index register. These four combinations are legal:

```
NAMEPROMPT[BX][SI]
NAMEPROMPT[BX][DI]
NAMEPROMPT[BP][SI]
NAMEPROMPT[BP][DI]
```

There are several ways to specify a combination. The combination of BX and SI, for example, can be written as [BX][SI], [SI][BX], [SI + BX], or [BX + SI].

Why use registers to modify addresses? You saw one reason in NAMEX (NAMEX is printed in Figure 3.12): a situation in which we needed to move an end-of-text marker ($) to an address that was unknown at the time we coded the program. The exact displacement of "$" from the beginning of OUTNAME couldn't be known until a name was input during program execution.

Later in this book, you will see programs in which modified addresses are used within loops so that each repetition affects a different address. Here's an example, part of a routine to move spaces to a 132-character printline:

```
          MOV   CX,132
          MOV   BX,0
CLEARIT:
          MOV   PRINTLINE[BX],' '
          INC   BX              ; ADDS 1 TO CONTENTS OF BX
          LOOP  CLEARIT
```

You haven't learned INC yet; don't worry about it now. It simply increases the value in BX by 1. You can see that each time the loop is repeated, a space is moved to the byte following the byte affected by the previous repetition. BX is often used to move through a data field in this way.

When would you use two registers in an operand? Most often in nested loops, such as in routines that are repeated for every occurrence of a two-dimensional array.

How do you decide whether to use BX, BP, SI or DI to modify an address? Sometimes one of these registers already contains the required value. For example, you know that DI points to the destination of a string move (MOVSB). At the end of the move, DI holds the offset of the byte following the last one to which data was moved. If you need to address that next byte (to move "$" into it, for example), it makes sense to use DI as the modifying register. If you are using SI, DI, and BP for other purposes, you will use BX in your address operand. Most of the time it's not so clearcut; the choice between BX, BP, SI, and DI is arbitrary.

An address operand can consist of a register (or two) in brackets, but without a variable name. The register(s) will previously have been loaded with an address, and that address will be the EA. These instructions,

```
LEA    BX , ONECHAR
. . .
MOV    AL , [BX]
```

result in moving the contents of the byte at ONECHAR to AL. Notice the difference between this and:

```
MOV AX , BX
```

which copies the one-word contents of BX into AX.

Displacements in Address Operands

An address can also be modified by a specific displacement. You can code the address of the fourth byte following NAMEPROMPT, for example, as NAMEPROMPT + 4. You can also put the displacement within brackets or combine it with a modifying register, like this:

```
NAMEPROMPT[4]
NAMEPROMPT[4][BX]
NAMEPROMPT[BX + 4]
NAMEPROMPT + 4[BX]
```

The last three of these examples are interchangeable; they all produce the same EA.

Various arithmetic operations can also be used in specifying a displacement, as in:

```
NAMEPROMPT[28 / 7]
```

Generally, however, we recommend that you stick to the simplest possible methods of indicating displacements. We usually code address operands using the following format:

```
variable+displacement[base][index]
```

You can't use a displacement alone as an address, even in brackets. An operand like 4 or [4] will be treated as immediate data rather than as an address. A displacement can, however, be combined with a modifying register. These three operands:

```
4[BX]
[BX][4]
[BX+4]
```

are each treated as an address operand, resulting in an EA computed by adding 4 to the contents of BX.

Segment Overrides

One more thing: in most cases an address operand is assumed to point to an offset in the data segment. There are exceptions, however. Here are the rules:

1. If a variable name is included, the segment is the one in which the variable is defined (that's usually the data or the extra segment).

2. If no variable name is included, and BP is one of the registers involved, the offset is assumed to be in the stack segment.

3. If no variable name is included, and BP is *not* one of the registers involved, the offset is assumed to be in the data segment.

Rules 2 and 3 can be overriden by specifying a segment within the operand. Look at Figure 6.1. Here we have defined variables in both the data and extra segments. In the code segment, operands such as [DI],

```
            . . .
THE_DATA SEGMENT 'DATA'
TEST1    DB 1,2,3,4,5
TEST2    DB 6,7,8,9,10
THE_DATA ENDS
;
THE_EXTRA SEGMENT 'XTRA'
TEST3    DB 11,12,13,14,15
TEST4    DB 16,17,28,19,20
THE_EXTRA ENDS
            . . .
```

Figure 6.1 Defining Data in Two Segments

TEST1, TEST2[BP], [BX][SI], DS:[BP], and DS:4[BP] are interpreted as offsets within the data segment, while operands such as TEST3, TEST4[BP], ES:[BX], and ES:4[BP][SI] point to offsets within the extra segment. Operands such as [BP], [BP][SI], 4[BP][SI] and SS:[BX] represent offsets within the stack segment.

What happens if you try to override a segment with a variable operand? The operand ES:TEST1 shows up in the object code generated by the assembler as an offset of 0 within the extra segment. But, the linker produces an error message indicating that the object code contains an impossible address. Don't try to override segment assignments of variables.

There's one more thing to watch about segment assignments. As you have learned, the destination of a string operation must be within the extra segment. You cannot use a segment override to change that assignment. That's why we usually put the same segment number in DS and ES; we want the same fields to occur at the same offsets within both segments.

A Matter of Terminology

Addresses that consist simply of a data or variable name are called **simple variable** operands. Those that include modifiers in brackets are called **indexed variable** operands. An indexed variable using two registers is called a **double indexed variable** operand. If you are familiar with other microcomputer assembler languages, you have seen references to addressing modes such as "direct", "indirect", "indirect indexed", and so on. Such terms are not really very useful in MASM. All you really need to remember is that an address can consist of combinations of these four elements:

1. Variable name

2. Displacement

3. Base register

4. Index register

The displacement can be specified in various complex forms, but the assembler always computes it and adds it to the offset specified by the variable name. The contents of the base and index registers are added into the effective address at run time.

Review Questions

Refer to these definitions to answer the review questions:

```
THE_DATA   SEGMENT
           'DATA'
EMPNAME    DB            30 DUP(' ')
EMPADDR    DB            50 DUP(' ')
EMPPHONE   DB             8 DUP(' ')
             . . .
THE_DATA   ENDS
```

In questions 1-5, code each operand to meet the specifications in the simplest possible form.

1. An operand referring to the first byte of the employee address.

2. An operand referring to the last byte of the employee phone number.

3. An operand using the contents of a base register to modify the address from question 1.

4. An operand using the contents of an index register to modify the address from question 2.

5. An operand using the contents of an index register to modify the address from question 3.

6. Some of these operands are incorrect. Which are incorrect and why?

   A.   ES:VARY

   B.   VARY[BX][SI]

   C.   VARY[AX]

   D.   VARY[BX][BP]

   E.   [BX]

Answers

1. EMPADDR   **2.** EMPHONE + 7   **3.** EMPADDR[BX] or
EMPADDR[BP]   **4.** EMPHONE + 7[SI] or EMPHONE + 7[DI]   **5.**
EMPADDR[BX][SI] or EMPADDR[BX][DI] or EMPADDR[BP][SI] or
EMPADDR[BP][DI]

You could have rearranged the parts involved in these answers in many
ways; the answer to question 4, for example, could be EMPHONE[SI + 7].
Throughout the book, however, we will code operands in the preferred
format:

```
variable+displacement[base][index]
```

6. A. Don't override a segment with a variable operand. C. AX cannot be
used as a modifying register. D. You can't use two base registers in an
operand. B and E are correct.

Symbolic Names for Constants

A variable has a value that may change during the course of the program's
execution. A constant has a value known at the time the program is
assembled; it does not change when the program is executed. Constants are
used in many ways in MASM source code. In each of these instructions, for
example, 4 is a constant:

```
MOV    AL , 4
MOV    AL , OUTNAME + 4
MOV    AX , 4[BX]
```

Immediate data operands are always constants. This instruction:

```
MOV    OUTMESS + 32 , 24H
```

moves an immediate data value to an address in storage. In this instruction
24H is a constant. It is coded directly in the source code and never changes
and is included in the object code instruction created by the assembler.

A symbolic name or label can be assigned to a constant by using the EQU pseudo-op. This pseudo-op has the format:

```
name EQU expression
```

where expression is the value assigned to the name. This is not the same as defining a variable; no space is reserved and the value assigned to the name cannot be changed. The assembler keeps track of names and values assigned by EQU instructions. When it encounters such a name in the rest of the program, it replaces the name by the assigned expression. In contrast, when the assembler encounters a variable name (one defined by DB, DW, and so on), the assembler replaces the name by the variable's offset within its segment.

24H, the ASCII code for "$", is frequently used as an end-of-text mark; let's assign it to the name EOT:

```
EOT                     EQU 24H                 ;EOT is $
```

In the source code, the EQU must occur before the first use of EOT. When the assembler encounters the instruction:

```
MOV    OUTMESS+32,EOT
```

it replaces EOT by 24H and assembles the instruction as though it were written:

```
MOV    OUTMESS+32,24H
```

Suppose we include this EQU for EOT in our NAME2 (see Figure 5.5) program and use EOT in the source code like this:

```
NAMEPROMPT    DB     OAH,ODH,'WHAT IS YOUR NAME? ',EOT
              . . .
              MOV    OUTNAME[BX],EOT
```

When the program is assembled, the assembler handles these instructions as in the original program:

```
NAMEPROMPT    DB      0AH,0DH,'WHAT IS YOUR NAME? ',24H
              ...
              MOV     OUTNAME[BX],24H
```

[**Note**: Throughout this example, we could have used '$' instead of 24H; the resulting object code would be the same. The assembler always replaces ASCII code characters, indicated by single quotes, by their numeric values.]

Why Use EQU?

EQUs are never necessary. Why bother with them, then? Because it's easier to code, read, and change programs using symbolic names for some of the constants. With most CRTs and printers, two common constants are those used to end a line and start a new one. We often assign these the names CR and LF:

```
CR    EQU    0DH    ; CARRIAGE RETURN (END LINE)
LF    EQU    0AH    ; LINE FEED (NEW LINE)
```

(On output, 0DH usually moves the cursor or carriage to the beginning of the current line, while 0AH moves it down one line without changing its horizontal position in the line. On input, 0DH generally indicates that the "return" or "enter" key was pressed, while 0AH has no universally accepted meaning.)

With these EQUs at the beginning of a program, you can use the symbolic names throughout the source code. It's much easier to remember the purpose of the first two characters in:

```
NAMEPROMPT DB LF,CR, . . . . . .
```

than in:

```
NAMEPROMPT DB 0AH,0DH, . . . .
```

You are also less likely to make errors in the source code when you use names that are meaningful to you instead of numeric values.

Another benefit of using EQU becomes evident when a constant must be changed. Consider a program that prints a report using the small (elite or compressed) typeface available on many printers. To turn on the desired typeface, you usually need to send a special code to the printer. For one commonly used printer, the code is 1CH. For another, the code is 0FH. Codes for setting and using tabstops, vertical formatting, underscoring, and other functions also vary considerably between printers. If you write your program initially to use one of these printers, you may want to change it later to use another. It is much simpler to change the values in a series of EQUs than to search through the entire program for every place that you may have used printer codes. You will still need to reassemble and relink the program, of course, so that the new values are incorporated in the run file.

An EQU Library

An EQU pseudo-op can be anywhere in the source code as long as it precedes the first use of the name being defined. Since the EQU itself does not become part of the object code or reserve any space, it does not have to be included within a segment.

You will find that you use the same EQUs over and over, especially those that define CRT and printer control codes. You can write these EQUs in a file and use INCLUDE to copy them into your programs in the same way that you copy the macro library file. This INCLUDE usually is best placed at the beginning of the program, before any macro definitions. That makes it possible to use common EQU names within the macros. Figure 6.2 shows a list of EQUs that should be useful for most programs.

Computer Exercise

Enter the EQUs from Figure 6.2 into your computer now. Use the filename EQULIB.LIB. Check your CRT and printer manuals to see if you need to change any of the EQUs to use them with your equipment.

```
BEEP      EQU    07H        ;BEEP OR BELL
CR        EQU    0DH        ;CARRIAGE RETURN
EOT       EQU    24H        ;END OF OUTPUT TEXT
ESC       EQU    1BH        ;BEGINS ESCAPE SEQUENCE
HOME      EQU    0BH        ;CURSOR TO HOME
LF        EQU    0AH        ;LINE FEED
NEW_PAGE  EQU    0CH        ;FORM FEED FOR MOST PRINTERS
NO        EQU    'N'
TABCHAR   EQU    09H        ;HORIZONTAL TAB
YES       EQU    'Y'
```

Figure 6.2 A Library of Common EQUs

Advanced Uses for EQU

In MOV OUTMESS + 32,EOT, both 32 and OUTMESS + 32 are also constants. We could code EQUs for either or both of these constants. Let's replace 32 by MESSAGE__END:

```
MESSAGE__END              EQU   32
                          . . .
                          MOV   OUTMESS + MESSAGE__END , EOT
```

Can we also define a name for OUTMESS + 32? Yes, here's one way to do it:

```
MESSAGE__END              EQU   32
LAST__CHAR                EQU   OUTMESS + MESSAGE__END
                          . . .
                          MOV   LAST__CHAR , EOT
```

Notice that we used one constant in the definition of the other one. That's ok, as long as MESSAGE__END is defined *before* it's used. In addition, OUTMESS must be defined in the program before LAST__CHAR; the assembler won't go looking through the program to find the value of OUTMESS when it's trying to evaluate LAST__CHAR.

What do we gain by using LAST__CHAR instead of OUTMESS + 32 or OUTMESS + MESSAGE__END? Probably nothing. I used this example to show you that it can be done, but there's no good reason to replace one variable name by another.

Another thing to notice in the example just discussed is that in this instance the name OUTMESS refers to OUTMESS's offset. In a code-segment instruction, such as:

```
MOV     AL , OUTMESS
```

the value moved would be the **contents** at offset OUTMESS. In a data definition or an EQU, however, a reference to a variable name always refers to the offset of the variable. Suppose OUTMESS is at offset 0002H. The definition:

```
SECOND_BYTE EQU OUTMESS +1
```

assigns the name SECOND_BYTE to the value 0003H. The definition:

```
SECOND_BYTE_ADD DW OUTMESS +1
```

reserves a one-word field and initializes it with the value 0003H.

So far, our EQU examples have assigned a numeric value of some kind to a name. Most of them have been 8-bit (one byte) values such as 0DH or 24H. EQU can't assign a number larger than 16 bits, a maximum of 0FFFFH.

EQU can, however, be used to assign new mnemonics for instructions (COPY EQU MOV) or symbolic names to signify complex address operands or parts of such operands (NEXT_ELEMENT EQU [BX + 8]), and so on. When you are ready for more advanced programming you can find information in the MASM manual about the uses of EQU.

Review Questions

1. Which statements are true of DB and which of EQU?

    _____ A. Reserves memory space for use during program execution.
    _____ B. Value cannot change during program execution.
    _____ C. Assigns a name to a variable.
    _____ D. Assigns a name to a constant.

2. A program uses a slash (/) as a separator in a date field. The program includes these instructions (CMP is a comparison):

```
TEXT__DATE    DB     8 DUP ( ' ' )
              . . .
              MOV    TEXT__DATE + 3 , '/'
              MOV    TEXT__DATE + 5 , '/'
              . . .
              CMP    TEXT__DATE[BX] , '/' ; DOES CHARACTER = '/' ?
              . . .
```

A. Code an instruction to assign the name "DATESEP" to '/'.

Where should this instruction be inserted in the program?

B. Rewrite the two MOVs and the CMP instructions above to use the symbolic name for the separator.

C. You decide to change the separator character to '-'. Assuming that the changes in A and B have been made, how many instructions must be changed? Code the revised instruction(s).

Answers

1. A. DB B. EQU C. DB D. EQU

2. A. DATESEP EQU '/' ;anywhere before the first use of DATESEP

   B. MOV TEXT__DATE + 3,DATESEP

   MOV TEXT__DATE + 5,DATESEP

   CMP TEXT__DATE[BX],DATESEP

   C. 1; DATESEP EQU '-'

Variable Attributes

Each variable defined in a MASM program has three attributes: a segment, an offset, and a type. You have already learned about the segment and offset attributes. The segment attribute identifies the beginning paragraph number of the segment within which the variable has been defined. The offset attribute identifies the location within the segment where the variable begins. The type attribute identifies the units which make up the variable, as determined by the variable's definition. A variable defined by DB will be of type "byte". One defined by DW (Define Word) will be of type "word". One defined by DD (Define Doubleword) will be of type "doubleword" and so on. All the variables you have used so far are of type "byte".

Remember that a variable name is the name of a data field. A label is a name assigned to a location in the code segment. A label also has segment, offset, and type attributes; a label's type, however, is either NEAR or FAR. (You may need to review the material about NEAR and FAR labels in Chapter 3.)

MASM provides five **value-returning operators** that can be used to code immediate operands with values that depend on a variable's attribute. One of these, OFFSET, we will discuss in detail. MASM also provides **attribute-override operators** that allow you to change an attribute in an instruction; you have already learned to use a segment-override operator (the ES is ES:[BX], for example). We will discuss one other attribute-override operator, PTR. You can find the other value-returning and override operators in the MASM manual when you are ready to use them in more advanced programming.

The OFFSET Operator

The OFFSET operator returns the offset of a variable or label. Look at this instruction:

```
MOV     AX , OFFSET NAMEPROMPT
```

The second operand is evaluated by the assembler as the offset of the variable NAMEPROMPT. If NAMEPROMPT starts at 00A2H, the assembler processes this instruction as:

```
MOV     AX , 00A2H
```

Notice that OFFSET is evaluated by the assembler. OFFSET is a value known at assembly time that cannot be changed, therefore, it is immediate data. The format for the OFFSET operator is:

```
OFFSET variable (or label)
```

The variable cannot be modified in any way. These instructions:

```
LEA      AX , NAMEPROMPT
MOV      AX , OFFSET NAMEPROMPT
```

have the same effect during program execution. But, if you want to use a modified address, as in:

```
LEA      AX , NAMEPROMPT[BX]
```

you cannot code an equivalent MOV using OFFSET NAMEPROMPT[BX] — you'll get an error message.

Where will you use OFFSET, then? For one thing, LEA must have a register destination, while MOV can use either a register or memory. There's no way to do this:

```
MOV      SAVE__ADDRESS , OFFSET CURRENT
```

in one instruction using LEA. You can use OFFSET anywhere you can use a word of immediate data. You haven't learned ADD yet, but this instruction:

```
ADD      AX , OFFSET CURRENT
```

does just what you might expect; it adds the offset of current to the value in AX.

The PTR Operator

The PTR (PoinTeR) operator overrides a variable's type. Its format is:

```
type  PTR  expression
```

Type can be BYTE, WORD, DOUBLEWORD; expression is an identifier whose attribute is being overriden. Let's look at some examples. Consider a variable that has been defined with DW and therefore is of type "word". If you want to access just the first byte of this variable, an instruction like this:

```
MOV     VARY , AL
```

will produce an assembler error message because you can't mix types in MOV. You can, however, override the type, like this:

```
MOV     BYTE PTR VARY , AL
```

Similarly, a variable of type "byte" can be treated as a word if you want to access two bytes of it at once:

```
MOV     AX , WORD PTR VBYTE
```

PTR can be very useful in identifying the type of an address without a variable. This instruction:

```
MOV     [BX] , 5
```

will produce an assembler error because the assembler can't tell if you are moving a byte or a word. Using PTR, as in:

```
MOV     BYTE PTR [BX] , 5
```

will avoid the error. When you run a program under DEBUG, you will often see unassembled instructions with the PTR operator. That's because the variable name you originally coded isn't in the object code, just the offset. Unless a register is one of the operands, DEBUG can only tell you whether a byte or a word is involved by using the PTR form for unassembly.

Computing Field Length Using the Location Counter

Sometimes we need to use the length of a field as an immediate operand—most often to initialize CX for a string operation. So far, we have just counted up the number of characters in the string, but we can make the assembler do the counting. This not only keeps us from making mistakes, but also makes sure that the count is changed if we change the message. Let's use this string for an example:

```
MESSAGE DB 'THIS IS AN ERROR MESSAGE'
```

During assembly, a **location counter** keeps track of the offset assigned to the next byte to be included in the object code. Suppose that MESSAGE starts at offset 0010H. When the assembler is ready to process the next instruction, the location counter is set at 0028H since MESSAGE took up 24 (0018H) bytes.

In the source code, the symbol $ can be used to refer to the current value of the location counter. (Notice that this is *not* the same as the end-of-text mark — that's a character enclosed in single quotes, '$' or 24H). We can get the assembler to compute the length of MESSAGE and save it like this:

```
MESSAGE DB 'THIS IS AN ERROR MESSAGE'
MESS_LEN EQU $-MESSAGE
```

Notice that we subtract the offset of MESSAGE from the current offset ($). Since EQU immediately follows MESSAGE in the source code, the location counter, and therefore $, has the value 0028H at the time the assembler begins processing MESS_LEN, and MESS_LEN is computed as a value 0028H − 0010H = 0018H or 24. By the way, since an EQU pseudo-op does not reserve any space in the object code, the location counter value is not changed; the next instruction to be assembled still begins at 0028H.

We can use MESS__LEN throughout the program whenever we need to refer to the length of MESSAGE. Then, if we revise MESSAGE, we don't need to change all the places we have coded the length. When we reassemble the program, the assembler will recompute the length and make the substitutions for us. That's why we do it this way instead of simply defining MESS__LEN as 24.

Review Questions

1.   Which statements are true?

A.   Both variables and labels have three attributes: segment, offset, and type.

B.   PTR changes a variable's type for one instruction.

C.   OFFSET changes a variable's offset.

D.   The type of a variable identifies the units of which it is composed.

E.   The type of a label depends on whether it names a called procedure or the target of a transfer of control.

F.   A value-returning operator is evaluated at execution time; it may produce a different value every time the program is run.

2.   Your program contains these definitions:

```
LAST__NAME  DB     30 DUP(' ')
ADDRESS     DB     30 DUP(' ')
CITY        DB     15 DUP(' ')
CODE__LIST  DB     1,7,8,3,2
```

A.   Code an instruction that will place the offset of LAST__NAME into AX (using MOV).

B.   Code an instruction that will place the first two bytes of CODE__LIST into SI.

C. Code a pseudo-op or an instruction that will assign the actual length of CODE_LIST to the name CODE_LENGTH.

Where should this instruction be placed in the program?

Code an instruction using CODE_LENGTH to move the length of CODE_LIST into AX.

What value will this instruction place into AX?

Answers

1. A, B, and D are true; here's what's wrong with the others: C. OFFSET returns (is replaced by) the value of a variable's offset. E. The type of a label depends on whether it is defined in the source code as NEAR or FAR. F. A value-returning operator produces a value that is known at assembly time and does not change during program execution. It is assembled as a constant. 2. A. MOV AX,OFFSET LAST_NAME B. MOV SI,WORD PTR CODE_LIST C. CODE_LENGTH EQU $-CODE_LIST ; immediately following the definition of CODE_LIST; MOV AX,CODE_LENGTH ; AX=5

Key Points From Chapter 6

In this chapter you have learned to use displacements and modifying registers to code more flexible address operands and to use symbolic names as constants in immediate and address operands. You have also learned to use the value-returning operator OFFSET, the attribute operator PTR, and the location counter symbol. Some of the most important points from this chapter are:

■ An address operand can include modifying registers. The contents of the modifying registers are added into the EA at execution time. The address operand may point to a different address each time the instruction is executed.

■ Each address operand may be modified by a base register (BX or BP), an index register (SI or DI), or a combination of one base and one index register.

■   A modifying register is coded within brackets in the address operand. Two modifying registers can be written in any order.

■   An address can be modified by a specific displacement represented by a constant. The displacement is usually written as a value attached to a variable name by "+".

■   There are many potential arrangements for coding the four possible parts of an address. We recommend this format:

```
variable+disp[base][index]
```

■   Each of the four parts can be omitted if necessary. Also, each of them, except the displacement, can stand alone as an address operand if necessary.

■   A symbolic name can be assigned to a constant by using the EQU pseudo-op. After processing an EQU, the assembler replaces the symbolic name by the constant anywhere the name is encountered in the source code.

■   The EQU pseudo-op has this format:

```
name EQU expression
```

where expression can be evaluated as a constant value to be assigned to the name.

■   A source-code file of commonly used EQUs can be treated as a library and included in a source-code program using the INCLUDE pseudo-op.

■   If a variable name is part of an address operand, the address is assumed to represent an offset in the segment in which the variable is defined (usually the data or the extra segment). If no variable name is included, and BP is used in the operand, the offset is assumed to be in the stack segment. Otherwise, the offset is assumed to be in the data segment.

■ A segment-override operator can be used to identify the segment of an address operand, overriding the default segment for the operand. The override operator should be used only in operands that do not include a variable name.

■ Each variable and label defined in a program has three attributes: segment, offset, and type.

■ The type attribute of a variable identifies the number of bytes per unit for the variable as indicated by the definition: 1 for a variable defined by DB, 2 for DW, and so on.

■ The type attribute of a label is NEAR or FAR, depending on the label's definition in the source code.

■ Attribute-override operators, including the segment-override operator, can be used to change a variable or label's attributes for one instruction.

■ Value-returning operators can be used to obtain the values of a variable or label's attributes; the values returned are treated by the assembler as constants.

■ The OFFSET value-returning operator's format is:

OFFSET variable

The variable cannot be modified by displacements or index or pointer registers.

■ The PTR attribute-override operator's format is:

type PTR expression

where type is BYTE, WORD, or DOUBLEWORD and expression points to a data field. The PTR operator overrides the defined type of the field (if known); during the execution of this instruction the operand's type will be the one specified.

■ The symbol $ can be used to refer to the current value of the location counter during assembly; this is the offset to which the next byte of object code will be assigned. The location counter symbol can be used to compute the length of a data field and assign that value to a symbolic name.

The review questions that follow will help you to be sure that you understand these key points.

Chapter Review Questions

Refer to these definitions to answer the questions:

```
THE__DATA      SEGMENT    'DATA'
FULL__NAME     DB         30 DUP ('  ')
TELEPHONE      DB         8 DUP ('  ')
CODE__LIST     DB         1 , 1 , 5 , 0 , 0
                 . . .
```

1. Code operands referring to:

    A. The first character of the telephone number.

    B. The fourth character of the telephone number.

    C. The character of the name pointed to by the contents of an index register.

    D. The fifth code in the code list.

    E. The contents of BP and DI added to the second character of the name.

2. Code instructions to assign the names CR, LF, and EOT to their usual values. For each instruction, include a comment indicating the meaning of the name.

3. Use the names defined in question 2 to define a prompting message asking for the telephone number. (Call the message TELEPROMPT).

4.   Code an instruction defining TP__LENGTH as the length of TELE-
     PROMPT (refer to question 3).

     Where should this instruction occur in the program?

5.   Code an instruction to move TELEPROMPT to OUTPROMPT. (Use
     the MOVE macro defined in Chapter 5.)

6.   Code a MOV instruction to place the offset of FULL__NAME into
     AX.

7.   Code an instruction to place the offset of CODE__LIST into
     SAVE__LIST.

8.   Code an instruction to place the EA computed from the offset of
     CODE   LIST and the contents of BX into AX.

9.   Code one instruction to place the first two bytes of CODE__LIST into
     AY.

10. Code an instruction to place the value 53 into the byte whose address
     is contained in BX.

Answers

1. A. TELEPHONE   B. TELEPHONE + 3 C. FULL__NAME[SI] or
FULL__NAME[DI] D. CODE__LIST + 4   E. FULL__NAME + 2[BP][SI]

2.   CR   EQU   0DH   ; CARR I AGE RETURN (END OF L I NE)
     LF   EQU   0AH   ; L I NE FEED (NEW L I NE)
     EOT   EQU   24H   ; END OF TEXT MARKER ("$ ")

   You probably worded your comments differently. You may have
   used decimal values (13, 10, and 36, respectively) instead of hexadecimal, or the ASCII value '$' instead of 24H.

3.   TELEPROMPT DB LF,CR, 'ENTER TELEPHONE NUMBER ',EOT

   You probably used a different message.

4.   TP__LENGTH EQU $-TELEPROMPT

   immediately following the definition of TELEPROMPT

5.   MOVE OUTPROMPT,TELEPROMPT,TP__LENGTH

6.   MOV AX,OFFSET FULL__NAME or LEA AX, FULL__NAME

7. · MOV SAVE__LIST,OFFSET CODE__LIST

8.   LEA AX,CODE__LIST[BX]

   Did you remember that you could not use OFFSET with a modified address?

9.   MOV AX,WORD PTR CODE__LIST

10.   MOV BYTE PTR [BX],53

7
Decisions and Repetitions

The design of any program can be described in terms of three types of logical structure. Figure 7.1 illustrates the logic involved in each of the three. The first and most obvious is a **sequential structure**—do a, then b, then c, then d, and so on. Sequential structures are not necessarily coded in a straight line. A CALL instruction, for example, may cause a branch to another part of the program. The order of execution, however, is always the same: first a, then b, then c, and so on.

The second logical structure is the **decision structure**. Based on a test of a current value, the program chooses one of two alternate paths to follow. (If x = y, do a; else do b.) Every time this part of the program is executed, one of the paths is followed and the other is skipped. One path may be "empty", that is, not involve any action. (If x = y, do a; otherwise don't do a.) We may call the test (x = y) a **condition** and say that a decision structure **evaluates a condition** and branches accordingly (if condition is true, do a; else do b.)

The third structure is the **repetition structure**, (often called a loop). In a repetition structure, a series of instructions is executed repeatedly until a condition is true. (Repeat a until count = 0). Sometimes, the repetition structure is described as being repeated *while* a condition is true (repeat a while count not = 0). For programming purposes, a repetition structure can be thought of as a special case of a decision structure; one path repeats the loop. (If condition is true, go on to b; else go back to a.)

A. Sequential

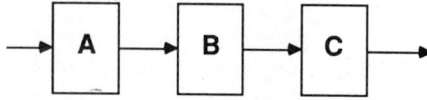

B. Decision

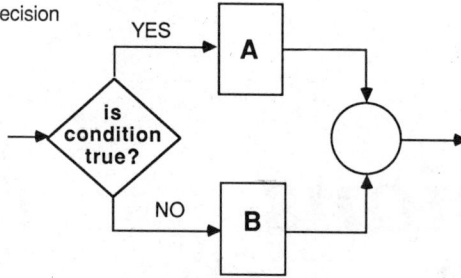

C. Repetition

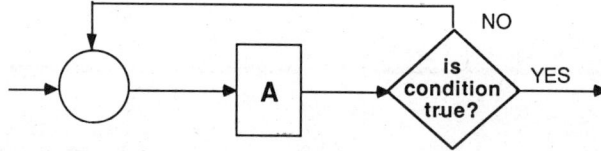

Figure 7.1 Logical Structures

The design of any program can be broken down into combinations of these three structures. The paths carried out by decisions and repetition structures are largely made up of step-by-step or sequential structures. Complex combinations are not uncommon, such as using decisions within repetitions, decisions within decisions, repetitions within repetitions, and so on. If you have been writing BASIC programs, you have been using these structures whether you realize it or not. Decision structures are usually coded in BASIC using IF..THEN..ELSE. Repetition structures can also be coded with IF..THEN..ELSE as well as with FOR...NEXT and WHILE...WEND.

Most of the coding you have done in MASM has involved sequential structures, although you have learned two instructions for repetition: LOOP and REP. In this chapter, you will learn other instructions from which you can build both decision and repetition structures. You will also learn some variations on LOOP and REP. By the time you have finished this chapter, you will be able to implement the logical structures for any program.

Making a Decision

When you plan a program, you often find situations where the current value of a variable or a register determines the next action to be taken. One example: in a checkbook program, if an entry is coded "D" add the amount to the balance; otherwise, subtract it. Another example: if a loop counter is not zero, go back to the beginning of the loop; otherwise, continue to the next part of the program. A third: if the user inputs END when asked for a name, branch to the program-ending routine; otherwise, do the regular input name processing. The LOOP and REP instructions both include a test of the current value of CX, the count register. When the value in CX is zero the loop or the string operation is not repeated; otherwise, it is repeated.

The decision making instructions in MASM, other than LOOP and REP and their variations, are **conditional jump instructions** such as JE (Jump if Equal), JA (Jump if Above), and so on. These instructions all have the following general format:

```
condjump target
```

where condjump is an instruction mnemonic and target is a label that identifies the next instruction to be executed if the condition is true. If the condition is not true, control falls through to the instruction following the conditional jump.

There are many conditional jump instructions, but at this point we will use only JE and JA as examples in our discussion of how conditional jumps work.

What's the Condition?

Consider the checkbook program mentioned above. We want to implement a decision structure as shown in Figure 7.2. If the transaction code is "D", transfer control to a deposit routine; otherwise, perform a withdrawal routine. The decision uses JE. If the deposit routine begins at DEPOSIT, the conditional branch instruction is:

```
JE DEPOSIT
```

But where is the condition? The only operand in the jump instruction is the target; how do you specify which fields are to be tested?

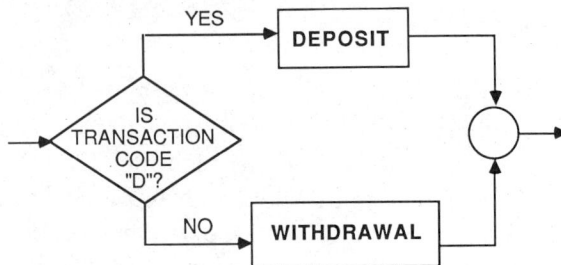

Figure 7.2 Checkbook Transaction Decision

The fact is that conditional jumps are always based on the status flags. (You may need to review the material on status flags in Chapter 2.) JE causes a jump if ZF = 1; if ZF = 0, control falls through to the next instruction. Similarly, JA tests the settings of CF and ZF. If both flags are set the jump is taken. If either is cleared (equal to zero) there is no jump. Other conditional jump instructions test other status flag combinations, but you don't really need to learn the combinations. As you will see, the instruction mnemonics reflect the effect of the instructions, so that you can use them without thinking about the flags used in the actual testing process.

How do the status flags get set (or cleared) before the jump? When certain MASM instructions are executed the status flags are always used to reflect the result. None of the instructions you have learned so far affects the flags. Generally speaking the results of arithmetic, bit manipulation, and comparison instructions are recorded in the flags. In this chapter we will concentrate on comparisons; in later chapters, you will learn about arithmetic and bit manipulation.

Comparing Two Operands

CMP (CoMPare) compares two operands. Its format is:

CMP dest , source

Notice the similarity to MOV's format. The first operand, dest, may be a register or an address. The second, source, may be a register, address, or immediate data. As with MOV, you cannot use addresses in both operands; the other five possibilities are all legitimate. If you need to compare data from two memory addresses, you will need to move the data from one address into a register to make the comparison. Also, as with MOV, both operands must be of the same size, either one byte or one word. If an immediate data byte is compared to a 16-bit register or variable, the immediate data is extended to 16 bits before the comparison is made.

A comparison is, in fact, a subtraction; the source is subtracted from the destination and the status flags (AF, CF, OF, PF, SF, and ZF) reflect the result. The subtraction takes place in a work area; neither operand actually changes. The only reason for using a comparison in a program is to prepare the flags for a decision.

The Two-Part Decision

Our transaction decision, then, requires two instructions: a comparison and a conditional jump. Assuming that all of the variables and labels have been defined, we could code the decision like this:

```
CMP       TCODE, 'D'
JE        DEPOSIT
```

We compare the transaction code to "D". If it matches, we jump (or branch) to a routine to handle deposits; otherwise, we continue on to handle a non-deposit transaction code.

Suppose the program allows a transaction code of A, B, C, or D? A code above D is an error. We can edit the input transaction code like this:

```
CMP       TCODE, 'D'
JA        CODE_ERROR
```

Here, we compare the transaction code to "D" again, but this time if the code is greater than "D" ("E" or above) we go to an error routine. If the code is "D" or less, we continue on to the next instruction.

Make sure you know the order in which the operands are compared. If "cond" is a conditional term such as ("equal to", "above", "less than", and so on,) a two-instruction decision:

```
CMP     dest,source
Jcond   target
```

means "jump to target if dest is cond source". It's important to keep this straight—testing for "a above b" produces different results than testing for "b above a". Remember, the results always reflect "dest cond source".

Where Can You Go with a Jump?

A conditional jump's target must always be within 128 bytes of the jump instruction in the object code. A target in this range is known as a **short label**. It's hard to judge this distance exactly in the source code; anything less than 30 instructions from the jump is usually safe. If the target is not close enough, you'll get an error message from the assembler.

Notice that in the source code the "condition not true" path from a decision must follow the decision. The source code for the checkbook transaction is arranged like this:

```
            CMP    TCODE , 'D'
            JE     DEPOSIT
WITHDRAW:
               . . .          ; WITHDRAWAL PROCESSING GOES HERE

DEPOSIT:
               . . .          ; DEPOSIT PROCESSING GOES HERE
CONTINUE:
               . . .          ; NEXT STEP AFTER TRANSACTION
```

If the withdrawal processing routine is too long, the JE instruction produces an assembler error; DEPOSIT won't be a short label. Probably the best way to avoid this problem is to code each process as a CALLed procedure. Then the conditional jump needs to go only to a CALL instruction, like this:

```
            CMP    TCODE , 'D'
            JE     DEPOSIT
WITHDRAW:
            CALL   WITHDRAW_ROUTINE
DEPOSIT:
            CALL   DEPOSIT_ROUTINE
CONTINUE:
               . . .
```

There's still one problem. When a withdrawal is processed, the withdraw routine returns control to the instruction following CALL. Then, control falls through to DEPOSIT, and the transaction is processed again, this time as a deposit. To avoid this, we need to include an instruction that *always* transfers control to CONTINUE after the withdrawal routine is through. An **unconditional jump**, JMP, is the answer. This instruction, like BASIC's GOTO, always transfers control to its target. The format is:

```
JMP    target
```

The target of an unconditional jump can be anywhere in the program; it doesn't have to be a short label. Our complete decision structure, then, looks like this:

```
           CMP    TCODE,'D'
           JE     DEPOSIT
WITHDRAW:
           CALL   WITHDRAW_ROUTINE
           JMP    CONTINUE
DEPOSIT:
           CALL   DEPOSIT_ROUTINE
CONTINUE:
           . . .
```

The unconditional jump is not only used to branch around an alternate path. Since it does not require a short label it is sometimes combined with unconditional jumps instead of using called procedures. The example above could be rewritten as:

```
           CMP    TCODE,'D'
           JE     DEPOSIT
           JMP    WITHDRAW
DEPOSIT:
           . . .   'the deposit routine goes here'
           JMP    CONTINUE
WITHDRAW:
           . . .   'the withdrawal routine goes here'
CONTINUE:
           . . .
```

You will find other uses for JMP as you continue to write programs.

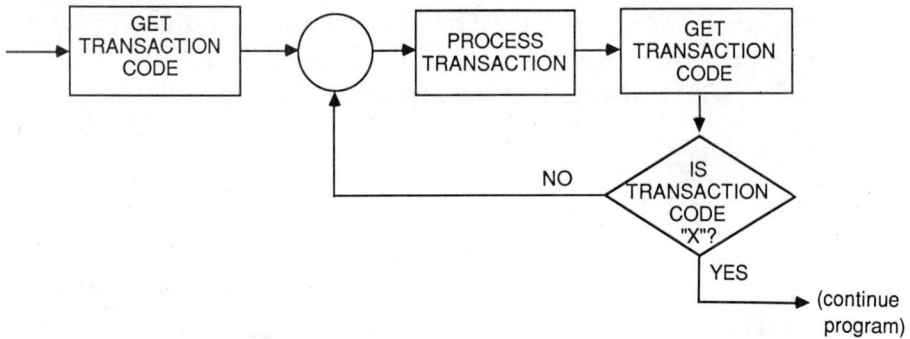

Figure 7.3 Checkbook Transaction Loop Structure

Deciding to Repeat

The same combination of instructions (CMP and a conditional jump) can be used to build a repetition structure. Figure 7.3 shows the logic for a repetition structure that includes our checkbook transaction processing. Transactions are processed until a transaction code of "X" is entered. Notice that the first transaction code is input before the loop begins. After the transaction is processed, a new transaction code is input and a decision is made either to repeat the loop or to continue to the next part of the program. Figure 7.4 shows the appropriate source code. The decision routine uses CMP, JE, and JMP. JE causes control to transfer out of the loop when the transaction code is "X"; otherwise, control falls through to JMP, which then repeats the loop. Another conditional jump, JNE (Jump if Not Equal) could be used in place of the combination of JE and JMP. JNE does require a short label, so it doesn't work if the loop being repeated is more than 128 bytes long.

```
            . . .
            CALL     GET_CODE
WHAT_TRANS:
            CMP      TCODE,'D'
            JE       DEPOSIT
WITHDRAW:
            CALL     WITHDRAWAL_ROUTINE
            JMP      CONTINUE
DEPOSIT:
            CALL     DEPOSIT_ROUTINE
CONTINUE:
            CALL     GET_CODE
            CMP      TCODE,'X'
            JE       TRANSACTIONS_DONE
            JMP      WHAT_TRANS
TRANSACTIONS_DONE:
            . . .
```

Figure 7.4 Source Code for Checkbook Transaction Loop

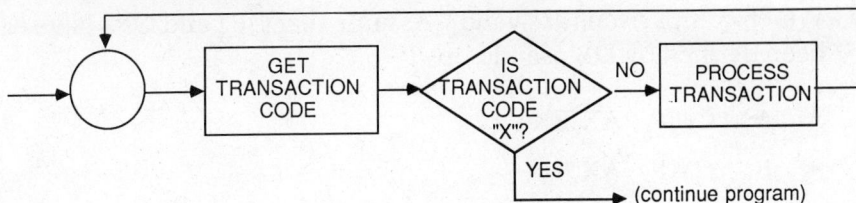

Figure 7.5 Logic and Source Code for Test at Beginning of Loop

Figure 7.5 shows the logic and source code for another way to handle the same situation. In this method, the loop begins by prompting for a transaction code and then testing the code. When the code is "X", control is transferred outside the loop. Otherwise, the transaction is processed and an unconditional jump gets back to the loop's beginning. Some programmers prefer to code repetition structures in this way, with the test at the beginning. Others prefer to test at the end, as in Figures 7.3 and 7.4. We usually use the end-of-loop test except when the first transaction may possibly be an end marker and therefore, should not be processed as a transaction; then, the beginning-of-loop test is safer. The repetition instructions you have learned, LOOP and REP, both test the loop count in CX at the end of their repetition cycles.

Review Questions

1. Which statements are true?

    A. A conditional jump transfers control to its target only if the condition is true.

    B. An unconditional jump always transfers control to its target.

    C. The target of either a conditional or unconditional jump must be within 128 bytes of the jump instruction.

    D. A conditional jump instruction compares its two operands to determine whether the condition is true.

2. Which comparisons are valid? (Assume that OP1 and OP2 have each been defined by DB pseudo-ops.)

    A. CMP AX,BX

    B. CMP AX,5

    C. CMP 15,BX

    D. CMP OP1,OP2

    E. CMP OP1,25

    F. CMP AL,OP2

    G. CMP OP2,BH

3. A. Code a decision that will branch to ALLDONE if TESTER is equal to AH.

   B. Code a decision that will branch to TOOHIGH if TESTER is above DL.

   C. Code a decision that will branch to ALARGE if AX is above TESTER.

   D. Code a routine that will call procedure ALLSAME if TESTONE equals TESTTWO, but will call procedure NOTSAME otherwise. Assume that TESTONE and TESTTWO have both been defined by DB pseudo-ops. (Be sure only one of the two procedures is called each time. Also, be sure that you use a valid pair of operands in your CMP instruction.)

Answers

1. A and B. Here's what's wrong with the others: C. The target of a conditional jump must be within 128 bytes of the jump instruction, but an unconditional jump's target can be anywhere within the program.   2. A, B, E, F, G. Here's what's wrong with the others: C. The destination (first operand) can be an address or a register, but not immediate data. D. Either operand can be an address, but not both.

3.   A. CMP   TESTER,AH
           JE   ALLDONE

Note: the comparison could just as well have been the other way around this time.

```
      B.   CMP       TESTER,DL
           JA        TOOHIGH
```

(Did you code the CMP operands in the right order?)

```
      C.   CMP       AX,TESTER
           JA        ALARGE
      D.   MOV       AL,TESTONE
           CMP       AL,TESTWO
           JE        CALLSAME
           CALL      NOTSAME
           JMP       CONTINX
CALLSAME:
           CALL      ALLSAME
CONTINX:
           ...
```

Note: Did you remember that you can't compare TESTONE and TESTTWO directly?

Other Jumps

Figure 7.6 shows the most useful conditional-jump instructions. The first column shows a mnemonic and its meaning; the second column shows an alternate mnemonic and its meaning. Both mnemonics represent the same 8088 instruction and produce the same translation into object code. It's your choice which one you use. Generally, I use the simpler versions from the first column. In the last group, I usually use JE and JNE after comparisons and JZ and JNZ after arithmetic instructions because it seems to make more sense when reading the code (if a = b ... for comparisons and if result is 0... for arithmetic).

The instructions in Figure 7.6 are divided into three groups. The first group (JA, JB, JNA, and JNB) are used after operations involving unsigned numbers. The second group (JG, JL, JNG, JNL) are used after signed number operations. The third group (JE and JNE) can be used after either signed or unsigned operations.

Signed and Unsigned

Let's review signed and unsigned numbers quickly. Remember that the high-order bit of a signed number is used to identify the number as positive or negative. A high-order bit with a value of zero indicates a positive

Group	Instruction		Alternate Version	
I: Unsigned	JA	(Jump if Above)	JNBE	(Jump if Not Below or Equal)
	JB	(Jump if Below)	JNAE	(Jump if Not Above or Equal)
	JNA	(Jump if Not Above)	JBE	(Jump if Below or Equal)
	JNB	(Jump if Not Below)	JAE	(Jump if Above or Equal)
II: Signed	JG	(Jump if Greater)	JNLE	(Jump if Not Less or Equal)
	JL	(Jump if Less)	JNGE	(Jump if Not Greater or Equal)
	JNG	(Jump if Not Greater)	JLE	(Jump if Less or Equal)
	JNL	(Jump if Not Less)	JGE	(Jump if Greater or Equal)
III: Any	JE	(Jump if Equal)	JZ	(Jump if Zero)
	JNE	(Jump if Not Equal)	JNZ	(Jump if Not Zero)

Figure 7.6 Conditional Jump Instructions

number, while a value of one indicates a negative number written in twos-complement format. One-byte (8-bit) signed numbers can range from −128 (80H) to +127 (7FH). 0FFH represents −1, so 0FFH is less than 0H when comparing signed numbers.

In unsigned numbers, all bits are used to represent magnitude (size or absolute value). Unsigned one-byte numbers can range from 0 (00H) to 255 (0FFH), so 0FFH is greater than 0H when comparing unsigned numbers.

How do you know whether you are dealing with signed or unsigned numbers? And how do you compare nonnumerics such as ASCII characters? Remember that ASCII code assigns a numeric value to each character. (Appendix A contains more information about ASCII character codes.) "A", for example, has a value of 65 (41H), while "a" is 97 (61H), and "$" is 36 (24H). This means that "a" is above "A", while "$" is below "A". Since IBM uses a full eight-bit ASCII code, the high-order bit is not a sign bit; you can compare ASCII coded characters as unsigned numbers. Because of the way that code values are assigned, you get the right results when you compare decimal digits to each other, or uppercase letters to uppercase letters, or lowercase to lowercase. It's not so simple to compare strings containing uppercase to lowercase, or letters to numbers, or special symbols. Even in these cases, however, it's easy to see whether or not two characters are the same; comparisons for "equal" or "not equal" work perfectly well.

Numbers stored in binary format can be signed or unsigned. If you know that a value is always positive, you can treat it as unsigned; if it might be negative, assume that you are dealing with a signed number. Handling numbers larger than 16 bits requires advanced techniques; we won't discuss them in this book.

Why do you need two sets of conditional jumps? What happens if you code the wrong one? CMP, like most other flag-setting instructions, affects all six of the status flags. You learned earlier, however, that SF and OF have meaning only when they reflect the result of a signed number operation, while CF has meaning only when it reflects the result of unsigned operations. (ZF is significant after both signed and unsigned operations. PF and AF are not relevant for this discussion.) JA, JB, JNA, and JNB test CF when deciding whether to branch. JG, JL, JNG, and JNL test SF and OF. If you code an inappropriate conditional jump there is no obvious error, but at execution time the wrong flags are tested and the wrong decision may be made. Look at this code:

```
CMP     AX,0FEH
JA      AHIGH
```

As an unsigned number, 0FEH is 254 (in IBM/PC ASCII code this is a special graphics character). If AX contains 0 the jump is not taken (0 is not greater than 254). If JG is used instead of JA, however, the test is based on a signed comparision. As a signed number, 0FEH is − 2. If AX contains 0, the jump is taken (0 > − 2). If you are testing a program and it doesn't seem to be branching correctly, make sure you are using the right conditional jumps.

Review Questions

1. Indicate whether each conditional jump is appropriate following operations on signed or unsigned numbers.

_____ A. JA
_____ B. JNL
_____ C. JZ
_____ D. JG
_____ E. JB
_____ F. JNA

2. Code a routine that will call procedure NOCAPS if an input character (INCHAR) is above "Z" and, otherwise, will call procedure CAPS.

3. Code a routine that will call procedure TOOLOW if the value in AL is less than 3 (note: the value in AL can range from − 128 to 127).

Answers

1. A. Unsigned B. Signed C. Both signed and unsigned D. Signed E. Unsigned F. Unsigned

2.
```
                CMP     INCHAR,'Z'
                JA      INCHAR__OVER__Z
                CALL    CAPS
                JMP     CONTINUE
INCHAR__  OVER__Z:
                CALL    NOCAPS
CONTINUE:
                ...
```

3.
```
                CMP     AL,3
                JL      UNDER3
                JMP     CONTINUE
UNDER3:
                CALL    TOOLOW
CONTINUE:
                ...
```

Notice the empty path when AL is not less than 3.

Comparing Strings

A special set of instructions is used to compare multi-byte strings just as a similar set is used to move such strings. (You may need to review the material on MOVSB and REP in Chapter 3.) The comparison instruction, CMPSB, has no operands. It compares the byte pointed to by DI to that pointed to by SI (thereby affecting the status flags, but not changing either byte) and then changes the contents of DI and SI by one. DI must point to a byte in the extra segment. This is similar to MOVSB, but with one major difference. For MOVSB, SI points to the source and DI to the destination of

```
1.  Compare bytes pointed to by SI and DI

2.  Set flags according to result of comparison

3.  If DF=0, increment SI and DI;

    If DF=1, decrement SI and DI

4.  Decrement CX

5.  If ZF = 0 go to step 8

6.  If CX = 0 go to step 8

7.  Go to step 1

8.  Comparison operation has ended; continue with program
```

Figure 7.7 Execution of REPE CMPSB

the move. For CMPSB, the roles of SI and DI are reversed. This is important when you consider how to interpret the result of CMPSB. This combination:

CMPSB
Jcond target

says "jump to the target if dest cond source," but dest is pointed to by SI and source by DI. Why this reversal? I don't know; I only know that that's how it works.

As with other string operations, a prefix is used to cause the operation to repeat. The comparison should be repeated until unmatched bytes are found or until the maximum number of bytes have been compared. CX is used as a repetition counter. The maximum number of bytes to be examined is loaded into CX before the string comparison begins. After each comparison (and change to SI and DI), CX is decremented; when CX reaches zero the comparison ends.

In order to cause the comparison to end when unequal bytes are compared, we use a variation of REP. REPE (REPeat while Equal) checks ZF, which reflects the result of the most recent comparison. If ZF is set, the bytes just compared are equal and the comparison continues (unless the last byte has been compared). If ZF is clear, the comparison ends. Figure 7.7 shows the steps in the execution of:

REPE CMPSB

```
        PAGE    ,132
;
        INCLUDE FIRSTLIB.LIB
;
PROG_STACK SEGMENT STACK 'STACK'
        DB      64 DUP ('STACK   ')
PROG_STACK ENDS
;
PROG_DATA  SEGMENT 'DATA'
NAMEPROMPT DB   0AH,0DH,'WHAT IS YOUR NAME? ',24H
OUTMESS DB      0AH,0DH,'HELLO, '
OUTNAME DB      255 DUP(' ')
INBUF   DB      255
INCOUNT DB      ?
INNAME  DB      255 DUP(' ')
ENDMESS DB      'END OF PROGRAM',24H
ENDINPUT DB     'END '
PROG_DATA  ENDS
;
PROG_CODE SEGMENT 'CODE'
MAIN_PROG PROC  FAR
        ASSUME  CS:PROG_CODE,DS:PROG_DATA,SS:PROG_STACK,ES:PROG_DATA
        STARTER
        CALL    PROMPTER                ;PROMPT FOR FIRST NAME
        CALL    GETNAME                 ;GET NAME INPUT
NAME_ROUTINE:
        CALL    MOVENAME                ;MOVE NAME TO OUTPUT LINE
        MOV     CX,5                    ;LOAD COUNTER FOR PRINTLOOP
PRINTLOOP:
        DISPLAY OUTMESS                 ;PRINT NAME MESSAGE
        LOOP    PRINTLOOP               ;      AND REPEAT CX TIMES
        CALL    PROMPTER                ;PROMPT FOR NEXT NAME
        CALL    GETNAME
        LEA     SI,INNAME               ;TEST FOR END OF INPUT
        LEA     DI,ENDINPUT.
        MOV     CX,4
        REPE CMPSB
        JE      ENDPROG
        JMP     NAME_ROUTINE
ENDPROG:
        CALL    FINAL
        RET                             ;THEN RETURN TO OPERATING SYSTEM
MAIN_PROG ENDP
;
;
FINAL   PROC
        LOCATE  24,0
        CURSOROFF
        DISPLAY ENDMESS
        RET
FINAL   ENDP
;
GETNAME PROC
        PUSH    AX
        PUSH    DX
        MOV     AH,0AH                  ;GET STRING FROM KEYBOARD/ECHO
        LEA     DX,INBUF                ;ADDRESS OF INPUT BUFFER
        INT     21H                     ;DOS
        POP     DX
        POP     AX
        RET
GETNAME ENDP
;
```

```
MOVENAME PROC
        PUSH    BX
        MOV     BH,0H                           ;SET COUNT FOR MOVE
        MOV     BL,INCOUNT
        MOVE    OUTNAME,INNAME,BX
        MOV     OUTNAME[BX],24H                 ;NEXT CHAR IS $
        POP     BX
        RET
MOVENAME ENDP
;
PROMPTER PROC
        CLS
        CURSORON
        LOCATE  10,0
        DISPLAY NAMEPROMPT
        RET
PROMPTER ENDP
;
PROG_CODE ENDS
        END     MAIN_PROG
```

Figure 7.8 NAMEX Repeated until Ended by User

When this instruction is used in a program, the instruction should be followed by one or more conditional jumps to determine the circumstances under which the comparison ended. If the comparison ends with ZF set, the compared strings are identical. If ZF is clear, they are not identical. Other tests can be made if you need to determine which string was above or below the other. SI or DI can be used to identify which bytes don't match. But, remember that both index registers have been changed and now point to the next pair of bytes, the ones which would have been compared next.

String comparisons can be used for a routine to recognize a predefined end message typed by a user in response to a prompt. Figure 7.8 shows NAMEX modified to use such a routine. The program will continue to prompt for names until you respond with "END ".

Figure 7.9 shows part of a sort routine. Two strings are compared; if they are out of order, an exchange procedure is called.

```
        . . .
        LEA     SI,CURR_STRING
        LEA     DI,NEXT_STRING
        MOV     CX,STRING_LENGTH
        REPE    CMPSB
        JNA     CONTINUE        ;IF CURR NOT ABOVE NEXT SKIP SWAP
        CALL    SWAP_STRINGS
CONTINUE:
        . . .
```

Figure 7.9 String Comparison for Sort Routine

Review Questions

1. Using the MOVE macro from your library as a guide, define a macro that can be used to compare strings. The definition should start with:

   COMPARE MACRO F I RST , SECOND , COUNT

   Remember to initialize SI, DI, and CX before making the comparision. Include this macro in your macro library.

2. Revise PHONER to continue prompting for names and telephone numbers until a predefined message is input. In our version, as shown in the answer to this question, the predefined message is "ALL DONE".

Answers

```
1 .    COMPARE    MACRO       F I RST , SECOND , COUNT
                  PUSH        S I
                  PUSH        D I
                  PUSH        CX
                  LEA         D I , SECOND
                  LEA         S I , F I RST
                  MOV         CX , COUNT
                  REPE CMPSB
                  POP         CX
                  POP         D I
                  POP         S I
                  ENDM
2 .    PAGE       , 132
       ;  I NCLUDE F I RSTL I B . L I B
       ;
       GETDATA    MACRO       I NBUF , COUNT
                  PUSH        AX
                  PUSH        DX
                  MOV         AH , 0AH        ; GET STR I NG FROM KEYBOARD/ECHO
                  LEA         DX , I NBUF     ; ADDRESS OF I NPUT BUFFER
                  MOV         I NBUF , COUNT  ; SET I NPUT S I ZE FOR NAME
                  I NT        21H             ; DOS
                  POP         DX
                  POP         AX
                  ENDM
       ;
       PROG__STACK
SEGMENT STACK 'STACK'
                              DB
```

```
64 DUP ('STACK   ')
    PROG_STACK
ENDS
    ;
    PROG_DATA
SEGMENT 'DATA'
    NAMEPROMPT              DB    0AH,0DH,'NAME: ',24H
    PHONEPROMPT             DB    0AH,0DH,'PHONE NUMBER; ',24H
    ENDMESSAGE              DB    'GOODBYE',24H
    OUTLINE                 DB    0AH,0DH
    OUTPHONE                DB    8 DUP(' ')
    OUTSPACE                DB    3 DUP(' ')
    OUTNAME                 DB    31 DUP(' ')
    INBUF                   DB    31
    INCOUNT                 DB    ?
    INDATA                  DB    31 DUP(' ')
    PROG_DATA ENDS
    ;
    PROG_CODE SEGMENT 'CODE'
MAIN_PROG PROC             FAR
ASSUME CS:PROG_CODE,DS:PROG_DATA,SS:PROG_STACK,ES:PROG_DATA
                STARTER
                CLS
                CURSORON
                LOCATE    10,0
                MOV       CX,3
MAINLOOP:
                CALL      GETNAME       ;PROMPT, INPUT, AND MOVE NAME
                CALL      GETPHONE      ;PROMPT AND INPUT PHONE
                DISPLAY   OUTLINE       ;DISPLAY LINE
                LOOP      MAINLOOP      ;   AND REPEAT PROCESS
                CALL      FINAL         ;THEN RETURN TO OPERATING SYSTEM
                RET
MAIN_PROG ENDP
    ;
FINAL           PROC
                LOCATE    23,10
                DISPLAY   ENDMESSAGE
                CURSOROFF
                RET
FINAL           ENDP
    ;
GETNAME         PROC
                PUSH      BX
                DISPLAY   NAMEPROMPT
                GETDATA   INBUF,31      ;PROMPT FOR NAME
                MOV       BH,0H         ;GET NAME IN BUFFER
```

```
                MOV     BL , INCOUNT              ; SET UP NAME COUNT
                MOVE    OUTNAME , INDATA , BX     ; MOVE NAME TO PRINT
                MOV     OUTNAME[BX] , 24H         ; NEXT CHAR IS $
                POP     BX
                RET
GETNAME         ENDP
;
GETPHONE        PROC
                DISPLAY  PHONEPROMPT              ; PROMPT FOR PHONE
                GETDATA  INBUF , 9                ; GET PHONE IN BUFFER
                MOVE     OUTPHONE , INDATA , 8    ; MOVE PHONE TO PRINT
                RET
GETPHONE        ENDP
;
PROG__CODE ENDS
                END      MAIN__PROG
```

Computer Exercise

Assemble, link, and test the new version of PHONER that you wrote in the answer to the preceding review question.

Other Variations for Repetition

REP has three other variations. The first, REPZ (REPeat while Zero) is an alternative mnemonic for REPE; it produces the same object code and is really the same instruction. REPNE (REPeat while Not Equal) can be used to find the first matching byte in two strings; it tests ZF and continues to repeat if ZF is cleared. Its alternative mnemonic is REPNZ (REPeat while Not Zero).

LOOP also has four variations: LOOPE, LOOPZ, LOOPNE, and LOOPNZ. These, like REP's variations, test both ZF and CX. LOOPE (LOOP while Equal) and its alternate LOOPZ (LOOP while Zero) end the loop when CX is zero or when an instruction within the loop clears ZF. LOOPNE (LOOP while Not Equal) and LOOPNZ (LOOP while Not Zero) also are alternates; they end the loop when CX is zero or when ZF is set.

```
          . . .
          MOV        CX,99
          CALL       GET_CODE
WHAT_TRANS:
          CMP        TCODE,'D'
          JE         DEPOSIT
WITHDRAW:
          CALL       WITHDRAWAL_ROUTINE
          JMP        CONTINUE
DEPOSIT:
          CALL       DEPOSIT_ROUTINE
CONTINUE:
          CALL       GET_CODE
          CMP        TCODE,'X'
          LOOPNE     WHAT_TRANS
TRANSACTIONS_DONE:
          . . .
```

Figure 7.10 Checkbook Transactions with LOOPNE

Figure 7.10 shows the routine from Figure 7.4 rewritten using LOOPNE. The checkbook routine now ends either when a transaction code of "X" is entered or when 99 transactions have been processed.

Key Points From Chapter 7

In this chapter you have learned to use comparisons, conditional jumps, and the unconditional jump instruction to implement decision and repetition structures. You have also learned to code string comparisons and to use variations of the repetition instructions REP and LOOP. Now you should be able to code the logical structure for any program. Some of the main points in this chapter are:

- ■ The status flags are set (or cleared) to reflect the result of a comparison, arithmetic, or bit manipulation instruction. A comparison is actually an implied subtraction of the second operand (source) from the first (destination) and affects the flags accordingly.

- ■ A conditional jump instruction tests the status flags. If the flag settings imply that the result of a previous operation matched the condition in the jump instruction mnemonic, the condition is true and the jump is made. Otherwise, control falls through to the next instruction.

- ■ The instructions JA, JB, JNA and JNB and their alternate forms test CF; they are used after flag-setting instructions involving unsigned data such as ASCII characters.

■   The instructions JG, JL, JNG, and JNL and their alternate forms test SF and OF; they are used after flag-setting instructions involving signed numbers.

■   The instructions JE, JNE, JZ and JNZ test ZF; they are used after any flag-setting instructions.

■   The target of a conditional jump must be a short label. A short label identifies an address within 128 bytes of the jump instruction in the assembled object code.

■   A decision requires the selection of one of two alternate paths based on the current value of a variable or register. One of the paths may be empty.

■   In MASM source code a decision requires two instructions; one sets the status flags based on a current value and the other is a conditional jump that tests the flags. When the condition is true, control is transferred to one of the alternate paths. When it is not true, control falls through to the other path.

■   An unconditional jump, JMP, transfers control every time it is executed. Such a jump can be used to avoid falling through from one alternate path to another.

■   A repetition structure can be coded as a special case of a decision structure. One alternate path is a repetition of the loop. The other path falls through to the instructions following the loop. Two special instructions, REP and LOOP with their variations, are used only for coding repetitions.

■   A multi-byte string can be compared using CMPSB. The beginning address of the source must be loaded into DI and that of the destination into SI before the comparison is made. The maximum number of bytes to be compared must also be loaded into CX.

■   One of the variations of REP must be coded as a prefix for the CMPSB instruction. The combination instruction will compare bytes until CX is 0 or until ZF is set (for REPNE and REPNZ) or cleared (for REPE and REPZ). The next instructions must test to see why the repetition ended.

■   LOOP also has variations similar to those for REP. They can be used to code loops that will end either after a given number of repetitions or when a specified condition is met.

Chapter Review Questions

1. Match each type of instruction to the appropriate phrases. Not all the phrases are used; some are used more than once.

   ___ A. Conditional   a. Affects flag settings
              jump   b. Test flag settings
   ___ B. Comparison   c. Transfers control if condition is met
   ___ C. Unconditional   d. Always transfers control
              jump   e. Two operands
                                  f. One operand
                                  g. Target must be within 128 bytes
                                  h. Target may be anywhere in program
                                  i. Always follows a comparison

2. Would JA or JG more likely be the correct instruction to follow CMP AX,-5?

   To follow CMP FIRST__CHAR,'Z'?

3. Code the appropriate routines for each of the situations below. Assume that all variables used in the decisions have been defined with DB pseudo-ops.

   A. Branch to OVERM if INCODE is above (or greater than) "M".

   B. Branch to TOOLOW if BALANCE is less than (or below) zero.

   C. Call YES procedure if INCODE is "Y"; otherwise call NO.

   D. Repeat a procedure that calls SETTOT until TOT equals seven.

4. Code a routine to compare two 5-byte strings, OLD__CODE and NEW__CODE. Don't use the COMPARE macro in this routine. If OLD__CODE is above NEW__CODE, perform procedure NEW__LESS before continuing to the rest of the program. (If OLD__CODE is equal to or below NEW__CODE, don't perform NEW__LESS, just continue with the program.)

Answers

1. A. b, c, f, g B. a, e C. d, f, h ; i is not used

2. JG; JA

3.
```
    A.   CMP    INCODE,'M'
         JA     OVERM
    B.   CMP    BALANCE,0
         JL     TOOLOW
    C.   CMP    INCODE,'Y'
         JE     CODE__NO
         CALL   YES
         JMP    CONTINUE
CODE__NO:
         CALL   NO
CONTINUE:
```

You undoubtedly used different names where I used CODE__NO and CONTINUE.

```
    D.
MAINLOOP:
         CALL   SETTOT
         CMP    TOT,7
         JNE    MAINLOOP
         LEA    SI,OLD__CODE
         LEA    DI,NEW__CODE
         MOV    CX,5
         REPE   CMPSB
         JA     NEW__LESS
CONTINUE:
         ...
```

4.

8

Using the Manual

You have learned instructions to provide the framework and structure of a MASM program, to transfer control both conditionally and unconditionally within the program, to use the stack, and to move and compare data. In Chapters 9 and 10 you will learn some arithmetic, bit testing and bit manipulation instructions. With all that, however, you still will not know all of the MASM instructions. Even some you do know have variations we are not covering. After Chapter 10, we will not present any new instructions. Instead, we will concentrate on presenting information and sample routines needed for functions, such as numeric conversions; other types of I/O, especially disk I/O; and how to interface MASM routines with BASIC programs.

How are you going to learn the rest of the MASM instructions and their variations? That's the point of this chapter. You will learn a few new instructions, but most importantly, you will learn to interpret the information in the MASM manual so that you can learn material not covered in this book.

A Look at the Manual

Let's look at what the MASM manual contains. We won't try to furnish page or chapter numbers. You may have a different version of MASM than we do, and the numbering may not correspond to ours. Your version may also include features not discussed in this chapter. But, you should still be able to find all the things that we mention.

Look at the table of contents. The manual contains chapters on formats, pseudo operations, and instruction mnemonics (among others). There is an appendix about messages, one that summarizes the instruction set, and one that summarizes the pseudo-ops. These six divisions (three chapters and three appendices) contain most of the information you need for MASM programming, so we'll look at each of them.

Assembler Language Format

Look in the table of contents at the headings under the Assembler Language Format chapter. You should recognize most them: Constants, Variables, Labels, Flag Registers, Operands, and so on. A quick glance through the chapter shows that it contains much that you already know, but there is some additional advanced material. Look at the section titled *Value Returning Operators*, for example. You will find the OFFSET operator, which you know, but you will also find others (SEG, TYPE, LENGTH, and SIZE) that you have not yet learned. Another section, *Record Specific Operators*, is all new to you; it describes operators that are to be used with data forms defined by the RECORD pseudo-op. We don't cover RECORD or record specific operators in this book. You may want to skim the entire chapter to make yourself familiar with terms used in the rest of the manual.

Pseudo-Operations

This chapter describes all of the MASM pseudo-ops. As you can see from the table of contents, these pseudo-ops are presented alphabetically within groups.

The first group, data pseudo-ops, includes those pseudo-ops used to define and handle data fields, names, and structures. You already know some of these: ASSUME, DB, END, EQU, INCLUDE, PROC (and ENDP), and SEGMENT (and ENDS). You can see that others not yet covered. Let's look at one that we have mentioned, but not covered in detail: DW (Define Word).

The DW Pseudo-Op

Turn to the description of DW. At the head of the page you will see the mnemonic and its meaning. Next, there is a short statement of the purpose of the pseudo-op. You can see that DW serves the same purpose as DB, except that DW allocates one word (two bytes) instead of one byte. Following the statement on purpose, you will find a generalized format for the pseudo-op. The format given for DW is:

```
variable-name    DW expression
```

The format is followed by remarks that clarify the purpose, format, and use of the pseudo-op. In this case, the remarks begin by telling you that variable-name is optional. When DW is used without a name, it simply reserves and possibly initializes memory space. When used with a name, it defines that name as a variable with the type attribute WORD.

The remarks also define possible ways to code the expression part of DW. The last part of the description contains source-code examples. You will find it easier to understand some of the remarks if you refer to the examples; the formal language used in the remarks section may be difficult to follow. Some pseudo-op definitions don't include examples. Usually, these have simpler or less variable formats.

Compare the remarks and examples for DW to those for DB. You will see that DW can be initialized as an address expression although DB cannot. (An address won't fit into one byte.) DB can be initialized with a character string ("ABCDE"), DW cannot. DB is limited to constants with a value of 255 or less, DW is not. Since you already know how to use DB, the information given for DW (and the contrasts to the information for DB) should enable you to use DW in your programs.

Other Pseudo-Ops

Other groups in this chapter include conditional, macro, listing, and false conditional pseudo-ops. Conditional and false conditional pseudo-ops are beyond the scope of this book. You have learned three macro psuedo-ops: MACRO, LOCAL, and ENDM. When you gain more MASM experience, you may find some of the other macro pseudo-ops useful in defining complex macros. The listing pseudo-ops control the assembler listing. You already know one of these: PAGE. Most of the others include or exclude portions of the program from the listing, print a heading on each page, and so on.

We'll skip over the instruction mnemonics chapter right now and come back to it after we discuss the three appendices.

Messages

This appendix begins by describing the messages that are printed by the assembler. Notice that if you use ASM, only error codes are displayed and printed; therefore, you will have to look up the codes in this appendix. With MASM, both error messages and codes are inserted in the listing and displayed on the screen.

For each error code, the appendix shows the message printed by MASM for that code and an amplified explanation of the error. In some instances, the explanation is not much different from the message, and, in any case, the message says it all. Look at code 9, for example. The error message is "Symbol not defined". The explanation is "A symbol is used that has no definition." In other cases, the explanation is a little more complete or provides an example. Look at Code 58. The message is "Byte register is illegal". The explanation provides an example, "PUSH AL". PUSH works only with 16-bit registers; the 8-bit registers (AL, AH, and so on) are illegal with this instruction.

The next section of the appendix deals with I/O handler messages. These are runtime errors. When one of these errors occurs in a program assembled with MASM, an error code, message and filename are displayed. With ASM, only the filename and code are displayed; you will need to look up the corresponding message in this appendix.

The last section of the appendix lists other runtime errors. These have no code numbers, they rarely occur, and you may never see them.

Instruction Set Summary

This appendix lists all of the MASM instructions. At the beginning of the appendix, you will find an explanation of the codes used in the summary. The instructions are arranged in alphabetical order by mnemonic. The first line for each instruction shows the mnemonic, followed by the operand field format, and then the meaning of the mnemonic. This is followed by a table showing possible operand combinations. For each combination, the table shows the number of bytes of object code generated by the instruction and an example of the instruction using this combination of operands. The final column in the table shows which, if any, of the status flags are affected by the instruction. This column is **not** related to the operand combinations. The same flags are affected regardless of the operands used.

When would you use this summary? When you're not sure of an instruction mnemonic, when you want to find out quickly whether an instruction exists that does what you want to do, when you want to see if a particular combination of operands is legal with a certain instruction, and when you want to know if an instruction affects the status flags. For more detail about the purpose, coding, and operation of an instruction, go to the instruction mnemonic chapter.

Pseudo-Operations Summary

This appendix lists the pseudo-ops in groups just as the pseudo-operations chapter does. It doesn't tell you much about them; it simply gives you the format for each one. For more detail, go to the pseudo-operations chapter.

Instruction Mnemonics

The chapter on instruction mnemonics contains descriptions of each MASM instruction. It starts, however, with two general information sections that explain the symbols and codes used in the descriptions. Let's look at these sections briefly before we look at the individual instructions.

Symbols and Notation

This section explains the abbreviations and symbols used in the descriptions. Some of the symbols are self-evident. By now you can recognize the meanings of AX, AH, AL, and so on. Some symbols are easy to understand once you look at the definition. REG8, for example, stands for any 8-bit register while REG16 stands for any 16-bit register.

Some of the symbols may not mean much to you even after you read the description. Look at r/m. The explanation says that r/m refers to bits 2, 1, 0 of the MODRM byte and that, combined with the mode and w fields, r/m defines EA. This will make more sense after the discussion of instruction fields, below.

Instruction Fields

In each individual instruction description there is an entry labeled "encoding". This entry describes the object-code instruction created by the assembler. The MASM programmer does not usually care about this information; after all, the purpose of using the assembler language is to avoid having to deal with or interpret object-code directly. If you do want to interpret the encoding entry, however, you will need the information about formats and codes found in the instruction field section. We'll look it over quickly and we'll see some examples in individual instructions.

An object-code instruction contains one to six bytes. They are, in order, an operation-code-byte, an optional addressing-mode-byte, an optional one- or two-byte displacement, and an optional one- or two-byte immediate data value.

The operation-code-byte corresponds to the specific 8088 instruction to be carried out. The operation-code-byte for JMP, for example, is 0FFH; for JE or JZ, 0E4H. The addressing-mode-byte describes the operands. The remaining bytes contain the address for an address operand and the immediate data for an immediate-data operand.

Both the operation-code-byte and the addressing-mode-byte can include subfields containing specific codes affecting the interpretation of the object code. The most common subfield in the operation-code-byte is the word field (w). When present, this field is usually in the low-order bit. When w is 0, the instruction involves 8-bit (one byte) operands; when w is 1, it involves 16-bit (one word) operands. For example: the operation-code-byte format for the instruction that moves immediate data to memory is 1100011w. This means that when a word is moved, the operation-code-byte is 11000111B (0C7H); when a byte is moved the operation-code-byte is 11000110B (0C6H). The encoding entries for some instructions show other subfields such as "d" or "reg" in the operation-code-byte. You can find the subfield's meaning in the symbols and notations section.

The second instruction byte, the addressing-mode-byte, is entirely built from subfields—usually mode, reg, and r/m. (The symbols and notation section contains definitions in which this byte is called the MODRM byte.)

The mode field is the two high-order bits of the addressing-mode-byte. The primary use of the mode field is to specify whether the instruction includes one, two, or no displacement bytes, and whether the displacement represents an address or immediate data. The three low-order bits of the addressing-mode-byte often contain a three-bit code called the register-/memory field, or r/m. (If the mode field is 11, then a three-bit register code is in this position instead.) The r/m code field identifies which combination of registers is used to modify the displacement when calculating EA. In many instructions, the three middle bits of the address-encoding-byte are not used; they contain zeros. Some instructions, however, require both a register and an r/m code. In these, the three middle bits contain the register code. This section of the manual lists both the register codes and the r/m codes. Register code 011, for example, refers to BX. R/m code 011 specifies that EA is calculated by adding the contents of BP and DI to the displacement.

We'll look at some specific instructions, including their encoding entries, after some review questions.

Review Questions

1. Where would you look for each of these items? Choose your answers from this list:

    a.   Assembler language format chapter

    b.   Pseudo operations chapter

    c.   Messages appendix

    d.   Instruction summary appendix

    e.   Pseudo operations summary appendix

_____ A.   An explanation of an error code from the assembly listing
_____ B.   The format of PAGE
_____ C.   A description of value returning operators
_____ D.   The flags affected by CMP
_____ E.   The meaning of a runtime error code
_____ F.   The mnemonic for a conditional jump instruction
_____ G.   A description of the use of PAGE

2. Which statements are true of DW and which of DB? (Some may be true of both DW and DB, some of neither.)

    A.   Reserves and optionally initializes memory

    B.   Can be initialized as an address expression

    C.   Can be initialized with a character string

    D.   Can be initialized with values over 255

    E.   Can define a variable name

3.   Match each phrase with its function. Some phrases may not be used.

_____ A.	Describes operands	a. Operation-code-byte
		b. Symbols and notations
_____ B.	Describes size of operation	c. Addressing-mode-byte
		d. Mode field
_____ C.	Defines instruction	e. Word field
		f. Register field
_____ D.	Indicates register	g. R/m field
_____ E.	Indicate EA computation	
_____ F.	Indicates presence of displacement bytes	

Answers

1.   A. c ;B. b or e ;C. a ;D. d ;E. c ;F. d ;G. b
2.   A. both ;B. DW ;C. DB ;D. DW ;E. both
3.   A. c ;B. e ;C. a ;D. f ;E. g ;F. d ; b is not used

Instruction Descriptions

The instruction mnemonic descriptions, like the pseudo-op descriptions, include purpose, format, and remarks entries. The descriptions also include the encoding entry and a flag entry, which lists the flags affected by the instruction's execution. Most descriptions also include source-code examples and a logic entry, which describes the steps taken in executing the instruction. Let's look at the descriptions of some instructions you have already learned.

A Description of LEA

Find the description of LEA. Look at the heading, purpose, format, and remarks entries. These serve the same function as similar entries in the pseudo-operations chapter. The logic entry reads "(REG)=EA". Turning back to the symbols and notation section, you will see that the parentheses indicate that the instruction is concerned with the contents of a register.

The logic entry, then, says that this instruction sets the contents of a register equal to an effective address. From the previous entries you will see that the register is specified in the first operand, while EA comes from the second operand.

The flags entry tells you that no flags are affected by LEA. The encoding entry shows two bytes for LEA's object code. The first, the operation-code-byte, is 10001101B (8DH). The second byte contains a mode field, a register field, and an r/m field in that order. Mode is always two bits and r/m three bits; this leaves three bits for the intervening register field. The addressing-mode-byte code for this instruction,

LEA BX , ADDER

would be 00011110. The instruction fields section of this chapter tells you that:

1.   the combination of mode 00 and r/m 110 means that EA comes from a two-byte displacement field and

2.   011 stands for register BX.

In the object code, the two-byte displacement field has the low-order byte first, and the high-order second. On the assembler listing the displacement is printed high-order first and is followed by R to remind you that this is a reversal of the actual object code. If ADDER is at offset 0123, then, the object code for our sample instruction is 8D 1E 23 01; the assembler listing shows it as 8D 1E 0123 R. The encoding entry mentions that the mode field for LEA should never be 11. The only way it could get set at 11 would be if you used DEBUG or a similar utility to play around with the object code.

The final entry for LEA contains several examples of valid source code using the instruction. Most instruction descriptions contain such examples. Some even include source code routines showing how the instruction can be used (see LOOP, for example).

Describing PUSH

Look at the description for PUSH. You have learned to use PUSH to place the contents of a register on the stack. It can also be used to place a word from memory on the stack. The purpose entry for PUSH says that there are three PUSH instructions. From a programmer's point of view, writing source code, there is only one PUSH instruction with a choice of two types of operand. The manual, however, looking at PUSH from the object-code standpoint, sees three separate instructions: one with a non-segment register operand, one with a segment register operand, and one with a memory (address) operand.

The purpose entry, the remarks entry, and the logic entry all tell you that execution consists of subtracting 2 from the stack pointer and then copying the contents of the source (the only operand) to the new location pointed to by SP. No flags are affected.

There are separate encoding and example entries for each of the three types of PUSH. Each of the examples includes the generated object code in the comments column. For the third type, only the first two bytes are shown; the actual object code would also include two displacement bytes.

Describing MOV

MOV is one of the first instructions you learned, and it may be the most often used instruction in MASM. It is not difficult to understand, to code, or to use correctly, yet its description is one of the longest in the manual. This is because MOV, like PUSH, is more complicated in object code than it is in source code.

For source-code purposes, MOV is one instruction with five possible operand combinations. As its purpose entry states, however, from an object-code standpoint there are seven different types of MOV, each with several possible variations. The remarks entry indicates that some of these MOV instructions may include a 1-bit destination subfield (d) (which is one if the destination is a register, and zero otherwise) as well as the word (w) subfield, previously discussed. Both subfields occur in the operation-code-byte.

Look at the seven types of MOV. Notice that moves involving the segment registers are different instructions than those involving other registers. Also, moves between memory and the accumulator (AX or AL) are different than moves between memory and other non-segment registers. On the other hand, the following moves are the same: moves from one register to another that do not involve segment registers; moves between a non-segment, non-accumlator register and memory; and moves between the accumlator and memory when the address does not include a variable name.

Look at the examples for these two instruction types: move to a register from immediate data, and move to memory-or-register from immediate data. In my copy of the manual, MOV BX,84 is an example in the second category. Why? Why isn't this an example of a move to a register? To try to understand it, I wrote a little program to see how the object code actually looks using this instruction as well as some moves of immediate data to memory. The relevant part of the assembler listing for the program is in Figure 8.1. Notice that the operation-code-byte for MOV BX,84 is BB. If this is compared to the encoding formulas, we see that MOV BX,84 is actually interpreted as a move to a register, not to a memory-or-register operand. The example in my manual is wrong. When you think you understand an entry in the manual fairly well, but one part of it just doesn't make sense, try out the instruction and operands in a short program to see how the assembler handles it. In this case, of course, it was simply a matter of curiosity. As long as we know that MOV BX,84 is a valid instruction, we don't care too much about how it is translated into object code.

Learning New Instructions

Let's use the manual to learn some new instructions. You really should know several more before you do much more programming. The new instructions include two string operations, STOSB (STOre String Byte) and SCASB (SCAn String Byte), and four instructions that affect flags: CLD (CLear Direction flag), STD (SeT Direction flag), CLI (CLear Interrupt), and STI (SeT Interrupt).

Storing a String

You won't find STOSB as a separate instruction in this chapter; instead, it is one of three instructions in the description headed STOS. The purpose entry tells you that these instructions (STOS, STOSB, and STOSW) copy

```
0000                    THE_DATA SEGMENT 'DATA'
0000   ??               ONEBYTE DB ?
0001   ????             ONEWORD DW ?
0003                    THE_DATA ENDS
                        ;
0000                    THE_CODE SEGMENT 'CODE'
                                ASSUME SS:THE_STACK,CS:THE_CODE,DS:THE_DATA,ES:THE_CODE
0000                    MAIN_PROC PROC FAR
0000   1E                       PUSH    DS
0001   B8 0000                  MOV     AX,0
0004   50                       PUSH    AX
0005   B8   ---- R              MOV     AX,THE_DATA
0008   8E D8                    MOV     DS,AX
000A   8E C0                    MOV     ES,AX

                        ;****** TEST CODE BEGINS HERE ***********
000C   C7 06 0001 R 01F4        MOV     ONEWORD,500
0012   C6 06 0000 R 32          MOV     ONEBYTE,50
0017   BB 0054                  MOV     BX,84
001A   CB                       RET
001B                    MAIN_PROC ENDP
```

Figure 8.1 Part of a Test Program

```
CLEAR     MACRO     CHAR_FIELD,COUNT
          PUSH      DI
          PUSH      AX
          PUSH      CX
          MOV       CX,COUNT
          MOV       AL,' '
          LEA       DI,CHAR_FIELD
          REP       STOSB
          POP       CX
          POP       AX
          POP       DI
          ENDM
```

Figure 8.2 The CLEAR Macro

data from the accumulator to a destination indicated by DI and then change the setting in DI. The format tells you that only STOS requires an operand. In this case, the operand is used by the assembler to determine whether a byte or a word is being copied. The real destination for the move is always indicated by DI. Neither STOSB nor STOSW require operands; information about the unit of data copied is included in the mnemonic.

Look at the descriptions for MOVSB and CMPSB. You will find that they follow the same pattern. They are a group of three instructions, one with operands (MOVS and CMPS), one specifying a byte-size operation (MOVSB and CMPSB), and one specifying a word-size operation (MOVSW and CMPSW). In each case, the notes at the end of the description tell you that the forms without operands are preferred.

Note the difference between string stores and string moves. In a move, both the source and destination are in memory and both DI and SI change when the instruction in repeated. In a store, only the destination is in memory and only DI changes; the source is always in the accumlator.

The string storing operations, like the string moves, are generally used with the repeat prefix (REP). STOSB is especially useful for filling a field with spaces, like this:

```
MOV CX,80
LEA DI,PRINTLINE
MOV AL,' '
REP STOSB
```

The macro in Figure 8.2 can be used to fill any field with spaces. This or a similar macro should become part of your macro library.

Scanning a String

SCASB is a variation of SCAS; let's look at that now. The manual says in the purpose statement that it "subtracts the destination byte or word from AL or AX and affects the flags but does not affect the result." In other words, it compares the destination to the accumulator.

The string scanning operations have the same relationship to the string comparisons that string stores have to string moves. The source is in the accumulator, the destination is pointed to by DI, and a repeat prefix is used, either REPE or REPNE. If REPE is used, the operation is repeated as long as the destination matches the source; if REPNE is used, as long as the destination does not match the source. The operation also ends when CX = 0, so the instructions following the scan must check the flags to find out why it ended.

In effect, then, we use SCAS and its variations to search for a particular byte (or word) in the destination. Here's a routine that looks for the first "-" in TELEPHONE, an eight-byte field:

```
     MOV     CX, 8
     MOV     DI, TELEPHONE
     MOV     AL, '-'
     REPNE SCASB
     JE      FOUND__DASH
NO__DASH: . . .
```

Controlling the Direction

All the string operations increment DI (and sometimes SI) when the direction flag, DF, is 0, but decrement the same register(s) when DF is 1. In effect, when DF is 0 the operation moves from left to right; when DF is 1, from right to left.

The instruction CLD clears the direction flag; look it up. It has no operands. Its only effect is to move zero to the direction flag. A similar instruction, STD, sets DF.

DF is usually zero when the computer is turned on. If nothing happens to change it, it will stay at zero. However, sometimes you may want to reverse the string operation. Here's a routine that searches for the **last** non-space character in an 30-byte NAME field:

```
     MOV        CX, 30
     LEA        DI, NAME + 29
     MOV        AL, ' '
     STD
     REPE       SCASB
     CLD
     JE         NAME__BLANK
FOUND__LAST:
     . . .
```

For safety, any program that changes DF using STD should include CLD before the program ends. If one program ends leaving DF set and assumes that DF is 0, the next program may not execute its string operations properly. It's not a good practice to make such an assumption; you should include CLD at the start of every program just in case it runs following a program that left DF set. It's best to CLD again at the end of any routine that sets DF, as we did in the above example.

Controlling the Interrupt Flag

The interrupt flag, IF, also affects the operation of your program. When IF = 0, external interrupts are disabled. This means that signals coming into the computer from the keyboard, printer, and so on may be ignored. When IF = 1, these interrupts are enabled; the system will pay attention to signals requesting service from outside sources. Many of the I/O interrupt routines, themselves, disable external interrupts and then enable them again before returning control to your program. As you learn more about system requirements and timing you will want to specifically enable and disable interrupts in your programs. For now, since you can't always be sure how the previous program left IF, enable interrupts at the beginning of a program, especially if it is one that uses the printer or keyboard. Looking through the instruction summary, you will find that you use CLI to clear (disable) interrupts and STI to set (enable) them. Neither instruction has operands. You can look up the details in the instruction mnemonics chapter, but neither requires much more explanation.

Review Questions

1. Answer these questions about CMP by looking at its description in the manual.

    A. Which entry or entries describes the operation of CMP?

    B. Which flags are affected by CMP?

    C. How many types of CMP instructions are listed?

    D. Which type is CMP AL,17?

    What is its operation-code-byte?

2. Look up the description of XCHG and answer these questions.

    A.   What does XCHG do?

    B.   Which operand is copied first?

        To where?

    C.   How many types of XCHG are there?

    D.   Which of these instructions are valid?

        a. XCHG AX,DX

        b. XCHG DS,ES

        c. XCHG NEW__FIELD,BX

        d. XCHG NEW__FIELD,OLD__FIELD

For questions 3-10, assume your program has defined these fields:

```
EMPLOYEE__NAME        DB   30 DUP(?)
EMPLOYEE__SSN         DB    9 DUP(?)
PRINT__LINE           DB   132 DUP(?)
```

and code an appropriate instruction or routine:

3. To clear PRINT__LINE (use the CLEAR macro defined in this chapter).

4. To find the first '-' in EMPLOYEE__SSN.

5. To find the last '-' in EMPLOYEE__SSN.

6. To fill EMPLOYEE__NAME with asterisks.

7. To enable interrupts.

8. To disable interrupts.

9. To fill EMPLOYEE__NAME with asterisks if EMPLOYEE__NAME is all spaces.

10. To move EMPLOYEE__NAME to the first 30 characters of PRINT__LINE and EMPLOYEE__SSN to the last 11 characters.

Answers

1. A. purpose, remarks, and logic B. AF, CF, OF, DF, SF, ZF C. 3 D. immediate operand with accumulator; 0011 1100 or 3AH

2. A. exchanges the source and destination operands B. destination; to an internal register C. 2 D. a,c; here's what's wrong with the others: b. segment registers cannot be operands of XCHG; d. at least one operand must be a register

Your answers to questions 3–10 will probably not be exactly the same as mine. Be sure that yours accomplish the same results.

3.  ```
    CLEAR  PRINT__LINE,80
    ```

4.  ```
          MOV    CX,11
          LEA    DI,EMPLOYEE__SSN
          MOV    AL,'-'
          REPNE  SCASB
          JNE    NO__DASH
    DASH__FOUND:
     . . .
    ```

Did you remember to load CX, DI, and AL? Did you remember to test ZF to see why the comparison ended?

5.  ```
          MOV    CX,11
          LEA    DI,EMPLOYEE__SSN+10
          MOV    AL,'-'
          STD
          REPNE  SCASB
          CLD
          JNE    NO__DASH
    LAST__DASH__FOUND:
          . . .
    ```

Did you remember to load CX, DI, and AL? Did you load DI with the address of the last byte of EMPLOYEE__SSN? Did you remember to use STD and then to clear DF with CLD? Did you test ZF to see why the comparison ended?
    ```

```
6.    MOV    CX , 30
      MOV    AL , '*'
      LEA    DI , EMPLOYEE__NAME
      REP    STOSB
```

Did you remember to load CX, DI, and AL?

```
7.    STI
```

```
8.    CLI
```

```
9.    MOV  CX , 30
      MOV  AL , ' '
      MOV  DI , EMPLOYEE__NAME
      REPE SCASB              ; SCAN TILL FIRST NON-SPACE
      JNE  CONTINUE
NAME__SPACES :
      MOV  CX , 30
      MOV  AL , '*'
      LEA  DI , EMPLOYEE__NAME
      REP  STOSB
CONTINUE :
      . . .
```

```
10.   MOV  CX , 30
      LEA  SI , EMPLOYEE__NAME
      LEA  DI , PRINT__LINE
      REP  MOVSB
      STD
      MOV  DX , 11
      LEA  SI , EMPLOYEE__SSN + 10
      LEA  DI , PRINT__LINE + 79
      REP  MOVSB
      CLD
```

Did you remember to clear DF after the move? You could have used the MOVE macro instead, like this:

```
MOVE   PRINT__LINE , EMPLOYEE__NAME , 30
STD
MOVE   PRINT__LINE + 79 , EMPLOYEE__SSN + 10 , 11
CLD
```

Key Points From Chapter 8

In this chapter, you have learned to find your way around the MASM manual and to use it to learn new pseudo-ops and instructions. You learned a new pseudo-op and several new instructions. You also obtained some new information about some instructions you already knew and learned the variations of the string operations. Some of the major points covered in this chapter were:

- The manual contains a chapter on Assembler-Language format. This chapter explains such things as constants, variables, labels, operands, operators, and so on.

- The manual also contains a chapter on pseudo operations. This chapter provides a full description of each pseudo-op, including its purpose and format, remarks that explain the pseudo-op and its format in detail, and examples when necessary to clarify the format and use.

- The manual's chapter on instruction mnemonics contains three sections. One section defines the symbols and notations used in other sections. Another section provides the general format and codes used in creating object-code instructions. The third and main section contains a description of each MASM instruction mnemonic.

- Each instruction mnemonic description includes a heading that lists the mnemonic (and sometimes variations) and its meaning, a purpose entry, a format entry, a remarks entry that amplifies the purpose and format, and a flags entry that describes the flags affected by the instruction. Most descriptions also include a logic entry that describes the steps that take place when the instruction is executed.

- A single instruction mnemonic may have several possible object-code translations depending on the operands used with it. The mnemonic's description presents these as separate instruction types. (For example, immediate data to register, register to register, and so on.) For each instruction type, an encoding entry describes how the object code is formatted; usually an example entry also presents several source-code examples for this instruction type.

- The first object-code byte for an instruction is the operation-code-byte. This byte may include subfields in the low-order bits. The most common is the word subfield, which specifies whether the operation involves a byte or a word. The operation-code-byte corresponds to the 8088 operation code for the instruction.

■ An addressing-mode-byte may follow the operation-code-byte. This byte describes the operands used in the instruction. It is also known as the MODRM byte.

■ Bits 7 and 6 (the two high-order bits) of the MODRM byte contain a mode subfield that primarily specifies the number and use of the following displacement bytes.

■ Bits 2, 1, and 0 (the low-order bits) of the MODRM byte may contain an r/m subfield. The three-bit code in this subfield specifies how EA is to be calculated.

■ If mode = 11, bits 2, 1, and 0 of MODRM contain a register code instead of an r/m code. If an instruction requires both a register and an r/m code (or two registers), bits 5, 4, and 3 of MODRM will also contain a register code.

■ The messages appendix of the manual contains assembler error codes, their corresponding messages, and explanations of the errors. It also contains error codes and messages generated by the I/O handling routines and other runtime messages.

■ The instruction summary appendix presents each of the instruction mnemonics with its format, all its possible operand combinations, possible object-code sizes for each combination, and a list of the flags affected by the instruction.

■ The pseudo-operations summary appendix lists the format of each of the MASM pseudo-ops.

■ The DW pseudo-op reserves and initializes one or more words of memory. It may also define a name as a variable-name associated with the beginning of the reserved area; the variable-name will have type attribute WORD.

■ String operations generally have three variations: a general instruction (MOVS or CMPS) used with either a byte or a word operand, a byte instruction (MOVSB or CMPSB) with no operands, and a word operation instruction (MOVSW or CMPSW) with no operands.

■ The operands in the general instructions (MOVS or CMPS) define whether a word or a byte is involved; the actual source and destination are the addresses pointed to by SI and DI.

■ The string store operations (STOS, STOSB, STOSW) are similar to the string move operations with the destination in DI and the source in the accumulator. They are usually coded with the REP prefix.

■ The string scan operands (SCAS, SCASB, SCASW) are similar to the string comparison operations; the destination in DI is compared to the source in the accumulator. They are usually coded with REPE or REPNE prefix or their equivalents (REPZ and REPNZ).

■ CLD is used to clear DF. When DF is cleared, string operations increment DI and SI.

■ STD is used to set DF. When DF is set, string operations decrement DI and SI.

■ CLI is used to clear IF. When IF is cleared, external interrupts are disabled.

■ STI is used to set IF. When IF is set, external interrupts are enabled.

Chapter Review Questions

Use the manual to answer questions 1–6.

1. A. Where will you find information about pass 1 and pass 2 of the assembler?

    B. Look at the section for Pass 1 and Pass 2. Read the paragraph titled *Forward Reference*. Why does the manual advise putting variable definitions at the beginning of the source code?

2. A. Where will you find information about attribute operators?

    B. Look at the section on attribute operators. Which operator could you use to indicate that the target of a JMP is a short-label?

3. Look up the COMMENT pseudo-op. (Hint: this is a data pseudo-op.) Read the description. Write a three-line comment describing the purpose of the program, the date it was written, and the author's name. The purpose could be something like this: "This program builds, maintains, and lists a name and phone-number file."

4. A. Look up the INC instruction in the instruction mnemonics chapter. Which entries tell you what the instruction does?

    What does it do?

    Which flags are affected?

    Is the carry flag ever changed by this instruction? How many types of the INC instruction are there

B. In the encoding formula of the first type, what does "reg" stand for? (Hint: look it up in symbols and notation.) If an INC instruction is encoded as 01000011B (43H), what was the operand in the source code version? (Hint: look up register codes in the instruction fields section.)

C. Your program includes these two variable definitions:

```
ATONE  DB  15
ATWO   DW  300
```

     What will be the operation-code-byte for INC AONE? For INC ATWO?

5. Error code 31 is displayed during the ASM assembly of a program. Where can you find the meaning of this code? What is the meaning of the code?

6. A. You want to use an instruction to decrement an operand. Where is the best place to look in the manual to find if such an instruction exists? (Hint: it's *not* the instruction mnemonic chapter.)

B. Can you find such an instruction? If so, what is it? How many operands does it have? Which flags does it affect? What kind of operands can it have?

For questions 7-11, code the appropriate instruction or routine using these data definitions:

```
NAME       DB   30 DUP (?)
ADDRESS    DB   30 DUP (?)
CITY       DB   10 DUP (?)
CODES      DB    5 DUP (?)
```

7. Move 0FFH into each byte of CODES.

8. Find the first space in ADDRESS.

9. Find the last "." in NAME.

10. Enable interrupts.

11. Disable interrupts.

Answers

1. A. Assembler language format chapter; B. It permits the assembler to generate more efficient code.

2. A. Assembler language format chapter; B. SHORT

3. COMMENT ! THIS PROGRAM BUILDS, MAINTAINS, AND LISTS

   A NAME AND PHONE NUMBER FILE

   4/17/00   DONNA N. TABLER

   (Your text, as well as your delimeter, are probably different from mine.)

4. A. Purpose, remarks, and logic; adds 1 to the operand; AF, OF, PF, SF, ZF; no; 2

   B. register; BX; C. 11111110 (0FEH); 11111111 (0FFH)

5. Messages appendix; operand types or sizes didn't match in a case where they must match.

6. A. Instruction summary appendix; B. Yes; DEC; 1; AF, SF, OF, PF, ZF; byte or word register or memory.

7.
```
    MOV    CX , 5
    LEA    DI , CODES
    MOV    AX , 0FFH
    REP    STOSB
```

8.
```
    MOV    CX , 30
    LEA    DI , ADDRESS
    MOV    AX , ' '
    REPNE  SCASB
    JE     SPACE__FOUND
NO__SPACE :
```

9.
```
    MOV    CX , 30
    LEA    DI , NAME + 29
    MOV    AX , ' . '
    STD
    REPNE  SCASB
    CLD
    JE     LAST__PERIOD
NO__PERIOD
```

10. ST I

11. CL I

Computer Exercise

Write a program called SSNPROG that will:

1. Prompt for a 30-character name

    a. Fill trailing blanks in name with asterisks

2. Prompt for an 11-character SSN

    a. If SSN does not have 11 non-space characters, repeat the prompt

3. Display name (including asterisks) and SSN on one line with 10 or more spaces in between

4. Repeat until no name is input (input count is 0)

Notes: After the name is input you will need to move it to the print line before prompting for SSN. Using the instructions you have learned so far to fill the trailing blanks of the name with asterisks, it is best to fill the entire print area for name with asterisks before copying the input name. When you move the name to the print area, you will need to use the input count to control the number of characters used. This count is a byte; it cannot be moved directly to CX. If you try to use the MOVE macro with the input count for character count you will get an assembler error. There are several ways to get around this. I chose not to use MOVE, but to code the move in the program, moving 0 to CH and the input count to CL.

If you need more hints, look at the program on the next page. Remember, though, that there are many correct ways to design a program. If you have thought of another way to write SSNPROG, try it.

Assemble, link, and run your program. If your source code is different from mine, but it works, take a few days away from it and then see whether it is easy to read and understand.

```
            PAGE    ,132
;
            INCLUDE MACLIB.LIB
;
            INCLUDE EQULIB.LIB
;
PROG_STACK SEGMENT STACK 'STACK'
            DB      64 DUP ('STACK   ')
PROG_STACK ENDS
;
PROG_DATA   SEGMENT 'DATA'
NAMEPROMPT DB       LF,CR,'NAME: ',EOT
SSNPROMPT  DB       LF,CR,'SSN:  ',EOT
ENDMESSAGE  DB      LF,CR,'GOODBYE',EOT
OUTLINE DB          LF,CR,80 DUP(' '),EOT
INBUF   DB          31
INCOUNT DB          ?
INDATA  DB          31 DUP(' ')
PROG_DATA   ENDS
;
PROG_CODE SEGMENT 'CODE'
MAIN_PROG PROC   FAR
            ASSUME  CS:PROG_CODE,DS:PROG_DATA,SS:PROG_STACK,ES:PROG_DATA
            STARTER
            STI
            CLD
            CLS
            CURSORON
MAINLOOP:
            CLEAR   OUTLINE+2,80            ;MOVE SPACES TO DISPLAY LINE
            CALL    GETNAME                 ;PROMPT AND INPUT NAME
            CMP     INCOUNT,0               ;IF NO NAME END PROGRAM
            JE      END_PROG
            CALL    MOVE_NAME               ;PUT ASTERISKS AND NAME IN LINE
            CALL    GETSSN                  ;PROMPT AND INPUT SSN
            MOVE    OUTLINE+42,INDATA,11    ;MOVE SSN TO LINE
            DISPLAY OUTLINE                 ;DISPLAY LINE
            JMP     MAINLOOP                 ;   AND REPEAT PROCESS
END_PROG:
            DISPLAY ENDMESSAGE
            RET                             ;THEN RETURN TO OPERATING SYSTEM
MAIN_PROG ENDP
;
GETNAME PROC
            DISPLAY NAMEPROMPT              ;PROMPT FOR NAME
            GETDATA INBUF,31                ;GET NAME IN BUFFER
            RET
GETNAME ENDP
;
GETSSN PROC
            PUSH    CX
            PUSH    AX
            PUSH    DI
GS01:
            DISPLAY SSNPROMPT               ;PROMPT FOR SSN
            GETDATA INBUF,12                ;GET SSN IN BUFFER
            CMP     INCOUNT,11              ;MUST BE 11 CHAR
            JNE     GS01
            MOV     CX,11
            MOV     AL,' '
            LEA     DI,INDATA
            REPNE   SCASB                   ;MUST HAVE NO SPACES
            JE      GS01
            POP     DI
            POP     AX
            POP     CX
            RET
GETSSN ENDP
```

```
;
MOVE_NAME PROC
          PUSH    CX
          PUSH    DI
          PUSH    SI
          PUSH    AX
          MOV     CX,30
          LEA     DI,OUTLINE+2
          MOV     AL,'*'              ;FIRST FILL WITH ASTERISKS
          REP     STOSB
          MOV     CX,0               ;THEN MOVE IN NAME
          MOV     CL,INCOUNT
          LEA     SI,INDATA
          LEA     DI,OUTLINE+2
          REP     MOVSB
          POP     AX
          POP     SI
          POP     DI
          POP     CX
          RET
MOVE_NAME ENDP
;
PROG_CODE ENDS
          END     MAIN_PROG
```

9

Arithmetic

In this chapter, you will learn the arithmetic instructions and routines. So far, our examples and practice programs have been limited by the lack of arithmetic instructions. When you can handle arithmetic, you will be able to write programs that cover a much wider range of situations.

MASM arithmetic operates with three types of numbers: binary, packed decimal, and unpacked decimal. (Packed and unpacked decimals are two varieties of binary coded decimals, often referred to as BCDs. If you need to review these formats, see Appendix A.) Remember that all information is stored in memory as binary digits. A string of binary digits, however, can be interpreted as a binary number, as a packed or unpacked decimal, or as a string of ASCII code characters. So far in this book, you have worked with binary numbers (signed and unsigned) and ASCII characters.

All arithmetic operations in the 8088 are performed using binary numbers. Special adjustment instructions are used to correct the results when the operands represent BCDs. We'll discuss binary arithmetic first and then the adjustments that are needed to work with packed and unpacked decimals.

Binary Addition and Subtraction

The arithmetic instructions for addition and subtraction are ADD, SUB, ADC (add with carry), and SBB (subtract with borrow). Figure 9.1 presents

Instruction Format	Operand Size(s)	Operand Combinations	Flags Affected	Remarks
ADD dest,source	Word,Byte	reg,reg reg,mem mem,reg reg,imm mem,imm	AF, CF, OF PF, SF, ZF	Adds source to dest Result in dest
ADC dest,source	Word,Byte	reg,reg reg,mem mem,reg reg,imm mem,imm	AF, CF, OF PF, SF, ZF	Adds source and CF to dest Result in dest
SUB dest,source	Word,Byte	reg,reg reg,mem mem,reg reg,imm mem,imm	AF, CF, OF PF, SF, ZF	Subtracts source from dest Result in dest
SBB dest,source	Word,Byte	reg,reg reg,mem mem,reg reg,imm mem,imm	AF, CF, OF PF, SF, ZF	Subtracts source from dest Result in dest

MUL source	Word,Byte	reg
		mem
			CF, OF	Unsigned multiplication of
				  source and accumulator
				Result is double source length
				With word operand:
				  source multiplied by AX
				  high-order word of result in DX
				  low-order word of result in AX
				With byte operand:
				  source multiplied by AL
				  high-order byte of result.in AH
				  low-order word of result in AL

IMUL source	Word,Byte	reg
		mem
			CF, OF	Signed multiplication of
				  source and accumulator
				Result is double length of source
				With word operand:
				  source multiplied by AX
				  high-order word of result in DX
				  low-order word of result in AX
				With byte operand:
				  source multiplied by AL
				  high-order byte of result in AH
				  low-order word of result in AL

DIV source	Word,Byte	reg
		mem
			none	Unsigned division of accumulator
				  and extension by source
				Result (quotient and remainder) in
				  accumulator and extension
				With word operand:
				  high-order word of dividend in DX
				  low-order word of dividend in AX
				  quotient in AX
				  remainder in DX

Instruction Format	Operand Size(s)	Operand Combinations	Flags Affected	Remarks

				With byte operand:
				  high-order byte of dividend in AH
				  low-order byte of dividend in AL
				  quotient in AL
				  remainder in AH

IDIV source	Word,Byte	reg
		mem
			none	Signed division of accumulator
				  and extension by source
				Result (quotient and remainder) in
				  accumulator and extension
				With word operand:
				  high-order word of dividend in DX
				  low-order word of dividend in AX
				  quotient in AX
				  remainder in DX
				With byte operand:
				  high-order byte of dividend in AH
				  low-order byte of dividend in AL
				  quotient in AL
				  remainder in AH

INC dest	Word, Byte	reg mem	AF, OF, PF SF, ZF	Adds 1 to operand
DEC dest	Word, Byte	reg mem	AF, OF, PF SF, ZF	Subtracts 1 from operand
NEG dest	Word, Byte	reg mem	AF, CF, OF PF, SF, ZF	Forms two's complement of dest Result in dest

Figure 9.1 Arithmetic Instructions

the formats and other information for these (and other) instructions. As we discuss their use, you should refer both to Figure 9.1 and to the instructions' descriptions in the manual.

ADD and SUB

Look at ADD and SUB in Figure 9.1. You can see that the formats and operand combinations are similar to those for MOV. The operation's result replaces the contents of the destination, which is the first operand. If both operands are bytes, the result is a byte. If both are words, the result is a word. You cannot mix operand sizes. (Exception: an immediate data byte can be used with a word destination. The immediate data is converted to a word.)

How do you add or subtract two variables? Since you cannot use two address operands, you must move one variable's contents into a register. When the destination is a register you will probably want to copy the result back to memory.

In this example, BALANCE, INCOME, and OUTGO have all been
defined with DW:

```
. . .
MOV      AX , BALANCE
ADD      AX , INCOME
MOV      BALANCE , AX
. . .
MOV      AX , OUTGO
SUB      BALANCE , AX
. . .
```

This example uses two different techniques. The addition destination is
moved to a register, and the result is moved back to the variable BAL-
ANCE. In the subtraction, the source is moved to a register, and the result
is already in BALANCE when the operation ends. Both operations use a 16-
bit register since the variables involved are words.

Here's another example of addition. For this one, the variables (IN1,
IN2, and SUM) have all been defined with DB, so we must use an 8-bit
register:

```
. . .
MOV      BL , IN2
ADD      IN1 , BL
MOV      SUM , BL
. . .
```

In this example, the result is moved to a new field (SUM), not one that is
used in the arithmetic. The original input variables (IN1 and IN2) are left
unchanged for later use.

All six status flags are set by addition and subtraction. In this book, we
are not concerned with PF. Before we continue our discussion, let's review
the meanings of the other flags in the context of arithmetic operations.

Significant Flags   ZF is set when an operation result is zero and cleared
when the result is not zero. SF is set when the result's high-order bit is one
and cleared when that bit is zero. This is significant in signed arithmetic
where the high-order bit represents the sign. OF is set when there is a carry
from or borrow to the next-to-high-order bit. In signed number arithmetic,
this means that the result would not fit in the destination, but overflows
into the sign bit. CF is set when there is a carry from or borrow to the high-

order bit. In unsigned arithmetic, this means that the result would not fit in the destination. AF is set when there is a carry from or borrow to the lower half of a byte; this flag is significant in BCD arithmetic.

Testing the Result   After addition or subtraction either CF or OF should be tested to ensure that the result fits the destination. There are conditional jumps for this purpose. After an unsigned operation, use JC (Jump if Carry) or JNC (Jump if Not Carry). After a signed operation, use JO (Jump if Overflow) or JNO (Jump if Not Overflow). When OF is cleared, which indicates a valid signed result, you will sometimes need to know whether that result was negative or positive. For this purpose, use JS (Jump if Sign set) or JNS (Jump if Not Sign set). Figure 9.2 shows the formats and other information for these conditional jumps. To find out if the result is zero, use JZ or JNZ. These instructions are equivalent to JE and JNE, which you have already learned.

Multi-Byte Numbers

So far, we have dealt with single byte or single word binary numbers, which limits us to numbers with a range of 0 through 65535 unsigned or -32768 through 32767 signed. These are the largest numbers that can be handled by the 8088 addition and subtraction instructions. We can, however, deal with larger numbers by using multiple bytes (or words), treating each one as a digit in a larger number. I'll restrict the discussion to multiple bytes, but remember that the same principles can be extended to multiple words.

Instruction Format	Operand Size(s)	Operand Combinations	Flags Affected	Remarks
JC short-label	n/a	n/a	none	Jumps to target if CF set
JNC short-label	n/a	n/a	none	Jumps to target if CF clear
JO short-label	n/a	n/a	none	Jumps to target if OF set
JNO short-label	n/a	n/a	none	Jumps to target if OF clear
JS short-label	n/a	n/a	none	Jumps to target if SF set
JNS short-label	n/a	n/a	none	Jumps to target if SF clear
CLC	n/a	none	CF	Clears CF
STC	n/a	none	CF	Sets CF

Figure 9.2 Miscellaneous Instructions Used with Arithmetic

Consider a variable called LIFETIME__PROFIT, which must range from -5,000,000 to +5,000,000. The binary equivalent of this range requires three bytes (six hexadecimal digits). You know that in a word-sized field the low-order byte comes first in memory and, the high-order byte comes last. It makes sense to use that principle in all multi-byte fields for two reasons:

1. compatibility with special numeric processors that define and handle multi-byte fields this way and

2. coding simplicity, since in most cases we process the low-order byte first and high-order last.

Let's define the field and initialize it to 2,500,000 (2625A0H):

```
LIFETIME__PROFIT              DB 0A0H,25H,26H
```

We can look at each byte in this number as having a place value 256 times that of the byte that logically precedes it, just as each digit in a hexadecimal number has a place value 16 times that of the preceding digit. LIFE-TIME__PROFIT's initial value, then, can be computed like this:

byte	digits	decimal value	place value	total value
low-order	0A0H	160	1	160
middle	25H	37	256	9472
high-order	26H	38	65536	2490368
		Total Value		2500000

Multi-Byte Addition We'll define another three-byte field, YEARLY__PROFIT, with an initial value of 0186A0H (100000):

```
YEARLY__PROFIT  DB  0A0H,86H,01H
```

We add YEARLY__PROFIT to LIFETIME__PROFIT just as we would manually. Add the low-order digits first. Then, the middle digits, including any carry resulting from the low-order addition. Then, the high-order digits, including any carry from the middle position. To perform these last two steps we use the instruction ADC (ADd with Carry). As you see in Figure 9.1, this differs from ADD in only one respect: it includes the value of CF in the addition. We can add the two numbers like this:

```
MOV     AL , YEARLY__PROF I T
ADD     L I FET I ME__PROF I T , AL
MOV     AL , YEARLY__PROF I T + 1
ADC     L I FET I ME__PROF I T + 1 , AL
MOV     AL , YEARLY__PROF I T + 2
ADC     L I FET I ME__PROF I T + 2 , AL
```

What about checking for overflow? There's no need to check after the first two additions. The sign bit for the whole number is the high-order bit of the high-order byte, so the first two additions involve unsigned numbers. A carry from these bytes is not an error, since in each case the carry will be added into a higher-order byte. The third addition uses signed numbers. If OF is set by this addition, the sum does not fit in the three bytes provided for LIFETIME__PROFIT. The last ADC should be followed by a conditional jump to an error routine such as JO TOO__BIG. If the addition uses unsigned numbers we would use JC instead of JO to check for a too-large result from the last byte addition.

Multi-Byte Subtraction   What about subtraction? Again, a special instruction, SBB (SuBtract with Borrow), uses CF if necessary to handle a situation in which a lower-order byte has borrowed from a higher one. Let's subtract the immediate data value 120000 (01D4C0H) from LIFE-TIME__PROFIT. This time we'll be sure to include a check for overflow when the subtraction finishes. We'll also test for a negative result.

```
          SUB     L I FET I ME__PROF I T , 0C0H  ; LOW ORDER BYTE
                  F I RST
          SBB     L I FET I ME__PROF I T + 1 , 0D4H  ; M I DDLE BYTE
          SBB     L I FET I ME__PROF I T + 2 , 01H  ; H I GH-ORDER
                  BYTE
          JO      BELOW__L I M I T
          JS      LOSS
PROF I T :
          . . .
```

In this example, you need not move the source or destination to a register since you can subtract an immediate operand directly from an address operand.

Looping through Multi-Byte Operations If we are sure that CF is clear before the low-order addition, we can use ADC (or SBB) there also, and then the entire procedure can be coded as a loop. A special instruction, CLC, clears the carry flag. It has no operands. As you might expect a similar instruction, STC, sets CF, if you should ever need to do that. You will find these instructions in Figure 9.2.

Here's our addition routine using a loop. (Notice the use of INC. You've seen this before, but we'll discuss it further later in the chapter.)

```
          CLC
          MOV     CX , 3
          MOV     BX , 0
ADDUP :
          MOV     AL , YEARLY__PROF I T[BX]
          ADC     L I FET I ME__PROF I T[BX] , AL
          I NC    BX
          LOOP    ADDUP
          JC      TOO__MUCH
          . . .
```

In this routine, CX is the loop counter. We want to add three bytes so CX is initialized to 3. BX starts at zero and is incremented each time the loop is repeated. The first time through, the bytes at YEARLY__PROFIT and LIFETIME__PROFIT are added; the second time, those at YEARLY__PROFIT + 1 and LIFETIME__PROFIT + 1; the third time, those at YEARLY__PROFIT + 2 and LIFETIME__PROFIT + 2. At the end of the third repetition, BX is 3 and CX is 0. LOOP ends when CX is 0.

With a three-digit operation, a loop doesn't really simplify matters; we have gone from six instructions to nine not including the conditional jump. In a longer operation, say eight or ten digits, the loop would make a big difference. The non-loop procedure requires two instructions per digit; the loop has the same nine instructions no matter how many digits are involved. Here is a macro that can be used to add multi-byte numbers:

```
B I NARY__ADDER   MACRO    DEST__BYTE , SOURCE__BYTE , COUNTER
                  LOCAL    NEXT__BYTE
                  PUSH     CX
                  PUSH     BX
                  PUSH     AX
                  MOV      CX , COUNTER
                  MOV      BX , 0
                  CLC
```

```
NEXT_BYTE:
                MOV        AL , SOURCE_BYTE[BX]
                ADC        DEST_BYTE[BX] , AL
                INC        BX
                LOOP       NEXT_BYTE
                POP        AX
                POP        BX
                POP        CX
                ENDM
```

To use this macro you must provide three parameters: the beginning address of the destination, the beginning address of the source, and the number of bytes to be added, like this:

BINARY_ADDER LIFETIME_PROFIT , YEARLY_PROFIT , 3

You may want to add this macro, or a similar one, to your macro library.

Review Questions

When answering the review questions use these definitions:

```
ONE_BYTE        DB   0          ; UNSIGNED
ONE_WORD        DW   0          ; UNSIGNED
BALANCE         DB   0,0,0      ; SIGNED
TRANSACT        DB   0,0,0      ; SIGNED
LIMIT           DW   0          ; UNSIGNED
```

1. Which instructions are incorrect? Why?

    A. ADD AX,ONE_WORD

    B. ADC AL,LIMIT

    C. SUB AH,BALANCE

    D. SBB BALANCE,10

    E. ADD BALANCE,TRANSACT

    F. ADC BALANCE+1,AL

    G. SUB LIMIT,CX

    H. SBB BALANCE+2,DH

2. Match each situation with its description. Not all descriptions are used.

___ A. SF is set.   a. Result of signed arithmetic fit in destination

___ B. OF is clear.   b. Result was zero

___ C. ZF is clear.   c. Result of unsigned arithmetic did not fit in destination.

___ D. CF is set.   d. Result of signed arithemetic was negative.

                        e. Result was not zero.

3. For each purpose, would you be more likely to use CLC, JO, JC, JS, or JZ?

_____ A. To test for overflow after unsigned addition

_____ B. To prepare for multi-byte subtraction

_____ C. To test for overflow after signed addition

_____ D. To test for a negative result after signed addition

4. Code a macro similar to BINARY__ADDER for multi-byte subtraction.

Answers

1. B. operand sizes don't match E. can't add 2 addresses; All of the others are correct.   2. A. d; B. a; C. e; D. c;b is not used.   3. A. JC; B. CLC; C. JO; D. JS 4. Here's my answer. You probably used different names but your logic should be about the same.

```
BINARY__SUB        MACRO     RESULT , SUB1 , COUNT
                   LOCAL     NEXT__SUB
                   PUSH      CX
                   PUSH      BX
                   PUSH      AX
                   MOV       CX , COUNT
                   MOV       BX , 0
                   CLC
NEXT__SUB:
                   MOV       AL , SUB1[BX]
                   SBB       RESULT[BX] , AL
                   INC       BX
                   LOOP      NEXT__SUB
                   POP       AX
                   POP       BX
                   POP       CX
                   ENDM
```

Other Binary Arithmetic

Looking at Figure 9.1, you see several other arithmetic instructions: MUL and IMUL for multiplication; DIV and IDIV for division; and three miscellaneous instructions, INC, DEC, and NEG. We'll discuss all of these.

Multiplication

There are two multiplication instructions: MUL for multiplying unsigned numbers and, IMUL for multiplying signed numbers. (The I in IMUL stands for Integer). Addition and subtraction are the same whether the numbers involved are signed or unsigned; the only difference lies in how to interpret carries from the two high-order bits. In multiplication and division, however, you get different results interpreting 0F2H, for example, as unsigned (a value of 242) rather than signed (a value of -14).

In multiplication, only the source is named in the instruction; it can be a register or address but not immediate data. The destination is always the accumulator: AL if the source is a byte, AX if it is a word. The result is twice the size of the destination. In a byte operation, the result is placed in AX. In this case AH is called the **accumulator extension**. In a word operation, DX is the accumulator extension; the low-order word of the result is placed in AX and the high-order word in DX.

Let's multiply WEEKS, an unsigned byte-sized variable, by seven to get DAYS, an unsigned word-sized variable. We can do it like this:

```
MOV     AL , 7
MUL     WEEKS
MOV     DAYS , AX
```

or like this:

```
MOV     AL , WEEKS
MOV     BL , 7
MUL     BL
MOV     DAYS , AX
```

Now let's redefine WEEKS as a signed word-size variable and multiply it by HOURS, another signed word-size variable.

To hold the result we will need a two-word variable:

```
TOT__HOURS          DW        2 DUP ( ? )
                    . . .
                    MOV       AX , WEEKS
                    MUL       HOURS
                    MOV       TOT__HOURS , AX
                    MOV       TOT__HOURS + 1 , DX
                    . . .
```

(Note that we store the result in TOT__HOURS with the low-order word first.)

The multiplication instructions affect only CF and OF. The extended accumulator is always large enough to hold the result; it cannot actually overflow. CF and OF are set, however, if the extension has significant digits. With MUL, that means that CF and OF are set if the extension is not zero. With IMUL, they are set if the extension's bits are not all zeros for a positive number or all ones for a negative number. If you want to move a multiplication result to a field that is the same size as the original operands, you will need to check CF or OF first to make sure you don't lose significant digits. Notice that CF and OF always match after multiplication; you can test either one.

Here's an example where DAYS, HOURS, and HOURS__WORKED are all defined by DB and hold unsigned numbers:

```
. . .
MOV       AL , DAYS
MUL       HOURS
JC        TOO__MANY
MOV       HOURS__WORKED , AL
. . .
```

Division

There are also two division instructions, as you can see in Figure 9.1: DIV for unsigned numbers and IDIV for signed numbers. The dividend is contained in the accumulator and in its extension (AL and AH for byte divisions, AX and DX for word divisions). The only operand for the instruction is the source, which serves as the divisor. As with multiplication, the source must be a register or an address operand. The quotient is put into the accumulator (AL for byte operations, AX for word); the remainder is put into the accumulator's extension (AH or DX). No flags are affected by division.

What happens if the quotient won't fit into the accumulator? An interrupt of type 0 is generated. Advanced MASM programmers may provide their own routines for type 0 interrupts; the system routine provided displays an error message (divide overflow) and stops the program. How can you avoid these errors? First, always include a check for a zero divisor in the source code because division by zero always causes a type 0 interrupt. Second, when you plan the program, make sure that the quotient can fit in the ranges shown in this table:

Operands	Range
Unsigned Byte	0 through 255
Signed Byte	− 128 through 127
Unsigned Word	0 through 65,535
Signed Word	− 32,768 through 32,768

Suppose you want to calculate average hours per day by dividing days into total hours. If days can range from 2 to 7 and hours from 10 to 250, then average hours per day range from 1 (10/7) to 125 (250/2). Each of these figures fits into an unsigned byte. If DAYS, HOURS, and AVERAGE are defined with DB, we can compute AVERAGE like this:

```
MOV     AH , 0
MOV     AL , DAYS
DIV     HOURS
MOV     AVERAGE , AL
```

Note that both the accumulator and its extension were initialized before dividing.

Here's another division example: we want to compute weekly cost by multiplying rate times hours and then dividing by days to get average cost per day. If hours can range from 1 to 125 and rate can go from 1 to 4, the total cost may range between 1 and 500. When we divide by days (from 2 to 7), our result will be between 0 and 250. We can code the routine in this way:

```
MOV     AL , HOURS
MUL     RATE
DIV     DAYS
MOV     AVERAGE , AL
```

The multiplication result prepared both AL and AX for the division. Now, suppose that hours and rate are such that the total cost may go up to 1,000.

Then, the average could range as high as 500 and cause a type 0 interrupt. We must use a word-size division to get the right result; DX will have to be initialized before the division. The revised routine looks like this:

```
MOV     AL , HOURS
MUL     RATE
MOV     DX , 0
DIV     DAYS
MOV     AVERAGE , AX
```

Both DAYS and AVERAGE now have to be defined with DW instead of DB.

When you prepare the accumulator extension for signed division you can't just move in zeros; you must copy the sign bit from the accumulator throughout the extension. Two special instructions, CBW and CWD, do exactly that. CBW extends a byte from AL through AH; CWD extends a word in AX through DX. Look up these instructions in Figure 9.2 or in the manual. Here is an example of a signed byte-size division. Note the test to avoid division by zero.

```
CHANGE   DB      ?   ; RANGE IS – 128 TO + 127
DAYS     DB      ?   ; RANGE IS 0 TO 30
AVERAGE  DB      ?   ; RANGE IS – 128 TO + 127
         . . .
         CMP     DAYS , 0
         JE      NO__DAYS
         MOV     AL , CHANGE
         CBW                         ; EXTENDS SIGN THROUGH AH
         IDIV    DAYS
         MOV     AVERAGE , AL
         . . .
```

INC, DEC, and NEG

You have already seen INC used in several examples, and you looked up DEC in one of the exercises in Chapter 8. Figure 9.1 provides a good description of each one. Each has only one operand, a destination, which may be an 8- or 16-bit register or address operand. INC adds 1 to the operand, DEC subtracts 1. Both operands set five flags, but not CF. I'll stick to INC in this discussion, but you should be able to apply most of what I say to DEC also.

Why bother with INC when you could use ADD ...,1? Well, you saw one reason in the multiple-byte addition routine. By using INC, we were able to add 1 to BX without affecting CF. If we had used ADD BX,1, the next loop's ADC would have used the carry from the addition to BX instead of the carry from the previous ADC.

NEG simply replaces the destination with its two's complement. The destination can be an 8- or 16-bit register or address operand. All six flags are set. This is the quickest way to change the sign of a number without changing its magnitude (absolute value). You will see NEG used in routines later in this book.

Review Questions

1. Which instruction would you use for each of these purposes?

    A. To multiply unsigned numbers

    B. To divide signed numbers

    C. To divide unsigned numbers

    D. To multiply signed numbers

2. CF and OF are set after a multiplication. Which statement best explains the significance of these settings?

    A. The result was too large to fit into the extended accumulator. Part of the answer has been lost.

    B. The result was too large to fit into the accumulator. The high-order portion of the result is in the accumulator extension; the low-order portion, in the accumulator.

    C. The result was too large to fit into the accumulator. The high-order portion of the result is in the accumulator, the low-order portion, in the accumulator extension.

3. Which statements are true?

    A. Multiplication and division instructions specify only one operand, the source.

B.   MUL multiplies the source by the accumulator.

C.   IMUL multiplies the source by the extended accumulator.

D.   In a word operation, the extended accumulator is AX and BX. In a byte operation it is DX.

E.   The low-order half of any multiplication result is put into the accumulator; the high-order half into the accumulator extension.

F.   Before DIV, the accumulator extension must always be initialized by extending the sign from the accumulator.

G.   After any division the quotient is put into the accumulator and the remainder is put into the extension.

H.   INC and DEC are especially useful in multi-byte arithmetic because they affect only the carry flag.

I.   NEG simply produces the two's complement of its operand.

Answers

1. A. MUL B. IDIV C. DIV D. IMUL   2. B.   3. A, B, E, G, I

Here's what's wrong with the others: C. IMUL multiplies the source by the accumulator, interpreting both as signed numbers. D. In a word operation the extended accumulator is AX and DX; in a byte operation, AX (AL and AH). F. Before any division, the accumulator and its extension must be initialized; this may be done by moving appropriate values into both fields. If the dividend is contained in the accumulator, the extension can be initialized by zero for DIV or by extending the accumulator sign for IDIV. H. INC and DEC are especially useful in multi-byte operations because they do *not* affect the carry flag.

Decimal Arithmetic

MASM uses the same arithmetic operations for packed and unpacked decimals as it does for binary arithmetic. These operations treat all numbers in the same way. They do not distinguish between decimal and binary numbers. In the decimal formats, however, a half-byte (four bits) can only represent digits 0-9. When two of these four-bit digits are added and the result is larger than 9 an adjustment must be made so that the result reflects the correct total. Similar adjustments are required in other operations. The adjustment instructions are shown in Figure 9.3. I will discuss their use,

Instruction Format	Operand Size(s)	Operand Combinations	Flags Affected	Remarks
AAA	n/a	none	AF, CF	Corrects AL after unpacked addition
AAS	n/a	none	AF, CF	Corrects AL after unpacked subtraction
AAM	n/a	none	PF, SF, ZF	Converts packed decimal in AL into two unpacked decimals in AH and AL. Used to adjust result of unpacked decimal multiplication
AAD	n/a	none	PF, SF, ZF	Converts two unpacked decimals in AX into packed decimal in AL. Used to prepare dividend for for unpacked division
DAA	n/a	none	AF, CF, PF SF, ZF	Corrects AL after packed addition
DAS	n/a	none	AF, CF, PF SF, ZF	Corrects AL after packed subtraction

Figure 9.3 BCD Adjustment Instructions

but will not go into much detail on how they make the adjustments. Before we discuss adjustments, though, let's look at how to define and initialize variables as packed and unpacked decimals.

Defining BCDs

Figure 9.4 shows some numbers represented as unsigned binary numbers, packed decimals, and unpacked decimals. Remember that these are formats for storing and manipulating numbers. They are *not* ways of representing values in your source code.

In source code, you use "B" to indicate that you are presenting a number in binary (0000 1011B), "H" for hexadecimal (0BH), "D" or no indicator for decimal (11). There is no indicator for packed or unpacked decimal format that is equivalent to "B" for binary or "H" for hexadecimal. A value of 11 in packed-decimal format can be written as 00010001B or as 11H. The decimal equivalent of 11H is 17, not 11. Similarly, 11 in unpacked-decimal format can be shown as 0000 0001 0000 0001B, or 0101H. The decimal equivalent of this is 257.

Notice that BCD digits are the same in binary as the hexadecimal digits 0-9. Suppose that you want to define a one-byte field to be used for packed decimals and to initialize it with the BCD digits 32. You could do it like this:

```
PACKED_FIELD DB 00110010B      ; PACKED BCD 32
```

Decimal	Binary	BCD Unpacked	BCD Packed
12	0000 1100 (0CH)	0000 0001 0000 0010 (0102H)	0001 0010 (12H)
27	0001 1011 (1BH)	0000 0010 0000 0111 (0207H)	0010 0111 (27H)
299	0001 0010 1010 (126H)	0000 0010 0000 1001 0000 1001 (020909H)	0010 1001 1001 (299H)

Figure 9.4 Binary and BCD Formats

Or, you could use the hexadecimal equivalent:

PACKED__F I ELD DB 32H   ; PACKED DCB 32

or the decimal equivalent:

PACKED__F I ELD DB 50   ; PACKED DCB 32

The hexadecimal version is the clearest and easiest to code. An unpacked field could be initialized similarly using hexadecimal notation:

UNPACKED__WORD DW 0302H   ; UNPACKED BCD 32

We could also have defined this field as two bytes:

UNPACKED__BYTE DB 02H , 03H   ; UNPACKED BCD 32

As usual we store the low-order byte first.

Many processors use a standard format for packed decimals. In the 8087, all packed decimals are 10 bytes long; they contain 18 digits in the low-order 9 bytes. The high-order bit of the high-order byte is a sign bit; the remaining seven bits are zeros. If you are planning files that will be used by such a processor, you may want to use this format. I will not discuss it any further. In fact, I will not deal at all with the subject of signed BCD's.

Addition and Subtraction Adjustments

To adjust the result of unpacked-decimal addition, use AAA (ASCII Adjust for Addition). AAA assumes that the addition result is in AL. If the result is greater than 9, either the four lower bits of AL are greater than 9, or AF is set, or both. In either case, AAA adjusts the four lower bits to show the correct decimal digit, clears the four upper bits, and sets both AF and CF.

To adjust the result of packed decimal addition, use DAA (Decimal Adjust for Addition). Again AL is adjusted but, in this case, adjustments may be made to both halves of the byte. If the lower four bits are greater than 9 or AF is set, the lower four bits are adjusted; if the upper four bits are greater than 9 or CF is set, the upper four bits are adjusted and CF is set. DAA, unlike AAA, also affects PF, SF, and ZF.

If ONE__BYTE and SUM__BYTE are unpacked decimals, then, you would need these instructions to add ONE__BYTE to SUM__BYTE:

```
MOV      AL , SUM__BYTE
ADD      AL , ONE__BYTE
AAA
MOV      SUM__BYTE , AL
```

We used AL for the destination of ADD since AAA expects to find the result there anyway. Unless this is the first step in a multi-byte addition, we would probably also want to include a JC after AAA. Then we can go to an error routine if the **adjusted** result is too large. If ONE__BYTE and SUM__BYTE were packed instead of unpacked decimals, the only change in the routine would be from AAA to DAA.

The subtraction adjustments, AAS for unpacked and DAS for packed decimals, are similar to the addition adjustments, as you can see from Figure 9.3.

Multi-Byte Decimals

Multi-byte addition and subtraction are the same for BCDs as for binary numbers, except that the routines must include the appropriate adjustments following ADC or SBB. Here's a macro for multi-byte unpacked decimal subtraction:

```
SUB__UNPACKED      MACRO      RESULT , IN1 , COUNT
                   LOCAL      NEXT__SUB
                   PUSH       CX
                   PUSH       BX
                   PUSH       AX
                   MOV        CX , COUNT
                   MOV        BX , 0
                   CLC
```

```
NEXT__SUB:
                    MOV          AL , RESULT[BX]
                    SBB          AL , IN1[BX]
                    AAS
                    MOV          RESULT[BX] , AL
                    INC          BX
                    LOOP         NEXT__SUB
                    POP          AX
                    POP          BX
                    POP          CX
                    ENDM
```

The count that is passed to this macro must be either in the form of immediate data or a word-sized variable; otherwise, MOV CX,COUNT will produce an error. BX is used to point to the bytes being operated on each time through the loop; the work is actually done in AL.

Decimal Multiplication and Division

AAM converts an unpacked multiplication result in AL into two unpacked decimals in AH and AL. AAM is also used in routines that convert binary numbers to unpacked decimals; we'll discuss its operation in more detail than we did the addition and subtraction adjustments.

Consider this routine, where M1 and M2 are one-byte unpacked decimals:

```
MOV        AL , M1
MUL        M2
AAM
```

If M1 = 3 and M2 = 7, AX contains 21 as a binary number after the multiplication. The contents of AH are 00000000, while AL contains 00010101. AAM actually divides AX by 10, putting the quotient (in this case 2) into AH and the remainder (1) into AL. After AAM in our example, AH contains 00000010 and AL contains 00000001. AX, then, contains 21 as a two-digit unpacked decimal.

AAD reverses AAM; it converts two unpacked-decimal digits in AH and AL into a binary value in AL and zeros out AH. It does this by multiplying AH by 10, adding the result to AL, and then moving zero to AH. AAD is used to **prepare** the accumlator for a byte division; the adjustment must be made **before** the division. AAD can be used any time you need to convert two unpacked-decimal digits to a binary number.

There are no packed multiplication or division adjustment instructions. If you must multiply or divide packed numbers you must convert them to unpacked decimal or binary format.

Why Use BCD?

Unpacked decimals are similar to ASCII code for the decimal digits. In ASCII code, each digit is one byte: the low-order four bits contain the binary representation of the digit and the high-order four bits contain 0011B (3). To convert digits that are input from the keyboard in ASCII code to unpacked decimals, you need to change the high-order four bits from 3 to 0. One way to do this is to subtract 30H from the ASCII character. To reverse the conversion so that you can display or print arithemetic results, change the high-order four bits from 0 to 3. For addition and subtraction, you don't even need to change the high-order bits; the unpacked-decimal adjustments (AAA and AAS) can handle ASCII characters directly. This compatibility with ASCII is the main reason for using unpacked decimals.

Figure 9.5 shows a program called ADDITION, which prompts for a number, adds it to a total field, displays the current total, and continues until no number is input. The working arithmetic fields are all unpacked decimals. The input number is restricted to five digits and the total to ten digits. The program calls a multi-byte unpacked addition macro similar to SUB_UNPACKED.

Packed decimals are usually used to save space. They take half the memory that unpacked decimals do. Also, each arithmetic instruction that involves packed decimals, handles two digits at a time instead of one. Therefore, they require only half as many operations as equivalent unpacked decimals. Some other processors handle packed decimals directly; the 8087 includes instructions that allow packed decimals to be converted to formats that are very efficient when used in the 8087's arithmetic operations. This kind of compatibility with other processors is one reason for using packed decimals in files and programs. We will not use them very much in our programs, however.

What About Decimal Places?

So far, all the examples have used integers exclusively. How does MASM handle decimal places? It doesn't. If you are going to use numbers that involve decimal places, you must handle them in the program as if they were integers. It is up to you to keep track of how many digits in each number actually represent decimal places, to add trailing zeros if necessary

```
        PAGE      ,132
;
        INCLUDE MACLIB.LIB
;
        INCLUDE EQULIB.LIB
;
PROG_STACK SEGMENT STACK 'STACK'
                DB        64 DUP ('STACK    ')
PROG_STACK ENDS
;
PROG_DATA   SEGMENT 'DATA'
NUMBER_PROMPT   DB        LF,CR,'PLEASE TYPE NEXT NUMBER: ',EOT
END_MESSAGE     DB        LF,CR,'GOODBYE',EOT
OUT_MESSAGE     DB        LF,CR,'CURRENT TOTAL: '
OUT_SUM         DB        10 DUP(' '),EOT
;
INBUF           DB        6
INCOUNT         DB        ?
INDATA          DB        6 DUP(' ')
;
IN1             DB        10 DUP(0)
SUM             DB        10 DUP(0)
PROG_DATA   ENDS
;
PROG_CODE SEGMENT 'CODE'
MAIN_PROG PROC   FAR
        ASSUME   CS:PROG_CODE,DS:PROG_DATA,SS:PROG_STACK,ES:PROG_DATA
        STARTER
        STI
        CLD
        CLS
        CURSORON
NEXT_NUMBER:
        DISPLAY           NUMBER_PROMPT
        GETDATA           INBUF,6
        CMP               INCOUNT,0
        JE                END_PROG
        CALL              ASCII_TO_UNPACKED
        ADD_UNPACKED      SUM,IN1,10
        CALL              UNPACKED_TO_ASCII
        DISPLAY           OUT_MESSAGE
        JMP               NEXT_NUMBER
END_PROG:
        DISPLAY           END_MESSAGE
        RET                                 ;THEN RETURN TO OPERATING SYSTEM
MAIN_PROG ENDP
;
ASCII_TO_UNPACKED         PROC              ;MOVES INPUT ASCII CHARACTERS TO
                                            ;   UNPACKED DECIMAL WORK AREA
        MOV               CX,10             ;FIRST CLEAR WORK AREA
        MOV               AL,0
        LEA               DI,IN1
        REP STOSB
        MOV               CH,0
        MOV               CL,INCOUNT        ;THEN CONVERT ASCII TO BCD
        MOV               BX,0
ASC1:
        SUB               INDATA[BX],30H   ;   BY CLEARING UPPER 4 BITS
        INC               BX
        LOOP              ASC1
        MOV               CH,0
```

```
            MOV         CL,INCOUNT       ;NOW MOVE INPUT TO WORK AREA
            MOV         SI,0             ;    PUTTING LOW-ORDER DIGITS
            MOV         DI,CX            ;    AT END OF WORK AREA
            DEC         DI
ASC2:
            MOV         AL,INDATA[SI]
            MOV         IN1[DI],AL
            INC         SI
            DEC         DI
            LOOP        ASC2
            RET
ASCII_TO_UNPACKED       ENDP
;
UNPACKED_TO_ASCII       PROC             ;MOVES UNPACKED SUM TO OUTPUT
                                         ;    AREA AND CONVERTS TO ASCII
            MOV         CX,10            ;FIRST MOVE SUM
            LEA         SI,SUM           ;SUM HAS HIGH-ORDER FIRST
            LEA         DI,OUT_SUM+9     ;   OUTPUT HAS HIGH-ORDER LAST
UNP1:
            MOV         AL,[SI]
            MOV         [DI],AL
            INC         SI
            DEC         DI
            LOOP        UNP1
            MOV         CX,10            ;NOW CONVERT TO ASCII
            MOV         BX,0
UNP2:
            ADD         OUT_SUM[BX],30H
            INC         BX
            LOOP        UNP2
            MOV         CX,10            ;NOW CLEAR LEADING ZEROS
            MOV         BX,0
UNP3:
            CMP         OUT_SUM[BX],'0'
            JNE         UNP4             ;QUIT WHEN FIRST NONZERO FOUND
            MOV         OUT_SUM[BX],' '
            INC         BX
            LOOP        UNP3
UNP4:
            RET
UNPACKED_TO_ASCII       ENDP
;
PROG_CODE ENDS
            END    MAIN_PROG
```

Figure 9.5 The ADDITION Program

for aligment for addition and subtraction, to round or truncate excess digits after multiplication, and to make adjustments for division. You must also edit printed and displayed numbers by inserting decimal points and other editing characters such as commas and currency signs in the proper places and by removing such excess characters from input numbers. The logic used in tracking and using decimal places is the same whether the arithmetic is performed manually or by a computer; we are not going to discuss it in detail in this book.

Review Questions

1. AH contains this value: 00000110 00000011.

    A.   What is this value if this is a binary number?

    B.   What is this value if this is an unpacked decimal?

    C.   What is this value if this is a packed decimal?

2. Code the definition of BINCODE if BINCODE is:

    A.   A three-digit unpacked decimal initialized as 173

    B.   A four-digit packed decimal initialized as 8175

    C.   A four-digit unpacked decimal initialized as 8175

3. Match each instruction with the appropriate phrase or phrases. Some phrases may not be used; some are used more than once.

    ___ A.   AAA

    ___ B.   DAA

    ___ C.   AAS

    ___ D.   DAS

    ___ E.   AAM

    ___ F.   AAD

    a.   Used before binary arithmetic instruction

    b.   Tests and affects AF

    c.   Affects CF

    d.   Adjusts packed decimals

    e.   Adjusts unpacked decimals

    f.   Converts binary value in AL to BCD digits in AH, AL

    g.   Converts two BCD digits in AH, AL to binary value in AL

    h.   Adjusts decimal point after multiplication

    i.   Used after addition

    j.   Used after subtraction

    k.   Adjusts byte in AL if necessary

4. Code a multi-byte unpacked-decimal addition macro similar to SUB_UNPACKED. The answer is the macro that is called in ADDITION (Figure 9.5). If yours is different, try writing a program similar to ADDITION to test it.

Answers

1. A. 1539 B. 63 C. 603   2. A. BINCODE DB 03H,07H,01H
   B. BINCODE DB 75H,81H or BINCODE DW 8175H C. BINCODE DB
05H,07H,01H,08H   3. A. b,c,e,i,k B. b,c,d,i,k C. b,c,e,j,k D. b,c,d,j,k E. e,f
F. a,e,g ; h is not used   4. Here's our macro:

```
ADD__UNPACKED        MACRO    RESULT , IN1 , COUNT
                     LOCAL    NEXT__ADD
                     PUSH     CX
                     PUSH     BX
                     PUSH     AX
                     MOV      CX , COUNT
                     MOV      BX , 0
                     CLC
NEXT__ADD :
                     MOV      AL , RESULT[BX]
                     ADC      AL , IN1 [BX]
                     AAA
                     MOV      RESULT[BX] , AL
                     INC      BX
                     LOOP     NEXT__ADD
                     POP      AX
                     POP      BX
                     POP      CX
                     ENDM
```

Key Points From Chapter 9

In this chapter, you learned the MASM arithmetic instructions and some additional instructions used to build arithmetic routines. You learned to do single and multi-byte addition and subtraction using both binary and decimal numbers and you learned to multiply and divide using binary and unpacked decimal numbers. Here are some of the main points from this chapter:

■ The general format for the addition and subtraction instructions is

```
opcode dest , source
```

and the result replaces dest. The operands can be words or bytes. Dest can be a register or address operand; source can be register, address, or immediate data. The combination address,address cannot be used.

■ Each of these instructions affects the status flags. SF and OF are significant after signed arithmetic, CF after unsigned arithmetic, AF in BCD arithmetic, and ZF in any arithmetic. When a significant flag is set the meaning is:

Flag	Meaning
SF	Result is negative
OF	Result overflows allowed space
CF	Result overflows allowed space
AF	Result overflows from low-order four bits
ZF	Result is zero

■ The addition instructions are ADD and ADC. ADC includes the original value of CF in the addition; ADD does not.

■ The subtraction instructions are SUB and SBB. Both subtract source from dest. SBB also subtracts the original value of CF from dest.

■ ADD and SUB are used in one-byte operations or with the low-order byte in a multi-byte-operation.

■ ADC and SBB are used with the other (not low-order) bytes in multi-byte operations.

■ Loops can be coded using ADC, and SBB can be used with all bytes in multi-byte operations, if CLC is first used to clear the carry flag. STC can be used to set CF if this is ever necessary.

■ After unsigned addition or subtraction, use JC or JNC to test the carry flag. After signed addition or subtraction, use JO or JNO to test the overflow flag and JS or JNS to test the sign flag. These tests should be made after a multi-byte operation or after the high-order byte in a multi-byte operation.

■ Multi-byte numbers should be stored with the low-order byte first, high-order last.

■ Division and multiplication use the accumulator and its extension. For a byte operation, AL is the accumulator and AH the extension. For a word operation, AX is the accumulator and DX the extension.

■ MUL is used to multiply unsigned numbers, IMUL to multiply signed numbers. Both require one operand, the source, which may be a word or a byte, a register or an address. The destination is always the accumulator (AL or AX). The result goes in the extended accumulator, with the high-order portion in the extension. CF and OF are set if the accumulator extension contains significant digits.

■ DIV is used to divide unsigned numbers, IDIV to divide signed numbers. Both require one operand, the source, which may be a word or a byte, a register or an address. The source is the divisor. The dividend is always the extended accumulator. The quotient is placed in the accumulator, the remainder in its extension. No flags are affected by division.

■ Before division, both the accumulator and its extension must be initialized with the dividend. If the dividend occupies only the accumulator, the extension can be initialized with zero for unsigned division. For signed division, the accumulator's sign can be extended into the accumulator extension by using CBW or CWD.

■ INC and DEC each has one operand, dest, which may be a word or a byte, an address or a register. The destination is incremented or decremented according to the instruction. All status flags except CF are affected.

■ NEG has one operand, dest, which may be a word or a byte, an address or a register. The two's complement of the destination replaces the destination. All status flags are affected.

■ BCD values can be initialized or coded as immediate by using hexadecimal digits, since the binary codes for 0–9 are the same for hexadecimal and BCDs.

■ AAA is used to adjust AL following addition of unpacked decimals. AAA places the correct unpacked-decimal digit in AL and sets AF and CF if necessary.

■ AAS is used to adjust AL following subtraction of unpacked decimals. AAS places the correct unpacked-decimal digit in AL and sets AF and CF if necessary.

■ DAA and DAS are used to adjust AL following addition and subtraction of packed decimals. Each of them places two correct packed-decimal digits in AL and affects all the status flags.

■ AAM is used to adjust AX following multiplication of unpacked decimals. The binary value in AL is divided by 10; the quotient is placed in AH and the remainder in AL. The effect is to convert the binary value in AL to two unpacked-decimal digits in AX.

■ AAD is used to adjust AX before division of unpacked decimals. The value in AH is multiplied by 10 and added to the value in AL; then, AH is cleared. The effect is to convert two unpacked-decimal digits in AX to a binary value in AL.

■ There are no adjustment instructions for multiplication or division of packed decimals. The packed decimals must be converted to unpacked decimals or binary for multiplication or division.

■ ASCII characters can be added and subtracted like unpacked decimals if desired. The conversion between ASCII characters and unpacked decimals is also very simple. To go from ASCII to unpacked, change the upper four bits of each byte from 3 to 0. To go from unpacked to ASCII, reverse the process.

Chapter Review Questions

Code instructions or routines to:

1. Add ABYTE to BBYTE. Both are one-byte binary values.

2. A. Go to ERROR__ROUTINE if an unsigned result overflows.
    B. Go to ERROR__ROUTINE if a signed result overflows.

    C. Go to BELOW__ZERO if a signed result is negative.

    D. Go to ZERO__BALANCE if a result is zero.

3. A. Add 250 to LOW__BALANCE, a one-byte unsigned binary number.

    B. Subtract 125 from DAYS, a one-byte signed number.

4. Add two eight-byte signed numbers, IN1 and IN2, putting the result in SUM. (Hint: code the addition as a loop.)

5. Subtract WITHDRAW from BALANCE; both are seven-byte unsigned numbers. If the result overflows, go to OVERDRAW.

6. Multiply WEEKS, a one-byte unsigned binary number, by seven; store the result in DAYS, also a one-byte number. If the result is too large for DAYS go to TOO__MANY instead of storing it.

7. Multiply PRICE and QTY, two one-word signed numbers; store the result in TOTAL__PRICE, a two-word number. If the significant digits of TOTAL__PRICE won't fit in one word, go to DISP__MESS after storing the result.

8. Multiply PRICE and QTY, two one-word signed numbers; divide the result by DAYS, a one-word signed number. Save the quotient in DAILY__AVE and the remainder in REMAIN. Make sure to include a check for a zero divisor. If DAYS is zero go to an error routine instead of performing the division.

9. Divide YEAR, a one-word unsigned number, by four. If the remainder is zero, go to LEAP__YEAR.

10. Divide TOTAL, a one-byte signed number, by three. Save the quotient in ONE__THIRD and the remainder in REMAIN.

11. A. Add INCOME to BALANCE and then subtract OUTGO. All three variables are five-digit unpacked decimals. Code the full routines as loops; don't use the macros developed in the chapter. If any operation overflows, go to ERROR__ROUTINE instead of continuing.

    B. Repeat A using ADD__UNPACKED and SUB__UNPACKED.

    C. Repeat A assuming all three variables are six-digit packed decimals.

12. Multiply M1 by M2 and move the result to R1. M1 and M2 are one-digit unpacked decimals; R1 is a two-digit unpacked decimal.

13. Divide D1, a two-digit unpacked decimal, by three. Store the result in M1 and the remainder in R1.

Answers

```
1.      MOV     AL , ABYTE
        ADD     BBYTE , AL
```

You may have used a different 8-bit register, or done the addition in the register and moved the result to BBYTE.

```
2.   A.   JC          ERROR_ROUTINE
     B.   JO          ERROR_ROUTINE
     C.   JS          BELOW_ZERO
     D.   JZ          ZERO_BALANCE or JE ZERO_BALANCE
3.   A.   ADD         LOW_BALANCE, 250
     B.   SUB         DAYS, 125
4.        MOV         CX, 8
          MOV         BX, 0
          CLC
     NEXT_ADD:
          MOV         AL, IN1[BX]
          ADC         AL, IN2[BX]
          MOV         SUM[BX], AL
          INC         BX
          LOOP        NEXT_ADD
5.        MOV         CX, 7
          MOV         BX, 0
          CLC
     NEXT_SUB:
          MOV         AL, WITHDRAW
          SBB         BALANCE, AL
          INC         BX
          LOOP        NEXT_SUB
          JC          OVERDRAW
6.        MOV         AL, 7
          MUL         WEEKS
          JC          TOO_MANY
          MOV         DAYS, AL
7.        MOV         AX, PRICE
          IMUL        QTY
          MOV         DX, TOTAL_PRICE   ;HIGH-ORDER FIRST
          MOV         AX, TOTAL_PRICE+1 ;LOW-ORDER LAST
          JC          DISP_MESS             ;OR JO
```

```
8.          MOV         AX,PRICE
            IMUL        QTY
            CMP         DAYS,0
            JE          ERROR__ROUTINE
            IDIV        DAYS
            MOV         DAILY__AVE,AX
            MOV         REMAIN,DX
9.          MOV         AX,YEAR
            MOV         DX,0           ;INITIALIZE EXTENSION

            MOV         BX,4


            DIV         BX
            CMP         DX,0           ;CHECK REMAINDER
            JE          LEAP__YEAR
10.         MOV         AL,TOTAL
            CBW                        ;INITIALIZES EXTENSION
            MOV         BL,3
            IDIV        BL
            MOV         ONE__THIRD,AL
            MOV         REMAIN,AH
11.   A.    MOV         CX,5
            MOV         BX,0
            CLC
      NEXT__ADD:
            MOV         AL,BALANCE[BX]
            ADC         AL,INCOME[BX]
            AAA
            MOV         BALANCE[BX],AL
            INC         BX
            LOOP        NEXT__ADD
            JC          ERROR__ROUTINE
            MOV         CX,5
            MOV         BX,0
            CLC
```

```
       NEXT__SUB:
               MOV        AL , BALANCE[BX]
               SBB        AL , OUTGO[BX]
               AAS
               MOV        BALANCE[BX] , AL
               INC        BX
               LOOP       NEXT__SUB
               JC         ERROR__ROUTINE
   B.  ADD__UNPACKED BALANCE , INCOME , 5
               JC         ERROR__ROUTINE
       SUB__UNPACKED BALANCE , OUTGO , 5
               JC         ERROR__ROUTINE
   C.          MOV        CX , 3            ; SIX PACKED DIGITS
               MOV        BX , 0
               CLC
       NEXT__ADD:
               MOV        AL , BALANCE[BX]
               ADC        AL , INCOME[BX]
               DAA
               MOV        BALANCE[BX] , AL
               INC        BX
               LOOP       NEXT__ADD
               JC         ERROR__ROUTINE
               MOV        CX , 3
               MOV        BX , 0
               CLC
       NEXT__SUB:
               MOV        AL , BALANCE[BX]
               SBB        AL , OUTGO[BX]
               DAS
               MOV        BALANCE[BX] , AL
               INC        BX
               LOOP       NEXT__SUB
               JC         ERROR__ROUTINE
12.            MOV        AL , M1
               MUL        M2
               AAM
               MOV        AL , R1           ; LOW–ORDER DIGIT FIRST
               MOV        AH , R1 + 1       ; HIGH–ORDER DIGIT LAST
```

```
13.      MOV      BL , 3
         MOV      AL , D1
         AAD
         MOV      AH , 0          ; INITIALIZE EXTENSION
         DIV      BL
         MOV      M1 , AL
         MOV      R1 , AH
```

10

Bit By Bit

This chapter presents instructions that test, change, and move individual bits within bytes or words. It's easy to describe these instructions and how they work, but it's not so easy to explain the reasons for using them. These bit manipulation instructions often are necessary when coding routines to perform complex functions that are beyond the scope of this book. As you gain programming experience, you will find situations in which one or another of these instructions is just what you need. In this chapter, however, I will generally discuss the "how" instead of the "why" of bit manipulation.

Logical Bit Operations

Figure 10.1 shows the formats of the logical bit operations: AND, OR, NOT, XOR, and TEST. In other contexts, these operators are described in terms of true and false:

- If both A and B are true, then A AND B is true; otherwise A AND B is false.

- If either A or B is true, then A OR B is true; otherwise A OR B is false.

- If A is true then NOT A is false; if A is false then NOT A is true.

- If either A or B is true, but not both, then A XOR B is true; otherwise, A XOR B is false.

Instruction Format	Operand Size(s)	Operand Combinations	Flags Affected	Remarks

AND dest,source	Word,Byte	reg,reg
		mem,reg
		reg,imm
		mem,imm
			CF, OF, PF
			SF, ZF
				Logical AND of bits of operands
				Result has bits set where both
				  operands had bits set
				  and all other bits cleared
				CF and OF are cleared

TEST dest,source	Word,Byte	reg,reg mem,reg reg,imm mem,imm	CF, OF, PF SF, ZF	Logical AND of bits of operands Neither operand changed CF and OF are cleared

OR dest,source	Word,Byte	reg,reg
		reg,mem
		mem,reg
		reg,imm
		mem,imm
			CF, OF, PF
			SF, ZF
				Logical OR of bits of operands
				Result in dest
				Results has bits cleared where
				  both operands had bit clear
				  and all other bits set
				CF and OF are cleared

XOR dest,source	Wor,Byte	reg,reg
		reg,mem
		mem,reg
		reg,imm
		mem,imm
			CF, OF, PF
			SF, ZF
				Logical XOR of bits of operands
				Result in dest
				Results has bits clear where
				  both operands had matching bit
				  and all other bits cleared
				CF and OF are cleared

NOT dest	Word,Byte	reg
		mem
			none	Changes each bit of operand
				Result in dest
				Result has bit set where
				  operand had bit cleared
				  and bit clear where operand
				  had bit set

Figure 10.1 Logical Bit Instructions

In these logical bit operations, corresponding operand bits are compared, and the result bit is set or cleared according to the rules above, using 1 for true and 0 for false. As with arithmetic operations, when the operation ends, the result replaces the destination operand.

NOT does not affect any flags. The others, AND, TEST, OR, and XOR, affect all the status flags except AF. When ZF is set, it means the result was zero; when SF is set, it means the high-order bit of the result was set. CF and OF are always cleared by these operations.

Let's look at the instructions in detail.

AND and TEST

AND looks at a bit position in the source and destination. If both operands have a 1 in this position, the corresponding position in the result is set; otherwise, it is cleared. The process is repeated until all bit positions in the result have been set or cleared.

You can use AND to force individual bits to be cleared. Where the source has 0 the result has 0; where the source has 1, the result matches the destination. Remember the routine used in Chapter 9 to change ASCII characters to unpacked decimals by subtracting 30H from each character? Another way to clear the upper half-byte is to use an AND, as shown:

```
AND dest , 0FH                        ; 0FH = 0000 1111
```

The lower four bits of the destination are preserved: 0 if they were already 0, 1 if they were already 1. The upper four bits are all cleared.

TEST is a special operation that performs an AND without changing the destination, just as CMP performs a subtraction without producing a result. Like CMP, TEST is used to prepare for a conditional jump, usually one that tests ZF. These instructions:

```
TEST    AL , 00000001B
JZ      EVEN_NUMBER
```

will cause a branch to EVEN__NUMBER any time the low-order digit of AL is zero and no branch if it is 1. In either case, the actual contents of AL are left undisturbed.

OR and XOR

OR also looks at corresponding bit positions in the source and destination, setting the result bit if either or both operands are set, clearing the result if both operands are clear. XOR (X stands for eXclusive) sets the result bit if only one, but not both, operands are set. In other words, if the operands match, the result is clear; if they differ, the result is set.

OR can be used to force result bits to be set. Where the source has 1, the result has 1; where the source has 0, the result is unchanged. This instruction:

```
OR      AL , 01H
```

will make sure that the low-order bit of AL is set and will leave the other bits undisturbed. Can you use it to convert unpacked decimals to ASCII, like this?

```
OR      AL , 30H
```

Yes, if you're sure that the original AL had zeros in the upper half. If AL originally contained 10000000B, this instruction would not produce a valid ASCII character since the high-order bit would remain set.

XOR forces the destination to change wherever the source is set and to remain the same wherever the source is cleared. This instruction, then:

```
XOR      AL,0FH
```

causes the lower half of AL to be reversed, while the upper half is untouched.

NOT

NOT simply changes each bit of the destination to form the result. It forms the one's complement of the destination. Remember that NEG forms the two's complement, changing each bit and then adding 1 to the result. If AL contains 0FFH, NOT AL changes AL to 00H, while NEG AL changes it to 01H. NOT does not affect any flags.

Review Questions

1. For each logical bit operation choose the phrase which best describes its effect on an individual result bit. Not all phrases are used.

___ A. AND   a. Reverses value
___ B. TEST   b. Set only if either or both operands set
___ C. OR   c. No effect
___ D. XOR   d. Set only if operands match
___ E. NOT   e. Set only if both operands set
                     f. Set only if operands don't match

2. Which sentences describe the effect of the AND, OR, XOR, and TEST on the flags? (More than one sentence should be chosen.) Which sentence(s) describe the effect of NOT?

    A. No status flags are affected.

    B. All status flags except AF are affected.

    C. All status flags except AF are cleared.

    D.   CF and OF are cleared.

    E.   ZF and SF are set.

    F.   ZF and SF reflect the result.

For questions 3 through 7 code the appropriate instructions or routines.

3.   Clear the upper half of BH leaving the lower half unchanged.

4.   Set the upper four bits of BH leaving the lower four unchanged.

5.   If bit 3 of CL is set, jump to EIGHT-BIT (count the low-order bit as bit 0).

6.   Change all the bits in the upper half of DL, leaving the lower bits unchanged.

7.   Change all the bits in DL.

Answers

1. A. e B. c C. b D. f E. a; d is not used.   **2.** B, D, F; A   **3.** AND AH,0FH   **4.** OR BH,0F0H   **5.** TEST CL,08H JNZ EIGHT-BIT   **6.** XOR DL,0F0H   **7.** NOT DL

Shift and Rotate

Figure 10.2 shows the shift and rotate instructions that move bits within a byte or word. All of these instructions move data within the destination. A right shift or rotate copies each bit to the next lowest position. The instruction determines what value is put into the high-order bit. A left shift or rotate copies each bit to the next highest position; the instruction determines what is put into the low-order bit.

Left Shift

Part A of Figure 10.3 illustrates a 1-bit left shift. Each bit is shifted to the left. The high-order bit replaces CF, the low-order position is filled by 0. The SAL instruction, or its equivalent SHL, produces such a shift. You can use this instruction to multiply a binary value by 2, just as in decimal arithmetic you can multiply by 10 if you shift digits to the left and insert a trailing 0. If CF is set, the multiplication has overflowed; the result is too large for the original destination. OF is set if the new CF does not equal the new high-order bit. What does this mean? It means that the high-order bit

Instruction Format	Operand Size(s)	Operand Combinations	Flags Affected	Remarks

SAL dest,count
SHL dest,count
	Word,Byte	reg,1
		mem,1
		reg,CL
		mem,CL
			CF, OF, PF
			SF, ZF
				Each bit of dest shifted to left
				Result in dest
				CF = original high-order bit
				Low-order bit = 0
				Original CF lost
				Rotation repeated count times
				OF set if new high-order bit
				    don't match new CF
				    and count = 1

SAR dest,count	Word,Byte	reg,1 mem,1 reg,CL mem,CL	CF, OF, PF SF, ZF	Each bit of dest shifted to right Result in dest CF = original low-order bit High-order bit unchanged Original CF lost Rotation repeated count times OF set if new high-order 2 bits don't match and count = 1
SHR dest,count	Word,Byte	reg,1 mem,1 reg,CL mem,CL	CF, OF, PF SF, ZF	Each bit of dest shifted to right Result in dest CF = original low-order bit High-order bit = 0 Original CF lost Rotation repeated count times OF set if new high-order 2 bits don't match and count = 1

RCL dest,count	Word,Byte	reg,1
		mem,1
		reg,CL
		mem,CL
			CF, OF	Each bit of dest shifted to left
				Result in dest
				CF = original high-order bit
				Low-order bit = original CF
				Rotation repeated count times
				OF set if high-order 2 bits of
				    original dest not matched and
				    count=1

RCR dest,count	Word,Byte	reg,1
		mem,1
		reg,CL
		mem,CL
			CF, OF	Each bit of dest shifted to right
				Result in dest
				CF = original low-order bit
				High-order bit = original CF
				Rotation repeated count times
				OF set if high-order 2 bits of
				    result not matched and
				    count=1

ROL dest,count	Word,Byte	reg,1
		mem,1
		reg,CL
		mem,CL
			CF, OF	Each bit of dest shifted to left
				Result in dest
				CF = original high-order bit
				Low-order bit =
				        original high-order bit
				Original CF lost
				Rotation repeated count times
				OF set if new high-order bit
				    doesn't match new CF and
				    count=1

```
ROR dest,count  Word,Byte   reg,1         CF, OF      Each bit of dest shifted to right
                            mem,1                     Result in dest
                            reg,CL                    CF = original low-order bit
                            mem,CL                    High-order bit =
                                                            original low-order bit
                                                      Original CF lost
                                                      Rotation repeated count times
                                                      OF set if new high-order 2 bits
                                                         don't match and count = 1
```

Figure 10.2 Bit Moving Instructions

has changed. If a signed number was shifted, the sign has changed and the new value is not necessarily twice the original. Suppose, for example, that AL contains 01000001B, or 65. A left shift changes AL to 10000010B with CF cleared. If AL represents an unsigned number this value is 130, but as a signed number the value is -126. If you are using the shift for signed multiplication it has produced the wrong answer.

Notice (in Figure 10.2) that SAL has a second operand that contains a count of digits shifted. This operand can be either 1 or CL. If you want to repeat the left shift, you can put the number of positions to be shifted into CL and then code SAL with CL for the count. The shift is repeated CL times, but CL is not decremented. The meaning of OF is uncertain after a multiple shift. Also, CF will hold only the last digit shifted out. You can't tell if other significant digits have been shifted. If AL contains 01000001B (65) and CL contains 3, then the instruction:

```
SAL        AL,CL
```

leaves CF cleared and AL with a value of 00001000B (8), whereas three multiplications by 2 should produce a value of 520. Unless you are working with small numbers multiple shifts are not reliable for multiplication. However, you will find them useful in other ways.

Right Shifts

Part B of Figure 10.3 shows a 1-bit right shift. Such a shift is produced by SHR with count = 1. Each digit shifts to the right; the low-order digit replaces CF and the high-order position is filled by 0. This is called a **logical shift**, as opposed to the **arithmetic shift** described below. With unsigned numbers a logical right shift is equivalent to division by 2. As with the left shift, OF is set if the high-order bit changes.

A. Left shift (one bit) --SAL or SHL

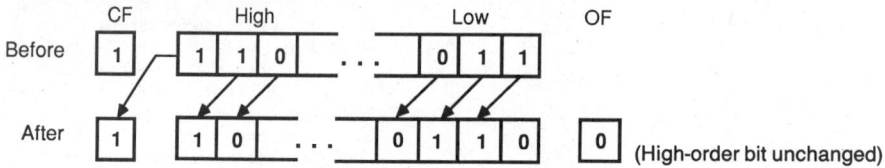

B. Right shirt (one bit)--Logical (SHR)

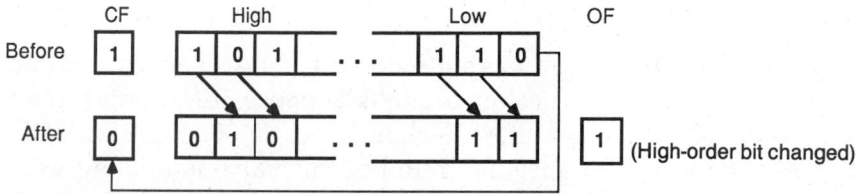

C. Right shirt (one bit)--Arithmetic (SAR)

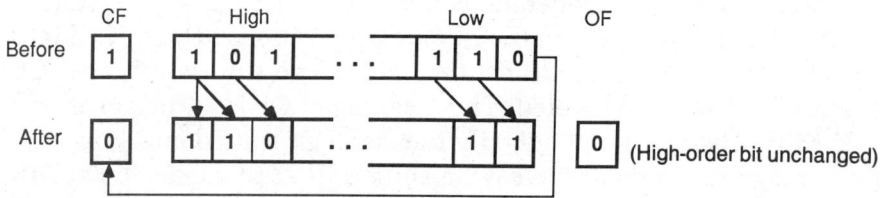

Figure 10.3 Bit Shifts

Part C shows a 1-bit arithmetic right shift. SAR is the instruction. Again, each digit shifts to the right and the low-order digit replaces CF. But, in an arithmetic right shift the high-order digit is not changed. You can use SAR to divide by 2 without changing the sign. The manual says that OF is set if the new high-order bit doesn't match the new next-to-high-order (that is, if the high-order bit changes), but it's hard to see how that can happen.

Both SAR and SHR allow multiple shifts using CL. Again, if you use multiple shifts, the value in CF is the last digit shifted out. OF is undefined after a multiple logical shift; it is always cleared by a multiple arithmetic shift.

Left Rotation

Figure 10.4 illustrates the rotation instructions. Part A shows a 1-bit left rotation through the carry flag; the instruction is RCL. The difference between a left shift and a left rotation is in how the low-order bit is filled. In a shift, it is always filled with 0. With RCL, the low-order bit is filled by the

A. Left Rotation (one bit) through CF (RCL)

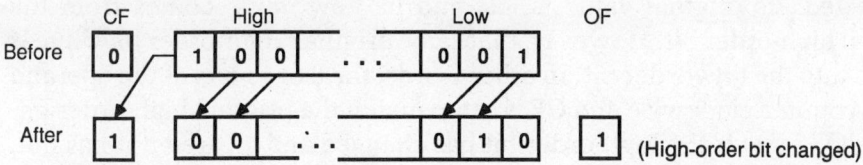

B. Right Rotation (one bit) throug CF (RCR)

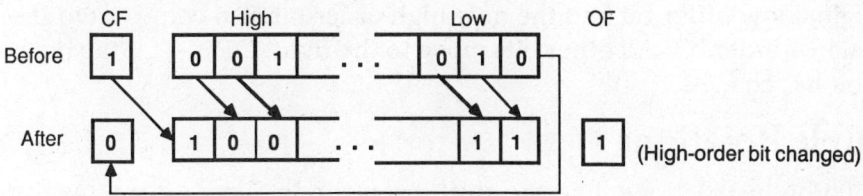

C. Left Rotation (one bit) not through CF (ROL)

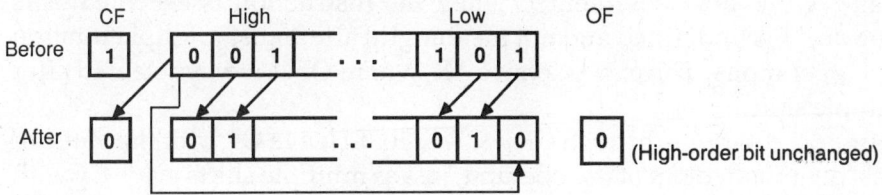

D. Right Rotation (one bit) NOT through CF (ROR)

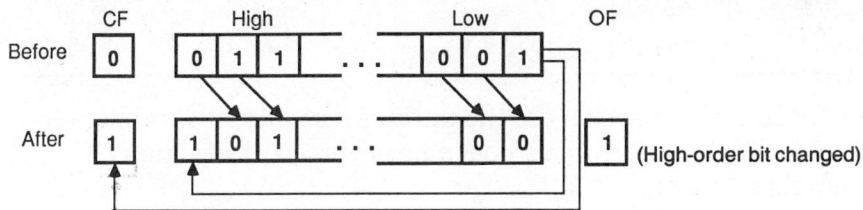

Figure 10.4 Bit Rotations

original value of the carry flag. If you think of the operand including CF as arranged in a circle, RCL simply moves each bit value one position in a counter-clockwise direction. If the high-order bit changes, OF is set; otherwise, it is cleared.

Part B illustrates a 1-bit right rotation through the carry flag (RCR). Each bit shifts to the right. The original CF shifts into the high-order bit, and the low-order bit goes into CF. If RCL is a counter-clockwise rotation, RCR is a clockwise rotation. If the high-order bit has changed, OF is set.

Part C illustrates a 1-bit left rotation that does not involve CF (ROL). CF is affected; its original value is lost and its new value comes from the original high-order bit. However, that same original, high-order bit value is copied into the low-order bit. In other words, the 8 or 16 bits of the operand rotate counter-clockwise and CF is set to match the original high-order bit. Again, OF is set if the high-order-bit has changed and cleared if it has not.

Part D shows a 1-bit right rotation, ROR, that does not go through CF. Again, CF's original value is lost. In this case, CF's new value comes from the original low-order bit and the new high-order bit also comes from the original low-order bit. All other bits move to the right. OF is set if the high-order bit has changed.

Multiple Rotations

The rotation instructions, like the shift instructions, have a count as the second operand. If the count is 1, one bit is rotated. For rotations of more than one bit, the count must be put into CL, and CL specified as the count operand. CL is not decremented when the instruction is executed. The setting of OF is undefined and not meaningful after most multiple rotation or shift operations. The exception is SAR, where OF is always cleared after a multiple shift.

Multiple rotations through CF (RCR or RCL) leave CF with the value of the last digit rotated out of the operand, just as multiple shifts leave CF with the last digit shifted out. A multiple rotation that uses ROL will leave CF matching the current low-order digit. After ROR is used, OF will match the current high-order digit.

Review Questions

1. For each instruction choose the phrases that describe its operation. There may be more than one phrase for an instruction. Not all phrases are used.

   ____ A. SAL   a. Digits move left.

   ____ B. SAR   b. Digits move right.

   ____ C. SHR   c. High-order filled by 0.

   ____ D. RCL   d. Low-order filled by 0.

   ____ E. RCR   e. High-order filled by original CF.

   ____ F. ROL   f. Low-order filled by original CF.

   ____ G. ROR   g. High-order unchanged.

                                  h. Low-order unchanged.

                                  i. Low-order filled by original high-order.

                                  j. High-order filled by original low-order.

2.   What does CF contain

    A.   after a 1-bit right shift or rotation

    B.   after a 1-bit left shift or rotation

3.   After a 1-bit shift OF is set. What is the significance of this?

4.   What is the effect on OF of a multiple shift or rotation?

Answers

1. A. a,d B. b,g C. b,c D. a,f E. b,e F. a,i G. b,j; h is not used.   **2.** A. the original low-order bit B. the original high-order bit.   **3.** The high-order bit has changed.   **4.** Undefined; OF has no significance after a multiple shift or rotation.

Key Points From Chapter 10

In this chapter you have learned five logical bit instructions and seven bit-moving instructions. You will see many of these instructions used in the next part of this book, especially in the data conversion routines. As you develop your own application programs, you will find many more occasions when you will use logical instructions to change individual bits in a byte or word, or when you can simplify a routine by shifting or rotating bits one or more positions. Here are some of the major points from this chapter:

■ The logical bit instructions AND, TEST, OR, and XOR have the general format

    opcode dest , source

■ Legal operand combinations are the same as for MOV. The operands may be bytes or words, as long as they match. (Exception: an immediate data byte can be used with a word register or address operand.)

■ The logical bit instruction NOT has only one operand, an 8- or 16-bit register or address operand.

■ These instructions, AND, TEST, OR, XOR, and NOT, use the corresponding operand bits to affect the result bit in the same position according to the rules listed on the following page.

INSTRUCTION	RULES
AND	If both operands set, result set.
	Otherwise, result clear.
TEST	Same as AND.
OR	If either or both operands set, result set.
	If both clear, result clear.
XOR	If operands don't match, result set.
	If both set or both clear, result clear.
NOT	If operand set, result clear.
	If operand clear, result set.

■   NOT does not affect any flags. Each of the other logical bit operations (AND, TEST, OR, and XOR) clears CF and OF and changes SF, ZF, and PF to reflect the result.

■   The result of TEST is not saved. The result of each of the other logical bit operations (AND, OR, XOR, and NOT) replaces the destination.

■   AND can be used to force bits to be cleared. Each bit cleared in the source will be cleared in the result.

■   OR can be used to force bits to be set. Each bit set in the source will be set in the result.

■   XOR can be used to force bits to be changed. Each bit set in the source will be changed in the result.

■   The shift and rotate instructions have the general format:

```
opcode dest , count
```

■   Dest is a register or address operand, either 8- or 16-bit. Count is either 1 or CL. When bits are to be moved one position within dest, count should be 1. For multiple moves, CL should be loaded with the number of moves and count should be CL.

■   On a left 1-bit shift or rotation, each bit shifts to the next high-order position. The high-order bit is copied to CF. The low-order bit is filled as follows:

INSTRUCTION	LOW-ORDER
SAL, SHL	0
ROL	original high-order bit value
RCL	original CF

■ On a right 1-bit shift or rotation, each bit shifts to the next low-order position. The low-order bit is copied to CF. The high-order bit is filled as follows:

INSTRUCTION	HIGH-ORDER
SHR	0
SAR	unchanged
ROR	original low-order bit value
RCR	original CF

■ After any 1-bit shift or rotation OF is set if the value of the high-order bit has changed.

■ A multiple shift or rotation repeats the 1-bit operation as indicated by CL. CL is not decremented. OF is not significant after a multiple shift or rotation.

Chapter Review Questions

For these questions, code the appropriate instructions or routines.

1. Clear the two low-order bits of AL.

2. Set the two low-order bits of AL.

3. If the lower-order bit of AH is 0, go to EVEN__NUMBER.

4. Change each of the upper four bits of DH.

5. Move each bit of BL three positions to the right, putting zeros in the high-order position.

6. Move each bit of SI four positions to the left, filling the low-order bits from CF.

7. Move each bit of AH one position to the right, keeping the sign bit unchanged.

8. Move each bit of AH two positions to the left, filling the low-order bits with 0.

9. Move each bit of BX one position to the left, filling the low-order bit from the original high-order bit.

Answers

1. AND   AL,0FCH
2. OR   AL,03H
3. TEST   AH,01H
   JZ   EVEN-NUMBER
4. XOR   DH,0F0H
5. MOV   CL,3
   SHR   AL,CL
6. MOV   CL,8
   RCL   SI,CL
7. SAR   AH,1
8. MOV   CL,2
   SAL   AH,CL or SHL AH,CL
9. ROL   BX,1

2

Reference Routines

In the first part of this book you learned to use Macro Assembler to write programs. When you begin to plan your own programs, though, you will find that you need more than a list of instructions in order to do what you want.

How do you convert a binary number to ASCII so you can display a total or a page number? How do you use the printer? How do you store and retrieve data from disk files? Can your MASM program read files written by BASIC? These problems, and others like them, can't be solved by learning new MASM instructions. They are handled using instructions you already know. However, you must have additional information about such instructions as the I/O interrupt that sends characters to the printer.

This part of the book presents information that you need in order to handle some common situations in MASM programs and provides sample routines for them. Many of the samples are presented as macros that you can incorporate into your own libraries.

Since this part of the book presents reference material rather than actual instruction in MASM, I won't provide review questions or summaries. Occasionally, I will suggest a program to use and test the material being covered.

11

Data Format Conversions

Four major data formats are used in MASM: binary, packed decimal, unpacked decimal, and ASCII. In this chapter I will discuss conversions between some of these forms, leaving other conversions for you to code for yourself.

ASCII and Unpacked

Most input and output data are in ASCII characters. Numeric data in ASCII is stored with the high-order digit first, and the low-order, last. Although we can add and subtract ASCII digits as if they were unpacked decimals, the arithmetic and other macros expect unpacked decimals to be stored low-order first. The conversion routine is simply a matter of moving digits from one place to another, clearing the upper four bits of each byte as we go. Figure 11.1 shows our routine coded as a macro. Calling the macro requires naming the destination (the unpacked number), the source (the ASCII variable), and the count of digits to be converted. Move each ASCII character to AL, clear the upper four bits, and move the result to the appropriate place in the unpacked decimal. The last ASCII character becomes the first unpacked digit, and so on.

```
ASC2UNP MACRO       UNPNUM,ASCHAR,COUNT
        LOCAL       NEXT_DIGIT
        PUSH        AX
        PUSH        CX
        PUSH        SI
        PUSH        DI
        MOV         SI,COUNT        ;LOW-ORDER SOURCE DIGIT
        DEC         SI
        MOV         DI,0            ;LOW-ORDER DEST DIGIT
        MOV         CX,COUNT        ;NUMBER OF DIGITS
NEXT_DIGIT:
        MOV         AL,ASCHAR[SI]
        AND         AL,0FH          ;UPPER 4 BITS = 0
        MOV         UNPNUM[DI],AL
        INC         DI
        DEC         SI
        LOOP        NEXT_DIGIT
        POP         DI
        POP         SI
        POP         CX
        POP         AX
        ENDM
```

Figure 11.1 ASCII to Unpacked

You may want to amplify this macro by adding a check for nonnumeric characters. If a comma, decimal point, or currency sign shows up in the ASCII field, just skip over it. You may want special handling for other nonnumerics also.

The reverse situation, conversion from unpacked decimals to ASCII, is pretty straightforward also. Try coding your own solution before you look at the macro in Figure 11.2.

```
UNP2ASC MACRO       ASCHAR,UNPNUM,COUNT
        LOCAL       NEXT_DIGIT
        PUSH        AX
        PUSH        CX
        PUSH        SI
        PUSH        DI
        MOV         SI,COUNT        ;HIGH-ORDER SOURCE DIGIT
        DEC         SI
        MOV         DI,0            ;HIGH-ORDER DEST DIGIT
        MOV         CX,COUNT        ;NUMBER OF DIGITS
NEXT_DIGIT:
        MOV         AL,UNPNUM[SI]
        OR          AL,30H          ;UPPER FOUR BITS = 3
        MOV         ASCHAR[DI],AL
        INC         DI
        DEC         SI
        LOOP        NEXT_DIGIT
        POP         DI
        POP         SI
        POP         CX
        POP         AX
        ENDM
```

Figure 11.2 Unpacked to ASCII

```
PACK2UNP MACRO  UNPNUM,PACKNUM,DIGITS
         LOCAL  NEXT_DIGIT,P2U_DONE
         PUSH   AX
         PUSH   CX
         PUSH   DX
         PUSH   SI
         PUSH   DI
         MOV    DX,DIGITS           ;DX HOLDS COUNT OF UNP DIGITS
         MOV    SI,0                ;LOW-ORDER PACKED BYTE
         MOV    DI,0                ;LOW-ORDER UNPACKED DIGIT
NEXT_DIGIT:
         AND    AX,0
         MOV    AL,PACKNUM[SI]
         MOV    CL,4
         SHL    AX,CL
         SHR    AL,CL
         MOV    UNPNUM[DI],AL       ;LOW-ORDER DIGIT FROM BYTE
         INC    DI
         DEC    DX
         JZ     P2U_DONE
         MOV    AH,UNPNUM[DI]       ;HIGH-ORDER DIGIT FROM BYTE
         INC    DI
         DEC    DX
         JZ     P2U_DONE
         INC    SI
         JMP    NEXT_DIGIT
P2U_DONE:
         POP    DI
         POP    SI
         POP    DX
         POP    CX
         POP    AX
         ENDM
```

Figure 11.3 Packed to Unpacked

Packed and Unpacked

Converting packed to unpacked data is mostly a matter of moving a byte of
packed data to a register and splitting it into two bytes, which are then
copied back to the unpacked data field. Figure 11.3 shows a macro that can
do this for any number of packed bytes. The count passed to the macro as
DIGITS is the number of unpacked digits—twice the number of packed
bytes.

In this macro we assume that the packed data is in the standard form of
two low-order digits first and two high-order last. Also assume that the
unpacked data will be low-order first as well. Notice the use of SHL and
SHR in this macro. Let's look at how it works. If AX contains zero and AL is
then loaded with 32H, AX's bits will look like this: 0000 0000 0011 0010.
SHL moves all of AX four bits to the left so it looks like this: 0000 0011 0010
0000. Then, SHR is used to shift the lower byte four bits to the right, leaving
AH unchanged; now AX is 0000 0011 0000 0010. AH contains 3H, AL

contains 2H. We have split the two packed digits into two unpacked digits in AH and AL. Now all that remains is to move AL and AH to the appropriate places in the unpacked number.

Why did we use DX instead of CX for the count in this routine? In the first place, we need CL for the shift count. We could get around this by PUSHing CX before the shifts and POPping it after. Notice, however, that we process *two* digits in every loop; you will find DEC DX two places. A LOOP using CX would only decrement CX once.

Unpacked to Packed

Converting from unpacked to packed is not quite the reverse of converting from packed to unpacked. For one thing, the unpacked decimal may have an odd number of digits, in which case we will need to fill our highest-order packed digit with 0. Figure 11.4 contains our version of a macro for this conversion. Again, DIGITS refers to the number of unpacked bytes. Basically, the macro puts an unpacked digit into AL, shifts it into the upper four bits, and then adds the next digit to AL so that it goes into the lower four bits. This works because the unpacked decimal's upper four bits will

```
UNP2PACK MACRO   PACKNUM,UNPNUM,DIGITS
            PUSH    AX
            PUSH    CX
            PUSH    DX
            PUSH    SI
            PUSH    DI
            MOV     DX,DIGITS                ;COUNT OF UNP DIGITS LEFT
            MOV     SI,0
            MOV     DI,0
HIGH_DIGIT:
            MOV     AL,0
            CMP     DX,1
            JE      LOW_DIGIT
            MOV     AL,UNPNUM+1[SI]
            MOV     CL,4
            SHL     AL,CL
            DEC     DX
LOW_DIGIT:
            ADD     AL,UNPNUM[SI]
            MOV     PACKNUM[DI],AL
            INC     DI
            ADD     SI,2
            DEC     DX
            JNZ     HIGH_DIGIT
            POP     DI
            POP     SI
            POP     DX
            POP     CX
            POP     AX
            ENDM
```

Figure 11.4 Unpacked to Packed

always be zero, as will the lower four bits of AL at this point. Nothing will be added or carried to the upper four bits. Work out a few examples for yourself and see. Notice that SI, the pointer to the unpacked digits, has to be increased by 2 every time the loop repeats. We pick up two unpacked digits each time. Again, we use DX instead of CX for reasons similar to those for the preceding routine.

Unpacked and Binary

To convert unpacked to binary, multiply each unpacked digit by an appropriate power of 10 (the proper power depends on its place value) and then add the result into the binary number. This is easy to accomplish manually, but in MASM it's much simpler to use the logic followed in the macro in Figure 11.5. Here, the high-order digit is added to the binary number, the binary number is multiplied by 10, the next high-order added, the entire number is multiplied by 10, and so on until the low-order digit is added and not multiplied. If you work it out on paper, you will see that the same effect has been achieved. Each digit has been multiplied by the nth power of 10, where n is the number of digits of lower-order.

In our macro we have restricted ourselves to a one-word binary value, requiring exactly five decimal digits. You may want to think about changing the macro to allow for more or fewer digits or to check that a five-digit number is within the one-word range.

```
UNP2BIN MACRO    BINUM,UNPNUM
        LOCAL    NEXT_DIGIT
        PUSH     AX
        PUSH     BX
        PUSH     CX
        PUSH     SI
        MOV      AX,0            ;INITIALIZE AX FOR DEST
        MOV      CX,5            ;ALWAYS 5 DIGITS
        MOV      SI,4            ;POINT TO HIGH-ORDER SOURCE DIGIT
        MOV      BX,10           ;MULITPLIER ALWAYS 10
NEXT_DIGIT:
        MUL      BX              ;MULTIPLY CURRENT BINUM BY 10
        ADD      AL,UNPNUM[SI]   ;ADD IN NEXT LOW-ORDER DIGIT
        DEC      SI
        LOOP     NEXT_DIGIT
        MOV      BINUM,AX
        POP      SI
        POP      CX
        POP      BX
        POP      AX
        ENDM
```

Figure 11.5 Unpacked to Binary

The problem of converting from binary to unpacked is again a matter of tens. We divide the binary digit by 10, and the remainder is the low-order decimal digit. We repeat the division to find the next digit. We could stop after four divisions and use the fourth quotient as the high-order digit, but it's simpler to code when we just loop through five times using the remainder each time. Our macro is in Figure 11.6. Try coding your own before you look at this one, or you may want to improve on this by allowing for binary values of more than one word.

Other Conversions

What about going between ASCII and binary? ASCII and packed? Packed and binary? You can do any of these things by combining macro calls, as in:

```
ASC2UNP            UNPACK,ASCII,10
UNP2PACK           PACKED,UNPACK,10
```

If you frequently have use for one or more of these conversions write your own routines using ours as a guide.

Testing the Conversion Macros

Figure 11.7 contains a short program that has no purpose except to test the six conversion macros shown in this program. I stored the macros in CONVLIB.LIB. I included addition routines in some spots just so you could

```
BIN2UNP MACRO     UNPNUM,BINUM
        LOCAL     NEXT_DIGIT
        PUSH      DX
        PUSH      CX
        PUSH      BX
        PUSH      AX
        PUSH      DI
        MOV       CX,5              ;ALWAYS 5 DIGITS
        MOV       DI,0              ;POINT TO LOW-ORDER DEST DIGIT
        MOV       AX,BINUM          ;DIVIDEND IN AX
        MOV       BX,10             ;DIVISOR ALWAYS 10
NEXT_DIGIT:
        MOV       DX,0              ;SET EXTENSION TO 0
        DIV       BX
        MOV       UNPNUM[DI],DL     ;REMAINDER DIGIT TO DEST
        INC       DI
        LOOP      NEXT_DIGIT
        POP       DI
        POP       AX
        POP       BX
        POP       CX
        POP       DX
        ENDM
```

Figure 11.6 Binary to Unpacked

```
        PAGE     ,132
;
        INCLUDE MACLIB.LIB
;
        INCLUDE CONVLIB.LIB
;
        INCLUDE EQULIB.LIB
;
;
PROG_STACK SEGMENT STACK 'STACK'
        DB        64 DUP ('STACK    ')
PROG_STACK ENDS
;
PROG_DATA  SEGMENT 'DATA'
NPROMPT DB        LF,CR,'NUMBER: ',EOT
ENDMESSAGE  DB  LF,CR,'GOODBYE',EOT
OUTLINE DB        LF,CR,5 DUP(' '),EOT
INBUF    DB       6
INCOUNT DB        ?
INDATA   DB       6 DUP(' ')
UNUMBER DB        5 DUP(0)
PNUMBER DB        3 DUP(0)
BNUMBER DW        0
ONEADD   DB       1,0,0,0,0
PROG_DATA   ENDS
;
PROG_CODE SEGMENT 'CODE'
MAIN_PROG          PROC   FAR
        ASSUME  CS:PROG_CODE,DS:PROG_DATA,SS:PROG_STACK,ES:PROG_DATA
        STARTER
        STI
        CLD
        CLS
        CURSORON
MAINLOOP:
        CLEAR             OUTLINE+2,5      ;MOVE SPACES TO DISPLAY LINE
        CALL              GETNUMBER        ;PROMPT AND INPUT NAME
        CMP               INCOUNT,0        ;IF NO NAME END PROGRAM
        JNE               CONT
        JMP               END_PROG
CONT:
        ASC2UNP           UNUMBER,INDATA,5
        ADD_UNPACKED      UNUMBER,ONEADD,5
        UNP2PACK          PNUMBER,UNUMBER,5
        ADD               PNUMBER,1
        ADC               PNUMBER+1,0
        ADC               PNUMBER+2,0
        PACK2UNP          UNUMBER,PNUMBER,5
        ADD_UNPACKED      UNUMBER,ONEADD,5
        UNP2BIN           BNUMBER,UNUMBER
        ADD               BNUMBER,5
        BIN2UNP           UNUMBER,BNUMBER
        ADD_UNPACKED      UNUMBER,ONEADD,5
        UNP2ASC           OUTLINE+2,UNUMBER,5
        DISPLAY           OUTLINE
        JMP               MAINLOOP         ;  AND REPEAT PROCESS
END_PROG:
        DISPLAY           ENDMESSAGE
        RET                                ;THEN RETURN TO OPERATING SYSTEM
MAIN_PROG ENDP
;
GETNUMBER PROC
        DISPLAY           NPROMPT          ;PROMPT FOR NUMBER
        GETDATA           INBUF,6          ;GET NUMBER IN BUFFER
        CMP               INCOUNT,0
        JE                GET1
```

```
          CMP               INCOUNT,5
          JNE               GETNUMBER
GET1:
          RET
GETNUMBER  ENDP
;
PROG_CODE          ENDS
          END
```

Figure 11.7 Conversion Test Program

see that data actually went in and got changed. The program reads a five-digit number, manipulates it through six conversions with several additions along the way, and displays the updated number on the screen. The updated number is nine more than the original input. You should enter the conversion routines into your system as a macro library; you may also want to include the test program from Figure 11.6. If you try the program out, make sure that both the original and the updated number fit in the unsigned one-word range.

12

I/O Interrupts

You have learned to use interrupt 21H to read from the keyboard and display character strings on the CRT. You have also written a few macros using BIOS interrupt 10H to control certain video functions. In this chapter I will discuss some other functions of these interrupts as well as some other BIOS interrupts. I'll discuss keyboard, printer, CRT, and communications I/O, as well as functions to get and set the date and time.

BIOS and DOS Interrupts

As you know, an interrupt transfers control to a routine that is provided as part of BIOS or DOS. Most interrupt routines are part of BIOS. Interrupts 20H through 3FH are reserved for DOS routines. Not all of the DOS interrupts were available in DOS 1.0; many were implemented in later versions. In some cases you can choose between a DOS or a BIOS interrupt to perform similar functions. You can write one character on the printer, for example, using function 5 of DOS interrupt 21H or function 0 of BIOS interrupt 17H. Which is best? IBM recommends using DOS functions whenever possible. We will follow that recommendation, but in a few cases we must use BIOS functions. Function 2 of interrupt 17H, for example, reads the printer status; there is no equivalent DOS function.

You will find all of the DOS interrupts described in an appendix of your DOS manual. We are interested in DOS 21H only. You will find its functions listed in the same appendix following the list of interrupts. The function descriptions begin at a section labelled FUNCTION CALLS. In this chapter and in the next two, we will describe many 21H functions. You should be able to learn the others from the manual if you need them.

What about the BIOS interrupts? We will teach you only a few of them in this chapter; there are many more. They are found in the IBM *Technical Reference Manual*, but they are not easy to find or interpret. You should be able to handle most I/O using DOS. If you need functions that DOS does not provide and that are not covered in this chapter, such as graphics or sound control, consider programming in a high-level language.

Reading From the Keyboard

Figure 12.1 summarizes the keyboard interrupts that will be discussed in this chapter. You have learned to use function 0AH of interrupt 21H to read a string of characters ending with CR (0DH) from the keyboard into a program-defined input buffer. Your program must specify the maximum number of characters to be read, including CR, in the buffer's first byte.

In Order To	Use INT	Function (In AH)	Other Preparation Required	Results and Remarks
Read one character with echo and Ctrl-Break check	21H	1	none	Character in AL
Read one character; no echo and no Ctrl-Break check	21H	7	none	Character in AL
Read one character; no echo but Ctrl-Break check	21H	8	none	Character in AL
Read string ending with CR	21H	0AH	Buffer offset in DX Max. char (inc. CR) in first byte of buffer	Count of char. read in (not inc. CR) in second buffer byte Characters (inc. CR) start at third byte
Check if character available in keyboard buffer	21H	0BH	none	If typed, AL = 0FFH else AL = 00
Clear buffer and call another function	21H	0CH	Function # in AL (1, 6, 7, 8, or A)	Depends on second function called
Get keyboard status byte	16H	2	none	Byte in AL

Bit	Meaning if Set
7	Insert On
6	Caps Lock On
5	Num Lock On
4	Scroll Lock On
3	Alt Key Pressed
2	Ctrl Key Pressed
1	Left Shift Pressed
0	Right Shift "

Figure 12.1 Keyboard I/O

Preparation for calling the interrupt includes putting the function number in AH, as with all interrupts; putting the buffer's offset into DX; and putting the character count into the buffer's first byte. The interrupt routine puts the count of characters actually read (not including CR) into the second buffer byte; the characters themselves (including CR) are copied into the buffer starting at the third byte. Notice that since the character count must fit into one byte, the maximum number of characters that can be read is 254 (not including CR).

Single-Character Input Functions

Several functions of 21H read a single character, putting it into AL. I will discuss three of them: functions 1, 7, and 8. Preparation for each of these functions consists simply of putting the function number into AH. Function 1 echoes the character on the CRT and checks to see if you pressed Ctrl-Break. If Ctrl-Break is pressed, interrupt 23 is automatically called and ends your program. Function 7 of 21H does not echo the character or check for Ctrl-Break. Function 8 of 21H checks for Ctrl-Break, but does not echo; it is similar to BASIC's INKEY$.

Clearing the Keyboard Buffer

Characters typed on the keyboard are actually put into a 15-character keyboard buffer. Characters read by functions 1, 7, 8, or 0AH are really taken from this keyboard buffer. If the keyboard buffer is empty when a character is needed, the program will pause until one is available.

Function 0CH of 21H clears the keyboard buffer and then performs the function whose number has been placed in AL. This second function may be 1, 6, 7, 8 or 0AH. (I don't cover function 6 in this book.) Using function 0CH prevents you from accidentally or intentionally typing a key before the program is waiting for one.

Here is a routine using 0CH:

```
DISPLAY     KEY_PRESS_PROMPT
MOV         AH,0CH
MOV         AL,08H
INT         21H
```

KEY_PRESS_PROMPT is a message such as "press any key to continue". You could use this routine to force a program pause so the user can read a display before the screen is cleared. Notice that the actual input function is 8, which does not echo the typed character, but does check for Ctrl-Break.

If you don't want the user to be able to end the program at this point, you could use function 7 instead of 8.

Checking for a Key

Function 0BH of 21H simply checks to see if a key has been pressed. If a character is available, the function puts 0FFH into AL; otherwise, 00. The function does perform a Ctrl-Break check; interrupt 23 is called if Ctrl-Break is detected. Otherwise, the character is not read and it remains in the keyboard buffer. To read a character you will need to use functions 1, 7, or 8. You could use 0BH to end a loop, telling the user to press any key to stop the current operation and continue the program, like this:

```
            . . .
            DISPLAY      HOW__TO__STOP
NEXT__TIME:
            . . .                     ;operation such as
            . . .                     ;displaying a dot
            MOV          AH,0BH
            INT          21H
            OR           AL,0    ;IS AL ZERO?
            JZ           NEXT__TIME
```

Checking Keyboard Status

Interrupt 16H, a BIOS interrupt, also deals with keyboard operations. Two of its functions, 0 and 1, deal with reading a character and determining if a character is available, which you already know how to do using DOS functions. Function 2 of 16H, however, is unique. It reads a byte of keyboard status information, called KBFLAG, into AL. Each of the eight bits in this byte describes the status of a particular key. The description of interrupt 16H, function 2, in Figure 12.1 includes a table that shows the meaning of each bit when set, and numbers the bits from high-order (bit 7) to low-order (bit 0). Notice that the two shift keys are represented by separate bits. Your program can check each bit in AL. Suppose that you need to know whether the caps lock key is on; that's bit 6. You could use this routine:

```
            . . .
            MOV     AH,2
            INT     16H
            TEST    AL,40H        ;0100 0000
            JNZ     CONTINUE
NO__CAP__ON:    . . .
```

If your program requires all uppercase input, you might now prompt the user to turn on CAPS LOCK and repeat the check until you find that it is turned on.

Extended Keyboard Codes

You know from BASIC that some keys generate a two-byte code with the first byte 00. The function keys, for example, use these extended codes. If you read a character and find it is 00, you need to read again to find out which of the extended-code keys was pressed. Or, if your program does not use the extended code keys, you may simply consider this an error, clear the buffer, and require the user to type another key.

Using the CRT

Figure 12.2 summarizes the CRT (or video) functions discussed in this chapter. You already know many of them. You have used function 9 of interrupt 21H to display a string of characters on the screen; the string's end is marked by "$" (24H). To prepare for this function, you must load the string's beginning offset into DX. There is no limit on the number of characters displayed.

Displaying One Character

Function 2 of 21H displays one character at the cursor position on the CRT. The character must be loaded into DL. The cursor is advanced as each character is displayed. To display more than one character you can use a loop, but you will need to know in advance how many characters are to be displayed. This function is especially useful when the characters displayed include "$" or when, because of the way they are used elsewhere in the program, it is not convenient to end the string with "$". Figure 12.3 shows a macro that could be used to display any number of characters using function 2. Function 2, by the way, checks for Ctrl-Break after each character is output, so the user can end the program during this display.

BIOS Video Interrupt Functions

Interrupt 10H is the BIOS interrupt for video (CRT) functions. It has 15 functions but we will deal with only six of them in this book.

Setting the Video Mode   Function 0 sets the video mode for the color/graphics adaptor; in BASIC, this job is done using a combination of

In Order To	Use INT	Function (In AH)	Other Preparation Required	Results and Remarks
Display one character	21H	2	Character in DL	none
Display a string	21H	9	DX points to string	String must end in 24H
Set video mode	10H	0	Mode in AL	Modes -- see box A
Define cursor	10H	1	Start line in CH lower four bits On,Off in CH bit 4 (set 4 for off) End line in CL	none
Set cursor position	10H	2	Row in DH Column in DL Page in BH	Row is 0-24 Column is 0-79
Read cursor position	10H	3	Page in BH	Row in DH, Column in DL
Scroll page up	10H	6	AL=number of lines to be scrolled within window CH,CL row,column for window's upper left DH,DL row,column for window's bottom right BH = attribute for blank lines scrolled in	AL=0 for entire window See box B below for B/W attributes See Technical Reference Manual for color attributes
Scroll page down	10H	7	Same as function 6	

```
A.  Video Modes

0 = 40x25 B/W Text
1 = 40x25 Color Text
2 = 80x25 B/W Text
3 = 80x25 Color Text
4 = Med. Res. Color
5 = Med. Res. B/W
6 = High Res. B/W
```

```
B.  Attributes for B/W

    White on black  = 07H (7)
    Black on white  = 70H (112)
    Black on black  = 00H (0)
    White on white  = 77H (119)

    Add 8H (8) for high-intensity
    Add 10H (128) for blink
```

Figure 12.2 CRT I/O

WIDTH and the first two parameters of the SCREEN statement. As Figure 12.2 shows, there are seven possible modes. The mode number must be placed in AL in preparation for the interrupt. The routine:

```
MOV    AH,0
MOV    AL,1      ;40 char color text
INT    10H
```

```
DISPLA$ MACRO     MESSAGE,COUNT
        LOCAL     NEXT_CHAR
        PUSH      AX
        PUSH      BX
        PUSH      CX
        PUSH      DX
        MOV       CX,COUNT
        MOV       BX,0
NEXT_CHAR:
        MOV       AH,2
        MOV       DL,MESSAGE[BX]
        INT       21H
        INC       BX
        LOOP      NEXT_CHAR
        POP       DX
        POP       CX
        POP       BX
        POP       AX
        ENDM
```

Figure 12.3 Display Loop Macro

is the equivalent of the BASIC instructions:

1000 WIDTH 40
2000 SCREEN 0 , 1

while using mode 5 (medium resolution b/w graphics) is equivalent to SCREEN 1,1.

Controlling the Cursor   We use function 1 to turn the cursor on and off in the CURSORON and CURSOROFF macros from Chapter 5. This function also controls the start and end lines for the cursor, thereby controlling the cursor's size. As Figure 12.2 shows, the start and end line numbers go into the lower four bits of CH and CL, respectively. When bit 4 (the low-order bit of the upper four bits) of CH is set, the cursor is invisible; when bit 4 is cleared, the cursor shows up on the screen. The start and end lines can range from 0 to 13 with the monochrome board and from 0 to 7 with the color/graphics board.

We used function 2 in the LOCATE macro. Function 2 sets the cursor position. DH must contain the row and DL the column for the new position. Remember that the count for rows and columns starts with 0,0 in the upper left corner of the screen and goes to 24,79 in the bottom right. BH must contain the number of the page on which output is being written, or the active page. In the monochrome board or in the graphics mode of the color/graphics board the page is always 0. In the color/graphics 40-column modes, you have a choice of pages 0 through 7; in the 80-column modes, 0 through 3. In this book I always use page 0.

Functions 1 and 2 combined serve the purpose of BASIC's LOCATE statement with its five parameters: row, col, cursoron, start, stop. The BASIC statement:

100 LOCATE 5 , 6 , 1 , 5 , 7

turns on a three-line cursor and places it at row 5, column 6. To do the same thing in MASM you could do this:

```
MOV    CH , 5     ; BEG I NN I NG OF CURSOR AND TURN ON
MOV    CL , 7     ; END OF CURSOR
MOV    AH , 1
I NT   1 OH       ; DEF I NE CURSOR
MOV    DH , 4     ; ROW 5
MOV    DL , 5     ; COLUMN 6
MOV    BH , 0     ; PAGE 0
MOV    AH , 2
I NT   1 OH       ; PLACE CURSOR
```

Reading the Cursor Position   Function 3 of 10H reads the cursor postion, like BASIC's CSRLIN and POS. Once again, page number must be specified in BH. The function returns the cursor row in DH and the column in DL. CH and CL are filled with the cursor type parameters, that is, the same information that you would put into CH and CL to set the cursor with function 1. (BASIC has no equivalent for this part of the function.)

Scrolling the Screen   We used function 6, which scrolls the active page up, to write the CLS macro in Chapter 5. It requires seven parameters passed through the registers, as shown in Figure 12.2. Function 7 is basically the same, except that it scrolls downward thereby bringing blank lines in at the top of the window.

Using the Printer

Figure 12.4 summarizes the printer I/O interrupts. Function 5 of DOS interrupt 21H sends one character to the printer. The character must be placed in DL. This is the only DOS printer function, and it's probably all you will need. Most printer functions, such as carriage return, form feed, underlining, and so on, are triggered by characters sent to the printer as if they themselves were to be printed. These are the same characters you

In Order To	Use INT	Function (In AH)	Other Preparation Required	Results and Remarks
Print one character	21H	5	Character in DL	none
Print one character and return status byte	18H	0	Character in AL Printer # in DX	Status byte in AH See box below for meaning of status
Initialize printer and return status byte	18H	1	Printer # in DX	Same as function 0
Return status byte	18H	2	Printer # in DX	Same as function 0

```
          Meaning of Status Byte

     Bit Set    Meaning
       7         Printer Busy
       6         ACKNOWLEDGE
       5         Out of Paper
       4         SELECTED
       3         I/O Error
       2         not used
       1         not used
       0         Time Out

     (7 is high-order bit, 0 low-order)
```

Figure 12.4 Printer I/O

send from BASIC using LPRINT CHR$(...). One difference: in MASM you will have to send CR, or LF, or both at the end of each line. BASIC does this automatically after each LPRINT that does not end with a semicolon.

Figure 12.5 contains a macro that can be used to send a number of characters to a printer. You will have to specify the number to print and make sure to include end-of-line characters. You might want to modify this macro to look for a specific end-of-text character instead of using a count.

Printing a Character with BIOS

BIOS interrupt 17H, function 0, also prints one character. In this case, however, the character goes in AL and the printer number in DX. BIOS allows for up to three printers, numbered 0, 1, and 2. If you have only one printer it will be printer 0. A byte of printer status information is returned to AH. We'll discuss this status byte when we discuss function 2 of this interrupt.

Initializing the Printer

Function 1 of 17H initializes the printer and returns the status byte in AH. Initializing resets all the printer options to their original values just as though you had turned the printer off and on again. You may find it useful to initialize your printer at the beginning of every program that uses it.

```
PRINTER MACRO      TEXT,COUNT
          LOCAL    NEXT_CHAR
          PUSH     AX
          PUSH     BX
          PUSH     CX
          PUSH     DX
          MOV      CX,COUNT
          MOV      BX,0
NEXT_CHAR:
          MOV      AH,5
          MOV      DL,TEXT[BX]
          INT      21H
          INC      BX
          LOOP     NEXT_CHAR
          POP      DX
          POP      CX
          POP      BX
          POP      AX
          ENDM
```

Figure 12.5 PRINTER Macro

The Printer Status Byte

Function 2 of 17H simply reads the status byte into AH. The meanings of the bits when set are shown in Figure 12.5. Some of them may require some explanation. ACKNOWLEDGE means that the printer has sent a signal to indicate that it has received data. SELECT means that the printer is on-line. TIME OUT means that the printer has returned BUSY signals for a long time and the system will no longer try to send it data.

Computer Exercise

Try writing a very primitive typewriter program. Here are the steps to follow:

1. Initialize the printer.

2. Clear the screen and put a prompt on it.

3. Read and echo a character from the keyboard.

4. If the character is an extended code (like a function key), end the program. Otherwise, continue.

5. Print the character.

6. If the character was CR, add LF on both the CRT and printer.

7. Go back to step 3.

In Order To	Use INT	Function (In AH)	Other Preparation Required	Results and Remarks
Get character from ASYNC	21H	3	none	Character in AL
Send character from ASYNC	21H	4	Character in DL	none
Get date	21H	2AH	none	CX = year; DH = month DL = day
Set date	21H	2BH	CX = year; DH = month; DL = day	AL = 0 if ok AL = 0FFH if invalid
Get time	21H	2CH	none	CH=hours; CL=minutes DH=seconds;DL=hund.
Set time	21H	2DH	CH=hours; CL=minutes DH=seconds; DL=hundredths	AL = 0 if ok AL=0FFH if invalid
Print Screen	5	none	none	none
Find DOS Version	21H	30H	none	Major version in AL minor in AH If AL = 0, version is pre-2.0

Figure 12.6 Miscellaneous I/O Functions

You'll find my version of this program (TYPER.ASM) at the end of the chapter. When you test your program don't worry if the first few characters typed don't print immediately. Many printers don't begin printing until their buffer is full or CR is sent.

Miscellaneous Functions

Figure 12.6 summarizes the remaining functions discussed in this chapter: those associated with communications, date and time, screen printing, and finding out under which version of DOS your program is running.

Communications Functions

DOS 21H function 3 receives input from the Asynchronous Communications Adapter. It waits for a character to be received and places that character in AL. Function 4 sends the character in DL to the Asynchronous Communications Adapter.

Date and Time

Function 02AH of interrupt 21H gets the system date. It puts the year (in binary) into CX, the month into DH, and the day into DL.

Function 02BH sets the date. To prepare for it, place the year into CX, the month into DH, and the day into DL. All three figures should be binary. The year must be between 1980 and 2099; the month, 1 to 12; and the date 1 to 31. The date is checked for range and validity; a date of 2/30/81 will be rejected since there is no such date. If the date is accepted, and the system date updated, the function returns 0 in AL. Otherwise, it returns 0FFH in AL.

Function 02CH gets the time of day as four one-byte quantities. CH has the hours (0 to 23). CL has minutes. DH has seconds and DL has hundredths of a second.

Function 02DH sets the time of day. CH, CL, DH, and DL must be prepared with the time in the same format as returned by 02CH. If the operation is valid, AL is returned as 00. If it is not valid, AL is returned as 0FFH.

Print Screen

BIOS interrupt 5 prints the screen. It serves the same function as Shift-PrtSc, but is started from your program instead of by the user.

DOS Version Number

Function 30 of interrupt 21H finds the DOS version number. The major number is returned in AL, and the minor number, in AH. If AL is 2 and AH is 1, for example, it means that your program is currently running under DOS 2.1. If AL is 0, you can assume that a version of DOS prior to 2.0 is being used.

```
          PAGE,132                        ;THIS IS TYPER.ASM
;                                         ; THE TYPING PROGRAM
          INCLUDE MACLIB.LIB             ;   FOR CHAPTER 12
;
          INCLUDE EQULIB.LIB
;
PROG_STACK        SEGMENT STACK 'STACK'
                  DB      64 DUP ('STACK    ')
PROG_STACK        ENDS
;
PROG_DATA         SEGMENT 'DATA'
INCHAR            DB
PROG_DATA         ENDS
;
PROG_CODE         SEGMENT 'CODE'
MAIN_PROG         PROC    FAR
                  ASSUME  CS:PROG_CODE,DS:PROG_DATA,SS:PROG_STACK;ES:PROG_DATA
                  STARTER
                  STI
                  CLD
                  MOV     AH,0      ;INITIALIZING PRINTER
                  MOV     DX,0
                  INT     17H
                  CLS
                  MOV     AH,2      ;DISPLAY PROMPT CHAR
                  MOV     DL,10H
                  INT     21H
INPUT_CHAR:
                  MOV     AH,1      ;INPUT WITH ECHO AND CHECK
                  INT     21H
CHECK_CHAR:
                  CMP     AL,0      ;IF ANY EXTENDED CODE
                  JE      END_PROG  ; END PROGRAM
OUTPUT_CHAR:
                  MOV     DL,AL
                  MOV     AH,5
                  INT     21H
                  CMP     AL,CR     ;CHECK FOR CR
                  JNE     INPUT_CHAR
                  MOV     DL,LF     ;IF CR ADD LF
                  MOV     AH,5
                  INT     21H
                  MOV     AH,2      ;  LF ON SCREEN ALSO
                  INT     21H
                  JMP     INPUT_CHAR
END_PROG:
                  RET
MAIN_PROG         ENDP
PROG_CODE         ENDS
                  END
```

Figure 12.7 Typing Program

13

Disk I/O Using File Control Blocks

In versions of DOS prior to 2.0, disk file handling requires the use of file control blocks (FCBs). DOS 2.0 and later versions have another way to access files that is both simpler and more flexible than the earlier one. This chapter describes file handling using FCBs. If your programs will always run under DOS 2.0 or later versions, you should not use this method. In fact, you should skip this chapter and go to Chapter 14, which covers the newer file-access method.

The File Control Block

An FCB is a 37-byte area defined in your program's data segment. It is divided into 10 fields that contain information to be passed between your program and the DOS disk-access routines. You will find a description of the FCB and its fields in an appendix of your DOS manual. (Note: an appendix in the BASIC manual also describes an FCB; this is a special BASIC FCB, *not* the DOS FCB.) Figure 13.1 shows a MASM program's description of an FCB. We'll discuss the fields in detail.

```
FILE_DRIVE       DB    0                  ;SET BEFORE OPEN
FILE_NAME        DB    'NAMEFILE'         ;SET BEFORE OPEN
FILE_EXT         DB    'DAT'              ;SET BEFORE OPEN
FILE_CURR_BLOCK  DW    0                  ;SET BY OPEN; CHANGE AS NEEDED
FILE_REC_SIZE    DW    0                  ;SET BY OPEN; CHANGE IF NEEDED
FILE_SIZE        DW    2 DUP (?)          ;SET BY SYSTEM; DONT CHANGE
FILE_DATE        DW    ?                  ;SET BY SYSTEM; DONT CHANGE
                 DB    10 DUP(?)          ;SET BY SYSTEM; DONT CHANGE
FILE_CURR_REC    DB    0                  ;SET BEFORE SEQ READ
FILE_REL_REC     DW    2 DUP (?)          ;SET BEFORE RANDOM READ
```

Figure 13.1 An FCB for NAMEFILE

File Identifiers

The first three fields, FILE__DRIVE, FILE__NAME, and FILE__EXT, identify the file. They must be initialized before the file is opened or used.

FILE__DRIVE is a one-byte field set to 1 for Drive A, 2 for Drive B, and
so on. When FILE__DRIVE is 0, as in Figure 13.1, it tells the system to use
the default drive; when the file is opened, the zero will be replaced by the
default drive's file number.

FILE__NAME is an eight-byte file name, left-justified, with trailing
spaces if necessary. FILE__EXT is the three-byte file extension, left-justified, with trailing spaces. (FILE__EXT may be all blanks.)

If the default drive is A when the program runs, the description in
Figure 13.1 tells DOS to use file A:NAMEFILE.DAT. Notice that there is no
provision for specifying a path in the FCB.

Current Block and Record

FILE__CURR__BLOCK and FILE__CURR__REC identify the record to be
accessed by read or write operations. A block is a group of 128 records. The
first block, which starts at the beginning of the file, is block 0. Since
FILE__CURR__BLOCK is one word and therefore has a maximum value of
65,535, you can't have more than 64K blocks in a file. Opening the file sets
the current block field to 0; the field does not need to be defined with an
initial value. Notice that the block always contains 128 records regardless
of the record size; the number of bytes in a block may be different for
different files.

FILE__CURR__REC can range from 0 to 127. This field identifies the
current record within the current block. The 129th record in the file is
record 0 of block 1. The current record field is *not* initialized when the file is
opened. The definition in Figure 13.1 gives the field an initial value of 0.
You may prefer to initialize it by moving 0 to FILE__CURR__REC before
the first read or write.

Record Size and File Length

FILE__REC__SIZE is a one-word field that identifies the size of the file's records. When the file is opened, the record size is always set to 80H (128). If this is not the right record size, you must change it after the file is opened, but before the first read or write. All records in the file are assumed to be the same size; there is no way to indicate variable length records.

FILE__SIZE indicates the length of the file in bytes. It's a two-word field and, as usual the low-order word is the first one. This field is initialized by DOS when the file is opened and should not be changed by the program.

File Date

The next word, FILE__DATE, indicates the date the file was last created or updated. This field is filled in when the file is opened and should not be changed by your program. The *five*, not four, low-order bits of the first byte contain the day of the month, a value ranging from 0 to 31. The three high-order bits, combined with the next byte's low-order bit, contain the month (0 through 12). The second byte's seven high-order bits contain a value between 0 and 119; add 1980 to get the actual year. Bit-by-bit, the date looks like this:

```
FILE_DATE:      y y y y y y y m
FILE_DATE+1:    m m m d d d d d
```

This layout makes a little more sense if you think of the word moved to a register, where the first byte (FILE__DATE) would go into the high byte and the second (FILE__DATE + 1) into the low byte. Then, numbering the register's bits from 0 (lowest) to 15 (highest), the date would look like this:

```
15  14  13  12  11  10  9   8   7   6   5   4   3   2   1   0
y   y   y   y   y   y   y   m   m   m   m   m   d   d   d   d   d
        HIGH                                            LOW
```

Relative Record Number

FILE__REL__REC, the last field in the description, is a two-word field identifying a record to be read or written by random access. If you want to read the 128th record in the file, for example, you would set this field to 128 before calling a random read function. Remember that this field, like other multiple-word fields, expects to find the low-order word first and the high-order word last. To read record 128, set FILE__REL__REC to 128 and FILE__REL__REC+1 to 0.

The Rest of the FCB

The 10 bytes between FILE__DATE and FILE__CURR__REC are used by DOS. No information is provided about what they contain or how they are used. Just make sure you leave room for them in the right place in the FCB.

The Disk Transfer Address

When a program reads a record, an area of the data-segment must be provided to hold the data read. Similarly, to write a record, the data to be written must first be placed in an area of the data segment. The data-segment address into which data is to be read or from which it will be written is called the **disk transfer address**, or **DTA**. You must identify the DTA before you can read or write any record. The records for NAME-FILE.DAT can be read into or written from this area:

```
LIST__NAME          DB   20 DUP(' ')
LIST__ID            DB   12 DUP(' ')
```

When you read or write NAMEFILE.DAT in your program, you will use the offset of LIST__NAME as the DTA.

Opening the File

Function 0FH of DOS interrupt 21H opens a file. DX must point to the file's FCB. The drive, name, and extension (if any) must be in the FCB before the interrupt is called.

The interrupt routine returns a status byte in AL. If AL is 0FFH, the file was not found; if AL is 0, the file was opened.

Make sure to test AL after using function 0FH.

When the open is successful, the drive field is set if necessary, the current block is set to 0, the record size is set to 80H, and the file size and creation/update date are filled in from the directory.

```
OPEN_FILE       PROC
                PUSH    AX
                PUSH    DX
                LEA     DX,FILE_DRIVE           ;FIRST BYTE OF FCB
                MOV     AH,0FH                  ;OPEN FILE FUNCTION
                INT     21H
                OR      AL,0                    ;IF AL = ZERO
                JZ      OPEN1                   ;    FILE WAS FOUND
                LEA     DX,FILE_DRIVE           ;OTHERWISE NEED TO CREATE IT
                MOV     AH,16H
                INT     21H
                OR      AL,0                    ;IF AX = ZERO CREATE OK
                JZ      OPEN1
                DISPLAY NO_ROOM                 ;IF NO ROOM IN DIRECTORY
                MOV     ERROR_CODE,1            ;SET ERROR CODE
                JMP     OPEN2                   ; AND RETURN TO MAIN LOOP
OPEN1:
                MOV     FILE_REC_SIZE,32        ;SET RECORD SIZE
                MOV     FILE_CURR_REC,0         ;AND CURRENT RECORD
OPEN2:
                POP     DX
                POP     AX
                RET
OPEN_FILE       ENDP
```

Figure 13.2 Opening NAMEFILE

Creating a New File

Function 16H of interrupt 21H creates a new file. Again, DX must point to the FCB and the file drive, name, and extension (if any) must be in the FCB before the function is called.

If the file directory lacks room for another entry, AL is returned with the value 0FFH. Otherwise, a directory entry is made for a zero-length file, the file is opened, and AL is returned with 0. Make sure you check AL after using function 16H.

Figure 13.2 presents a routine that opens NAMEFILE.DAT if it exists; otherwise, it creates the file and opens it. If the directory has no room, an error message is displayed and an error code field is set.

Sequential Writes

Function 15H writes a record from the area pointed to by the DTA. DX must point to the file's FCB. The record written is the one identified by the current block and record fields. Obviously a DTA must be established before function 15H is called. This is done by function 1AH, which sets the disk-transfer address. DX must point to the DTA.

```
WRITE_RECORD      PROC
                  PUSH      AX
                  PUSH      DX
                  LEA       DX,LIST_NAME             ;SET DISK TRANSFER ADDR
                  MOV       AH,1AH
                  INT       21H
                  LEA       DX,FILE_DRIVE            ;WRITE FROM DTA
                  MOV       AH,15H
                  INT       21H
                  OR        AL,0                     ;IF AL = 0 WRITE OK
                  JZ        WRITE1
                  DISPLAY   WRITE_FAILED             ;OTHERWISE NOT WRITTEN
                  MOV       ERROR_CODE,1
WRITE1:
                  POP       DX
                  POP       AX
                  RET
WRITE_RECORD      ENDP
```

Figure 13.3 Writing NAMEFILE

Function 1AH does not return a status byte, but the sequential write (function 15H) does return one in AL. If AL is 1, the disk is full. If AL is 2, it means that the area between the DTA and the end of the data segment was smaller than the FCB's record size. Probably, either the record description or the FCB has an error. If AL is 0, the write was successful and the FCB's current record (and current block if necessary) is incremented to point to the next record.

Figure 13.3 shows a routine to write records to NAMEFILE.DAT. The DTA is set every time the routine is called, but this is not necessary if the rest of the program never changes the DTA. The routine includes an error check, but it does not differentiate between the two types of write error.

Reading Sequentially

Function 14H performs a sequential read. DX must point to the FCB. A DTA must be established before the read. The record read is the one pointed to by the current block and record fields. AL is returned with a status byte. If AL is 1 or 3, end-of-file was encountered. A status of 1 indicates that no record was found and 3, that a partial record was read and filled out with zeros. A status of 2 indicates that the area between DTA and the end of the data segment was not large enough to hold the record read. After a successful read, indicated by AL = 0, the current block and record fields are incremented.

Random Reads and Writes

Function 21H performs a random read, while 22H performs a random write. For both, a DTA must have been previously established; DX must point to the FCB, and the FILE__REL__REC field must be set with the desired record number. The relative record number is used to compute the current block and record numbers which are actually used to access the file. The status byte returned in AL has the same meanings as it does with a sequential read or write. The current block and record, however, will *not* be incremented after a random operation.

Closing a File

Function 10H of interrupt 21H closes a file. DX must point to the file's FCB. A status byte is returned in AL. If AL is 0FFH, either the file is not in the current disk directory or its position there has changed. Usually this means that a disk has been changed since the file was opened. The directory cannot be properly updated when this happens; changes or additions to the file may be lost. If AL is 0, the file was successfully closed.

Computer Exercise

Figure 13.4 contains the entire program that writes NAMEFILE.DAT. Now write a program to list the file on the printer. My bare bones version of this program follows Figure 13.4. Your version may include refinements such as headings, page changes after 50 lines, and so on. Assemble and try both the write program and your listing program.

Remember the telephone number program you worked on in earlier chapters? Try revising that to save the names and phone numbers and then print a telephone number list.

The NAME13 Program

```
        PAGE    ,132
;
        INCLUDE MACLIB.LIB
;
        INCLUDE EQULIB.LIB
;
;
PROG_STACK      SEGMENT STACK 'STACK'
                DB      64 DUP (('STACK    '))
PROG_STACK      ENDS
;
PROG_DATA       SEGMENT 'DATA'
NAME_PROMPT     DB      LF,CR,'NAME: ',EOT
ID_PROMPT       DB      LF,CR,'ID:  ',EOT
NO_ROOM         DB      LF,CR,'NO ROOM IN DIRECTORY FOR NEW FILE',EOT
BAD_CLOSE       DB      LF,CR,'CANT CLOSE FILE: DID YOU CHANGE DISK?',EOT
WRITE_FAILED    DB      LF,CR,'CANT WRITE RECORD -- NO ROOM ON DISK',EOT
END_MESSAGE     DB      LF,CR,'GOODBYE',EOT
ERROR_CODE      DB      0
CCOUNT          DW      0
;
INBUF           DB      21
INCOUNT         DB      ?
INDATA          DB      21 DUP(' ')
;
FILE_DRIVE      DB      0               ;SET BEFORE OPEN
FILE_NAME       DB      'NAMEFILE'      ;SET BEFORE OPEN
FILE_EXT        DB      'DAT'           ;SET BEFORE OPEN
FILE_CURR_BLOCK DW      0               ;SET BY OPEN; CHANGE AS NEEDED
FILE_REC_SIZE   DW      0               ;SET BY OPEN; CHANGE IF NEEDED
FILE_SIZE       DW      2 DUP (?)       ;SET BY SYSTEM; DONT CHANGE
FILE_DATE       DW      ?               ;SET BY SYSTEM; DONT CHANGE
                DB      10 DUP(?)       ;SET BY SYSTEM; DONT CHANGE
FILE_CURR_REC   DB      0               ;SET BEFORE SEQ READ
FILE_REL_REC    DW      2 DUP (?)       ;SET BEFORE RANDOM READ
;
LIST_NAME       DB      20 DUP (?)
LIST_ID         DB      12 DUP (?)
;
PROG_DATA  ENDS
;
PROG_CODE       SEGMENT 'CODE'
MAIN_PROG       PROC    FAR
                ASSUME  CS:PROG_CODE,DS:PROG_DATA,SS:PROG_STACK,ES:PROG_DATA
                STARTER
                STI
                CLD
                CLS
                CURSORON
                CALL OPEN_FILE
                TEST    ERROR_CODE,1            ;IF ERROR CODE NOT ZERO
                JZ      MAINLOOP
                JMP     END_PROG                ;     END PROGRAM
MAINLOOP:
                CLEAR   LIST_NAME,32            ;MOVE SPACES TO OUTPUT AREA
                CALL    GETNAME                 ;PROMPT AND INPUT NAME
                CMP     INCOUNT,0               ;IF NO NAME END PROGRAM
                JE      CLOSE_UP
                MOVE    LIST_NAME,INDATA,CCOUNT ;MOVE NAME TO OUTPUT RECORD
                CALL    GETID                   ;PROMPT AND INPUT ID
                MOVE    LIST_ID,INDATA,CCOUNT   ;MOVE ID TO OUTPUT RECORD
                CALL    WRITE_RECORD
```

Figure 13.4 The NAME13 Program (continued)

```
                TEST    ERROR_CODE,1            ;IF ERROR CODE NOT ZERO
                JNZ     CLOSE_UP                ;   END PROGRAM
                JMP     MAINLOOP                ;ELSE REPEAT PROCESS
CLOSE_UP:
                CALL    CLOSE_FILE
END_PROG:
                DISPLAY END_MESSAGE
                RET                             ;THEN RETURN TO OPERATING SYSTEM
MAIN_PROG       ENDP
;
CLOSE_FILE      PROC
                PUSH    AX
                PUSH    DX
                LEA     DX,FILE_DRIVE
                MOV     AH,10H
                INT     21H
                OR      AL,0                    ;IF AL = 0
                JZ      CLOSE1                  ;   CLOSE WAS OK
                DISPLAY BAD_CLOSE               ;ELSE ERROR OCCURRED
                MOV     ERROR_CODE,1
CLOSE1:
                POP     DX
                POP     AX
                RET
CLOSE_FILE      ENDP
;
GETNAME         PROC
                PUSH    BX
                CLEAR   INDATA,21
                DISPLAY NAME_PROMPT             ;PROMPT FOR NAME
                GETDATA INBUF,21                ;GET NAME IN BUFFER
                MOV     BL,INCOUNT              ;MOVE INCOUNT TO WORD SIZE
                MOV     BH,0
                MOV     CCOUNT,BX
                POP     BX
                RET
GETNAME         ENDP
;
GETID           PROC
                PUSH    BX
GID01:
                DISPLAY ID_PROMPT               ;PROMPT FOR ID
                GETDATA INBUF,13                ;GET ID IN BUFFER
                MOV     BL,INCOUNT              ;MOVE INCOUNT TO WORD SIZE
                MOV     BH,0
                MOV     CCOUNT,BX
                POP     BX
                RET
GETID           ENDP
;
OPEN_FILE       PROC
                PUSH    AX
                PUSH    DX
                LEA     DX,FILE_DRIVE           ;FIRST BYTE OF FCB
                MOV     AH,0FH                  ;OPEN FILE FUNCTION
                INT     21H
                OR      AL,0                    ;IF AL = ZERO
                JZ      OPEN1                   ;   FILE WAS FOUND
                LEA     DX,FILE_DRIVE           ;OTHERWISE NEED TO CREATE IT
                MOV     AH,16H
                INT     21H
                OR      AL,0                    ;IF AX = ZERO CREATE OK
                JZ      OPEN1
                DISPLAY NO_ROOM                 ;IF NO ROOM IN DIRECTORY
```

```
                  MOV       ERROR_CODE,1          ;SET ERROR CODE
                  JMP       OPEN2                 ; AND RETURN TO MAIN LOOP
OPEN1:
                  MOV       FILE_REC_SIZE,32      ;SET RECORD SIZE
                  MOV       FILE_CURR_REC,0       ;AND CURRENT RECORD
OPEN2:
                  POP       DX
                  POP       AX
                  RET
OPEN_FILE         ENDP
;
WRITE_RECORD      PROC
                  PUSH      AX
                  PUSH      DX
                  LEA       DX,LIST_NAME          ;SET DISK TRANSFER ADDR
                  MOV       AH,1AH
                  INT       21H
                  LEA       DX,FILE_DRIVE         ;WRITE FROM DTA
                  MOV       AH,15H
                  INT       21H
                  OR        AL,0                  ;IF AL = 0 WRITE OK
                  JZ        WRITE1
                  DISPLAY   WRITE_FAILED          ;OTHERWISE NOT WRITTEN
                  MOV       ERROR_CODE,1
WRITE1:
                  POP       DX
                  POP       AX
                  RET
WRITE_RECORD      ENDP
;
PROG_CODE         ENDS
                  END       MAIN_PROG
```

Figure 13.4 The NAME13 Program

```
        PAGE    ,132
;
        INCLUDE MACLIB.LIB
;
        INCLUDE EQULIB.LIB
;
;
PROG_STACK      SEGMENT STACK 'STACK'
                DB      64 DUP ('STACK    ')
PROG_STACK      ENDS
;
PROG_DATA       SEGMENT 'DATA'
BAD_OPEN        DB      LF,CR,'CANT FIND FILE',EOT
BAD_CLOSE       DB      LF,CR,'CLOSE FAILED',EOT
BAD_READ        DB      LF,CR,'PROBABLE END OF FILE',EOT
ERROR_CODE      DB      0
;
FILE_DRIVE      DB      0               ;SET BEFORE OPEN
FILE_NAME       DB      'NAMEFILE'      ;SET BEFORE OPEN
FILE_EXT        DB      'DAT'           ;SET BEFORE OPEN
FILE_CURR_BLOCK DW      0               ;SET BY OPEN; CHANGE AS NEEDED
FILE_REC_SIZE   DW      0               ;SET BY OPEN; CHANGE IF NEEDED
FILE_SIZE       DW      2 DUP (?)       ;SET BY SYSTEM; DONT CHANGE
FILE_DATE       DW      ?               ;SET BY SYSTEM; DONT CHANGE
                DB      10 DUP(?)       ;SET BY SYSTEM; DONT CHANGE
FILE_CURR_REC   DB      0               ;SET BEFORE SEQ READ
FILE_REL_REC    DW      2 DUP (?)       ;SET BEFORE RANDOM READ
;
INPUT_NAME      DB      20 DUP (?)
INPUT_ID        DB      12 DUP (?)
;
OUTPUT_NAME     DB      20 DUP (' ')
                DB      10 DUP (' ')
OUTPUT_ID       DB      12 DUP (' ')
                DB      CR,LF
;
PROG_DATA  ENDS
;
PROG_CODE       SEGMENT 'CODE'
MAIN_PROG       PROC    FAR
                ASSUME  CS:PROG_CODE,DS:PROG_DATA,SS:PROG_STACK,ES:PROG_DATA
                STARTER
                STI
                CLD
                CLS
                CURSORON
                CALL    OPEN_FILE
                TEST    ERROR_CODE,1            ;IF OPEN FAILED
                JZ      MAINLOOP
                JMP     END_PROG                ;     END PROGRAM
MAINLOOP:
                CALL    READIN                  ;READ INPUT RECORD
                TEST    ERROR_CODE,1            ;IF END OF FILE
                JNZ     CLOSE_UP                ;     CLOSE FILE AND END
                MOVE    OUTPUT_NAME,INPUT_NAME,20   ;SET PRINT LINE
                MOVE    OUTPUT_ID,INPUT_ID,12
                CALL    PRINT_LINE              ;PRINT LINE
                JMP     MAINLOOP                ;ELSE REPEAT PROCESS
CLOSE_UP:
                CALL    CLOSE_FILE
END_PROG:
                RET                             ;THEN RETURN TO OPERATING SYSTEM
MAIN_PROG       ENDP
;
```

Figure 13.5 (continued)

```
CLOSE_FILE      PROC
                PUSH    AX
                PUSH    DX
                LEA     DX,FILE_DRIVE
                MOV     AH,10H
                INT     21H
                OR      AL,0                    ;IF AL = 0
                JZ      CLOSE1                  ;   CLOSE WAS OK
                DISPLAY BAD_CLOSE               ;ELSE ERROR OCCURRED
                MOV     ERROR_CODE,1
CLOSE1:
                POP     DX
                POP     AX
                RET
CLOSE_FILE      ENDP
;
OPEN_FILE       PROC
                PUSH    AX
                PUSH    DX
                LEA     DX,FILE_DRIVE           ;FIRST BYTE OF FCB
                MOV     AH,0FH                  ;OPEN FILE FUNCTION
                INT     21H
                OR      AL,0                    ;IF AL = ZERO
                JZ      OPEN1                   ;   FILE WAS FOUND
                DISPLAY BAD_OPEN                ;OTHERWISE NOT FOUND
                MOV     ERROR_CODE,1            ;SET ERROR CODE
                JMP     OPEN2                   ; AND RETURN TO MAIN LOOP
OPEN1:
                MOV     FILE_REC_SIZE,32        ;SET RECORD SIZE
                MOV     FILE_CURR_REC,0         ;AND CURRENT RECORD
OPEN2:
                POP     DX
                POP     AX
                RET
OPEN_FILE       ENDP
;
PRINT_LINE      PROC
                PUSH    CX
                PUSH    BX
                MOV     CX,44                   ;PRINT 44 CHAR
                MOV     BX,0
PRINT1:
                MOV     DL,OUTPUT_NAME[BX]      ;LOAD CHAR INTO DL
                MOV     AH,5                    ;FOR PRINT FUNCTION
                INT     21H                     ;   AND PRINT
                INC     BX                      ;POINT TO NEXT CHAR
                LOOP    PRINT1                  ;AND REPEAT
                POP     BX
                POP     CX
                RET
PRINT_LINE      ENDP
;
READIN          PROC
                PUSH    AX
                PUSH    DX
                LEA     DX,INPUT_NAME           ;SET DISK TRANSFER ADDR
                MOV     AH,1AH
                INT     21H
```

Figure 13.5 (continued)

```
                LEA     DX,FILE_DRIVE           ;READ TO DTA
                MOV     AH,14H
                INT     21H
                OR      AL,0                    ;IF AL = 0 READ OK
                JZ      READ1
                DISPLAY BAD_READ                ;OTHERWISE BAD READ
                MOV     ERROR_CODE,1
READ1:
                POP     DX
                POP     AX
                RET
READIN          ENDP
;
PROG_CODE       ENDS
                END     MAIN_PROG
```

Figure 13.5

14

Disk I/O Using File Handles

This chapter describes a method of disk I/O using interrupt 21H functions that were implemented with DOS 2.0. If your programs need to run with an earlier version of DOS, you cannot use this method. If they will run only under DOS 2.0 or later, this is the preferred method of disk I/O.

How It Works

In this method, when a file is opened it is assigned a 16-bit number called a **handle**. Your program must keep track of which handle has been assigned to which file. When you read, write, or close the file you place the handle in BX before calling the appropriate 21H function. When you read or write you also specify (in DX) a buffer address; that is, a offset in your data segment where input will be placed or from which output will be copied. Additionally, you specify in CX the maximum number of bytes to be read or written. DOS maintains a **read/write pointer** for each open file; this always points to the next byte to be accessed in the file. The pointer is set to 0 when the file is opened and is updated by the number of bytes actually handled by each read or write. You can also use a 21H function to change this pointer.

```
Error         Meaning
Code

  1           Invalid function number

  2           File not found

  3           Path not found

  4           Too many open files (no paths left)

  5           Access denied

  6           Invalid handle

 12           Invalid access code
```

Figure 14.1 Error Codes for File Handle Functions

The interrupt functions for this I/O method use CF to indicate whether an operation is successful. CF is cleared when an operation is successful and set if an error occurs. When CF is set an error code is placed in AX. You can find a list of error codes in the DOS appendix that describes 21H functions; the list is called the ERROR RETURN TABLE. The functions we describe in this chapter use only seven of these codes; Figure 14.1 contains a description of those seven codes.

I'll discuss the six most useful file handle functions in detail. Once you understand them you should be able to learn others from the DOS manual if you need them.

Create and Open

Function 3CH creates a new file. DX must point to a string that identifies the file. The string can include the drive, path, and filename, and must end with a byte of zeros. A character string ending in 00H is called an **ASCIIZ string**. In the ASCIIZ string identifying the new file, both drive and path are optional but the full filename, including any extension, is required. To create a file named NAMEFILE.DAT on the default drive and path, then, our program should include a definition like this:

```
NAME_FILE DB     'NAMEFILE.DAT',0
```

and load NAME_FILE's offset into DX before calling the interrupt. A file attribute must also be specified by a code in CX. A file's attribute code may mark it as a hidden file, a system file, a read-only file, a read-write file, and so on. You will find all possible attribute codes listed in another DOS manual appendix, the DOS Disk Allocation appendix. In this book, all files are straightforward read-write files, with attribute code zero. The routine to create NAME__FILE, then, could be:

```
LEA     DX,NAME__FILE
MOV     CX,0
MOV     AH,3CH
INT     21H
```

The create function creates a new file or truncates an old one so that it can be rewritten. It opens the file for read/write and assigns a handle which is returned in AX. If the file cannot be created, CF is set and the error code is put into AX. The possible error codes are 3, 4, and 5. (In this case access denied means either that the directory was full or that the file already exists and is read-only.) Function 3CH, then, should be followed by some type of error testing; if no error is found the file handle must be saved for later use.

An existing file is usually opened instead of re-created. Function 3DH of 21H opens a file. Again, DX points to an ASCIIZ string identifying the file. AL contains an access code: 0 to open the file for read only, 1 for write only, 2 for read/write. We usually open our files for read/write. This routine would open the existing NAME__FILE:

```
LEA     DX,NAME__FILE
MOV     AL,2
MOV     AH,3CH
INT     21H
```

Again, an error check should be made. Possible error codes from this function are 2, 4, 5, and 12. Access denied will usually mean that you are trying to open a read-only file for write or read/write. If the open is successful, the file handle is returned in AX and should be saved.

Figure 14.2 contains an OPEN macro which opens an existing file; if the file is not found, the macro creates a new one. To call the macro you must specify the variable that contains the filename, the variable that should contain the file handle, and a variable that can hold an error code. After using the macro you should check CF to see if the open was successful; if it was not, you can examine the error code and print an appropriate message, then end the program.

```
OPEN        MACRO     FNAME,HANDLE,ECODE
            LOCAL     SAVE_HANDLE,OPEN_DONE
            PUSH      AX
            PUSH      CX
            PUSH      DX
            LEA       DX,FNAME
            MOV       AH,3DH
            MOV       AL,2
            INT       21H
            MOV       ECODE,AL
            JNC       SAVE_HANDLE       ;IF NO ERROR JUMP
            CMP       AL,2              ;IF ERROR NOT FILE NOT FOUND
            JNE       OPEN_DONE         ;   QUIT
            MOV       CX,0              ;CREATE R/W FILE IF NOT FOUND
            LEA       DX,FNAME
            MOV       AH,3CH
            INT       21H
            MOV       ECODE,AL
            JC        OPEN_DONE         ;IF ERROR DONT SAVE HANDLE
SAVE_HANDLE:
            MOV       HANDLE,AX
OPEN_DONE:
            POP       DX
            POP       CX
            POP       AX
            ENDM
```

Figure 14.2 The OPEN Macro

Here's an example:

```
NAME_FILE     DB     'NAMEFILE.DAT'.0
NAME_HANDLE   DW     ?
ERROR_CODE    DB     ?
              . . .
              OPEN   NAME_FILE,NAME_HANDLE,ERROR_CODE
              JNC    OPEN_OK      ;CONTINUE PROGRAM
              CALL   ERROR_ROUTINE
              JMP    END_PROG
OPEN_OK:
              . . .
```

The error routine might simply display an error message that includes the error code or it might display a different message for every possible error code value.

Read and Write

To read a file, use function 3FH of interrupt 21H. Before you call this function, BX must contain the file handle; CX the number of bytes to read;

and DX the address into which the bytes are to be read. If we want to read 32 bytes from NAME__FILE into this area:

```
LIST__NAME      DB 20 DUP ( ? )
LIST__ID        DB 12 DUP ( ? )
```

we can do it like this:

```
MOV      BX , NAME__HANDLE
MOV      CX , 32
LEA      DX , LIST__NAME
MOV      AH , 3FH
INT      21H
```

This function reads from the indicated file starting at the current location of the read/write pointer; the bytes read are transferred to the area to which DX points. Possible error returns are 5 and 6. After a successful read, the read/write pointer will be updated by the number of bytes read and AX will contain that number. This is not necessarily the number of bytes that you asked for. If you try to read from the end-of-file, for example, you may get 0 bytes. DOS does not consider this an error, so CF will be clear and no error code will be passed.

In the READ macro in Figure 14.3 we test for end-of-file; if found, we set CF and pass 100 to the error code field. This allows us to handle end-of-file like any other error after using the macro. Notice that AX is *not* PUSHed and POPped; its value will be changed. This is done because there may be a need to know the the number of bytes actually read even when end-of-file is not found. You'll see an example later in the chapter.

To use the READ macro, you must identify the variables used for the file handle and input buffer, the number of bytes to be read, and the error code field. After READ you should test CF for an error condition. To read a record from NAME__FILE you could use this routine:

```
READ      NAME__HANDLE , LIST__NAME , 32 , ERROR__CODE
JNC       READ__OK
CALL      ERROR__ROUTINE
JMP       READ__DONE
```

```
;NOTE THAT THE READ MACRO DOES NOT PRESERVE AX
;
READ      MACRO     HANDLE,BUFFER,COUNT,ECODE
          LOCAL     CHECK_COUNT,READ_DONE
          PUSH      BX
          PUSH      CX
          PUSH      DX
          MOV       BX,HANDLE
          MOV       CX,COUNT
          LEA       DX,BUFFER
          MOV       AH,3FH
          INT       21H
          JNC       CHECK_COUNT
          MOV       ECODE,AL
          JMP       READ_DONE
CHECK_COUNT:
          CMP       AX,0
          JNE       READ_DONE
          MOV       ECODE,100        ;OUR CODE FOR EOF
          STC
READ_DONE:
          POP       DX
          POP       CX
          POP       BX
          ENDM
```

Figure 14.3 The READ Macro

```
WRITE     MACRO     HANDLE,BUFFER,COUNT,ECODE
          LOCAL     CHECK_COUNT,WRITE_DONE
          PUSH      AX
          PUSH      BX
          PUSH      CX
          PUSH      DX
          MOV       BX,HANDLE
          MOV       CX,COUNT
          LEA       DX,BUFFER
          MOV       AH,40H
          INT       21H
          JNC       CHECK_COUNT      ;IF WRITE OK CHECK COUNT WRITTEN
          MOV       ECODE,AL         ;OTHERWISE SET ERROR CODE AND QUIT
          JMP       WRITE_DONE
CHECK_COUNT:
          CMP       AX,COUNT
          JE        WRITE_DONE
          MOV       ECODE,99         ;OUR OWN ERROR CODE FOR DISK FULL
          STC                        ;  SET CARRY FLAG FOR ERROR
WRITE_DONE:
          POP       DX
          POP       CX
          POP       BX
          POP       AX
          ENDM
```

Figure 14.4 The WRITE Macro

To write to a file, use function 40H of interrupt 21H. This is similar to the read function. BX contains the file handle; CX contains the number of bytes to write; DX contains the address of the data to be written. Possible return error codes are 5 and 6. The read/write pointer is updated and AX contains the number of bytes actually written; this may not be the number requested. When the full number of bytes is not written it usually means that the disk is full.

The WRITE macro in Figure 14.4 requires that you specify the file handle, buffer area, count, and error code. After a write a check is made to see if all bytes were written; if not, CF is set and an error-code of 99 is returned from the macro.

Adjusting the Read/Write Pointer

Function 42H of interrupt 21H allows you to change the read/write pointer. As usual, BX contains the file handle. There are three methods of changing the pointer; the method is indicated by a code in AL. In each method, a two-word offset is specified in CX and DX, with the low-order word in DX, high-order in CX. This offset is a signed value; it may be negative.

If AL = 0, the offset is calculated from the beginning of the file. If the offset is 182, for example, the pointer is set to point to byte 182 of the file. To point to the beginning of the file, move 0 to CX, DX, and AL. Then the next read or write will start at the file's beginning.

If AL = 1, the new value of the pointer is computed by adding the specified offset to the current pointer value. In other words, the offset specifies how far (and in what direction) you will move from the current read/write position. If the offset is negative, you will move backwards through the file.

If AL = 2, the new location is computed by adding the offset to the end-of-file location. If the file's records are 32 bytes long, you can point to the last record in the file by moving 2 to AL, -32 to DX, and 0FFH to CX (to extend the negative sign through the high-order word). If you move 0 to CX and DX and 2 to AL, the pointer will be set at the end of the file, ready for you to append new records.

Possible error codes from this function are 1 and 6; in this case an error code of 1 means that AL didn't contain a valid method.

If the pointer is moved successfully, AX and DX will show the updated pointer value. AX has the low-order word, DX the high-order. (Remember that *before* the call, DX had the low-order word of the offset, while CX had the high-order word.) You can use method 1 with an offset of 0 to find the current value of the pointer; you can use method 2 with an offset of 0 to find out how long the file is.

```
FIND_END MACRO   HANDLE
         PUSH    AX
         PUSH    BX
         PUSH    CX
         PUSH    DX
         MOV     AH,42H
         MOV     AL,2
         MOV     BX,HANDLE
         MOV     CX,0
         MOV     DX,0
         INT     21H
         POP     DX
         POP     CX
         POP     BX
         POP     AX
         ENDM
;
;
POINT    MACRO   HANDLE,COUNT
         LOCAL   POINT1
         PUSH    AX
         PUSH    BX
         PUSH    CX
         PUSH    DX
         MOV     BX,HANDLE
         MOV     CX,0
         MOV     DX,COUNT
         CMP     DX,0
         JGE     POINT1
         NOT     CX
POINT1:
         MOV     AL,1
         MOV     AH,42H
         INT     21H
         POP     DX
         POP     BX
         POP     CX
         POP     AX
         ENDM
```

Figure 14.5 The FIND__END and POINT Macros

Figure 14.5 contains two macros that use function 42. FIND__END sets the pointer to the end of the file. When you plan to add records to an existing file, you could use FILE__END before beginning to write. POINT simply changes the pointer a specified number of bytes; POINT only asks for a value for DX so the macro can only be used with a range of -32,768 to 32,767 bytes. Notice the provision for setting CX to 0FFFFH if DX is negative, thus extending the sign of DX throughout CX. When you use either of these macros be sure to follow them with JC or JNC to check for errors.

Closing a File

Function 3EH of interrupt 21H closes a file. BX must contain the file handle. The only error code possible is 6. Figure 14.6 contains a CLOSE macro that could be used for any file.

```
CLOSE     MACRO    HANDLE,ECODE
          PUSH     AX
          PUSH     BX
          MOV      BX,HANDLE
          MOV      AH,3EH
          INT      21H
          MOV      ECODE,AL
          POP      BX
          POP      AX
          ENDM
```

Figure 14.6 The CLOSE Macro

Computer Exercise

Figure 14.7 contains a simple program using OPEN, FIND__END, WRITE, and CLOSE to write NAMEFILE.DAT. The macros from this chapter are included under the name FILEHAND.LIB. If you want to, you can use WRITENAM to create NAMEFILE.DAT and enter some data into it; then write a similar program using READ to read NAMEFILE.DAT and display each record on the screen. You'll find our version, READNAME.ASM, at the end of the chapter.

```
          PAGE     ,132
;
          INCLUDE MACLIB.LIB
;
          INCLUDE FILEHAND.LIB
;
          INCLUDE EQULIB.LIB
;
;
PROG_STACK          SEGMENT STACK 'STACK'
                    DB       64 DUP ('STACK    ')
PROG_STACK          ENDS
;
PROG_DATA           SEGMENT 'DATA'
NAME_PROMPT     DB       LF,CR,'NAME: ',EOT
ID_PROMPT       DB       LF,CR,'ID:  ',EOT
BAD_PATH        DB       LF,CR,'PATH NOT FOUND',EOT
TOO_MANY_FILES  DB       LF,CR,'TOO MANY FILES OPEN',EOT
ACCESS_DENIED   DB       LF,CR,'ACCESS DENIED',EOT
INVALID_HANDLE  DB       LF,CR,'INVALID HANDLE USED',EOT
DISK_FULL       DB       LF,CR,'DISK FULL',EOT
INVALID_ACCESS  DB       LF,CR,'INVALID ACCESS CODE',EOT
UNKNOWN_ERROR   DB       LF,CR,'UNKNOWN ERROR',EOT
END_MESSAGE     DB       LF,CR,'GOODBYE',EOT
ERROR_CODE      DB       ?
CCOUNT          DW       ?
;
INBUF           DB       21
INCOUNT         DB       ?
```

Figure 14.7 WRITENAM.ASM (continued)

```
INDATA              DB      21 DUP(' ')
;
NAME_HANDLE         DW      ?
NAME_FILE           DB      'NAMEFILE.DAT',0
;
LIST_NAME           DB      20 DUP (?)
LIST_ID             DB      12 DUP (?)
;
PROG_DATA           ENDS
PROG_CODE           SEGMENT 'CODE'
MAIN_PROG           PROC    FAR
                    ASSUME  CS:PROG_CODE,DS:PROG_DATA,SS:PROG_STACK,ES:PROG_DATA
                    STARTER
                    STI
                    CLD
                    CLS
                    CURSORON
                    OPEN    NAME_FILE,NAME_HANDLE,ERROR_CODE
                    JNC     POSITION                ;IF OPEN OK CONTINUE
                    CALL    ERROR_ROUTINE           ;ELSE    DISPLAY APPROPRIATE MESSAGE
                    JMP     END_PROG                ;        AND END PROGRAM
POSITION:
                    FIND_END NAME_HANDLE
                    JNC     MAINLOOP
                    CALL    ERROR_ROUTINE
                    JMP     CLOSE_UP
MAINLOOP:
                    CLEAR   LIST_NAME,32            ;MOVE SPACES TO I/O BUFFER
                    CALL    GETNAME                 ;PROMPT AND INPUT NAME
                    CMP     INCOUNT,0               ;IF NO NAME END PROGRAM
                    JE      CLOSE_UP
                    MOVE    LIST_NAME,INDATA,CCOUNT ;MOVE NAME TO OUTPUT RECORD
                    CALL    GETID                   ;PROMPT AND INPUT ID
                    MOVE    LIST_ID,INDATA,CCOUNT   ;MOVE ID TO OUTPUT RECORD
                    WRITE   NAME_HANDLE,LIST_NAME,32,ERROR_CODE
                    JNC     MAINLOOP                ;IF WRITE OK REPEAT LOOP
                    CALL    ERROR_ROUTINE           ;ELSE   DISPLAY APPROPRIATE MESSAGE
CLOSE_UP:
                    CLOSE   NAME_HANDLE,ERROR_CODE  ;CLOSE FILE
                    JNC     END_PROG                ;IF CLOSE OK END PROGRAM
                    CALL    ERROR_ROUTINE           ;ELSE DISPLAY APPROPRIATE MESSAGE
END_PROG:
                    DISPLAY END_MESSAGE
                    RET                             ;THEN RETURN TO OPERATING SYSTEM
MAIN_PROG           ENDP
;
ERROR_ROUTINE       PROC
                    CMP     ERROR_CODE,3
                    JNE     ERR1
                    DISPLAY BAD_PATH
                    JMP     ERR_END
ERR1:
                    CMP     ERROR_CODE,4
                    JNE     ERR2
                    DISPLAY TOO_MANY_FILES
                    JMP     ERR_END
ERR2:
                    CMP     ERROR_CODE,5
                    JNE     ERR3
                    DISPLAY ACCESS_DENIED
                    JMP     ERR_END
ERR3:
                    CMP     ERROR_CODE,6
                    JNE     ERR4
                    DISPLAY INVALID_HANDLE
                    JMP     ERR_END
```

Figure 14.7 WRITENAM.ASM (continued)

```
ERR4:
                CMP       ERROR_CODE,12
                JNE       ERR5
                DISPLAY   INVALID_ACCESS
                JMP       ERR_END
ERR5:
                CMP       ERROR_CODE,99
                JNE       ERR6
                DISPLAY   DISK_FULL
                JMP       ERR_END
ERR6:
                DISPLAY   UNKNOWN_ERROR
ERR_END:
                CLC
                RET
ERROR_ROUTINE   ENDP
;
GETNAME         PROC
                PUSH      BX
                CLEAR     INDATA,21
                DISPLAY   NAME_PROMPT       ;PROMPT FOR NAME
                GETDATA   INBUF,21          ;GET NAME IN BUFFER
                MOV       BL,INCOUNT        ;MOVE INCOUNT TO WORD SIZE
                MOV       BH,0
                MOV       CCOUNT,BX
                POP       BX
                RET
GETNAME         ENDP
;
GETID           PROC
                PUSH      BX
GID01:
                DISPLAY   ID_PROMPT                 ;PROMPT FOR ID
                GETDATA   INBUF,13                  ;GET ID IN BUFFER
                MOV       BL,INCOUNT
                MOV       BH,0
                MOV       CCOUNT,BX
                POP       BX
                RET
GETID           ENDP
;
PROG_CODE       ENDS
                END       MAIN_PROG
```

Figure 14.7 WRITENAM.ASM

File Handles for Keyboard, CRT, and Printer

Five handles have been pre-defined by DOS and are reserved for the use of input/output devises. These handles are:

0000   Input device; usually the keyboard.

0001   Output device; usually the CRT.

0002	Error output device; always the CRT.
0003	Auxiliary device (communications device).
0004	Standard printer (printer 0).

The first two can be redirected if desired. You can use these file handles with the read and write functions described above. You don't need to open or close these files and there are no read/write pointers for them. Keyboard input and CRT or printer output is very simple using these handles.

Figure 14.8 shows the typing program from Chapter 12 revised to use file handles for the keyboard and printer. Notice the EQUs that assign handle values to KEYBOARD, CRT, and PRINTER. You may want to add these to your EQU library.

There are a few things you should know about the keyboard input. As with function 0AH, CR signals the end of the input. If you ask for MAX characters, nothing but CR will be accepted after MAX-1. You can enter as many fewer than MAX as you like; CR will end the input. There is one other limitation: no matter how large MAX is, no more than 128 characters (including CR) will be accepted.

The maximum size of the input area, though, should be 129. That's because when CR is entered, both CR and LF are put into the input area. All input is echoed on the CRT, including the CR and LF. There is no need, then, to add LF after CR as in Chapter 12's version of TYPER. After the interrupt AX will contain the actual count of characters read, including CR and LF. In the typing program this count is used to set the number of characters to be printed after each input.

Just For Fun

Remember the telephone number program you worked on in early chapters of this book? You know enough now to revise the program so that names and telephone numbers are saved in a file and then to write a new program that prints the list. Go ahead and try these using the programs from this chapter as a guide. You may want to include headings and page breaks in your telephone list when you print it.

```
        PAGE,132
;
        INCLUDE MACLIB.LIB
;
        INCLUDE FILEHAND.LIB
;
        INCLUDE EQULIB.LIB
;
KEYBOARD        EQU     0
CRT             EQU     1
PRINTER         EQU     4
;
PROG_STACK      SEGMENT STACK 'STACK'
                DB      64 DUP ('STACK    ')
PROG_STACK      ENDS
;
PROG_DATA       SEGMENT 'DATA'
TYPE_BUFFER     DB 130 DUP('  ')
PROG_DATA       ENDS
;
PROG_CODE       SEGMENT 'CODE'
MAIN_PROG       PROC    FAR
                ASSUME  CS:PROG_CODE,DS:PROG_DATA,SS:PROG_STACK;ES:PROG_DATA
                STARTER
                STI
                CLD
                MOV     AH,0      ;INITIALIZING PRINTER
                MOV     DX,0
                INT     17H
                CLS
INPUT_STRING:
                MOV     BX,KEYBOARD
                MOV     AH,3FH
                MOV     CX,130
                LEA     DX,TYPE_BUFFER
                INT     21H
                CMP     TYPE_BUFFER,0
                JE      END_PROG
OUTPUT_STRING:
                MOV     CX,AX
                MOV     BX,PRINTER
                MOV     AH,40H
                INT     21H
                JMP     INPUT_STRING
END_PROG:
                RET
MAIN_PROG       ENDP
PROG_CODE       ENDS
                END
```

Figure 14.8 TYPER Program, Version 2

```
        PAGE    ,132
;
        INCLUDE MACLIB.LIB
;
        INCLUDE FILEHAND.LIB
;
        INCLUDE EQULIB.LIB
;
;
PROG_STACK      SEGMENT STACK 'STACK'
                DB      64 DUP ('STACK    ')
PROG_STACK      ENDS
;
PROG_DATA       SEGMENT 'DATA'
BAD_PATH        DB      LF,CR,'PATH NOT FOUND',EOT
TOO_MANY_FILES  DB      LF,CR,'TOO MANY FILES OPEN',EOT
ACCESS_DENIED   DB      LF,CR,'ACCESS DENIED',EOT
INVALID_HANDLE  DB      LF,CR,'INVALID HANDLE USED',EOT
INVALID_ACCESS  DB      LF,CR,'INVALID ACCESS CODE',EOT
END_OF_FILE     DB      LF,CR,'END OF FILE FOUND',EOT
UNKNOWN_ERROR   DB      LF,CR,'UNKNOWN ERROR',EOT
END_MESSAGE     DB      LF,CR,'GOODBYE',EOT
ERROR_CODE      DB      ?
CCOUNT          DW      ?
;
NAME_HANDLE     DW      ?
NAME_FILE       DB      'NAMEFILE.DAT',0
;
INPUT_NAME      DB      20 DUP (?)
INPUT_ID        DB      12 DUP (?)
;
OUTPUT_LINE     DB      CR,LF
OUTPUT_NAME     DB      20 DUP (' ')
                DB      10 DUP (' ')
OUTPUT_ID       DB      12 DUP (' ')
                DB      EOT
;
PROG_DATA       ENDS
;
PROG_CODE       SEGMENT 'CODE'
MAIN_PROG       PROC    FAR
                ASSUME  CS:PROG_CODE,DS:PROG_DATA,SS:PROG_STACK,ES:PROG_DATA
                STARTER
                STI
                CLD
                CLS
                CURSORON
                OPEN    NAME_FILE,NAME_HANDLE,ERROR_CODE
                JNC     MAINLOOP                ;IF OPEN OK CONTINUE
                CALL    ERROR_ROUTINE           ;ELSE    DISPLAY APPROPRIATE MESSAGE
                JMP     END_PROG                ;        AND END PROGRAM
MAINLOOP:
                READ    NAME_HANDLE,INPUT_NAME,32,ERROR_CODE
                JNC     READ_OK
                CALL    ERROR_ROUTINE
                JMP     CLOSE_UP
READ_OK:
                MOVE    OUTPUT_NAME,INPUT_NAME,20
                MOVE    OUTPUT_ID,INPUT_ID,12
                DISPLAY OUTPUT_LINE
                JMP     MAINLOOP
CLOSE_UP:
                CLOSE   NAME_HANDLE,ERROR_CODE  ;CLOSE FILE
                JNC     END_PROG                ;IF CLOSE OK END PROGRAM
                CALL    ERROR_ROUTINE           ;ELSE DISPLAY APPROPRIATE MESSAGE
```

Figure 14.9 (continued)

```
END_PROG:
                DISPLAY END_MESSAGE
                RET                                 ;THEN RETURN TO OPERATING SYSTEM
MAIN_PROG       ENDP
;
ERROR_ROUTINE   PROC
                CMP     ERROR_CODE,3
                JNE     ERR1
                DISPLAY BAD_PATH
                JMP     ERR_END
ERR1:
                CMP     ERROR_CODE,4
                JNE     ERR2
                DISPLAY TOO_MANY_FILES
                JMP     ERR_END
ERR2:
                CMP     ERROR_CODE,5
                JNE     ERR3
                DISPLAY ACCESS_DENIED
                JMP     ERR_END
ERR3:
                CMP     ERROR_CODE,6
                JNE     ERR4
                DISPLAY INVALID_HANDLE
                JMP     ERR_END
ERR4:
                CMP     ERROR_CODE,12
                JNE     ERR5
                DISPLAY INVALID_ACCESS
                JMP     ERR_END
ERR5:
                CMP     ERROR_CODE,100
                JNE     ERR6
                DISPLAY END_OF_FILE
                JMP     ERR_END
ERR6:
                DISPLAY UNKNOWN_ERROR
ERR_END:
                CLC
                RET
ERROR_ROUTINE   ENDP
;
PROG_CODE       ENDS
                END     MAIN_PROG
```

Figure 14.9

15

MASM With BASIC Files

If you have been programming in BASIC for a while, you probably have some data files that contain valuable information which you would just as soon not reenter from scratch for use with MASM programs. In this chapter, I will give you some hints on how to access data from BASIC files in MASM programs.

Sequential Files

As you know, BASIC can read and write two types of files: sequential and random. BASIC's sequential files are very simple to handle in BASIC, but not so simple in MASM. The main problem is that sequential files have variable-length records; in fact, each data item in the record is variable-length.

Let's look at a sequential file where each record contains a name (a string variable) followed by an integer. The maximum size for the name is 255. For the integer, it is six characters (including a possible leading sign). Strings are stored with quotation marks surrounding them. Numbers are stored in ASCII characters as BASIC's PRINT command would display them on the CRT. Fields are always separated by commas. The end of the record is always marked by CR and LF; and the end of the file, by 1AH. This means that each of our file's records may be as much as 266 bytes long, like this:

"A Name . . . up to 255 total . . .",-33001!@

where ! and @ represent CR and LF respectively. On the other hand, if the string is empty and the integer zero, the record could be as short as six characters: "",0!@

To read a BASIC sequential file in a MASM program, then, you must read an arbitrary number of bytes into a buffer and examine each byte. As you examine each byte, move meaningful characters to the appropriate fields, skip over quotation marks, look for commas that mark the ends of fields, keep track of how many characters were actually put into each field, skip but keep track of decimal points and signs, and look for CR and LF to mark the end of the last field in each record. You should be able to develop routines to do these jobs using the commands you already know.

Random Files

BASIC's random files have fixed-length records and fixed-length fields. A record written with this BASIC FIELD statement:

FIELD #1, 18 as NAM$, 2 as A$, 4 as B$, 8 as C$

is a 32-byte record that can easily be read into a MASM program. The input buffer might look like this:

```
IN__NAME     DB    18 DUP ( ? )
IN__A        DB    2 DUP ( ? )
IN__B        DB    4 DUP ( ? )
IN__C        DB    8 DUP ( ? )
```

The problem with random files is in handling the numeric data. As you know, BASIC handles integers, single-precision, and double-precision numbers. An integer in a random file is formatted by MKI$ and stored in a two-byte field, a single-precision number is formatted by MKS$ and stored in a four-byte field, and a double-precision number is formatted by MKD$ and stored in an eight-byte field. Integers really create no problems for MASM; MKI$ simply provides a two-byte (or one-word) signed binary number with the low-order byte first. If A$ represents an integer, you can handle IN__A as you would any two-byte binary signed number. Single- and double-precision are more complicated, however. I'll discuss single- precision in some detail, but first I'll quickly review some of the terms that we'll need in that discussion.

Mantissa, Exponent, and Base

The number 5,350 can be expressed in a form such as 5.35×10^3. In this form we say that the number has a **mantissa** of 5.35, an **exponent** of 3, and a **base** of 10. You can convert to other exponents and mantissas by multiplying or dividing the mantissa by 10. Each multiplication shifts the decimal point one place to the right and subtracts 1 from the exponent. Each division shifts the point to the left and adds 1 to the exponent.

In other words, $5.35 \times 10^3 = 53.5 \times 10^2 = 5350 \times 10^0 = 53500 \times 10^{-1}$.

Any number can be expressed as a mantissa, an exponent, and a base. The base that you pick determines the digits in the mantissa and the exponent. 5,350 is 14E6H. This can be written as $1.4E6H \times 16^3$. A positive exponent represents the number of times the mantissa must be multiplied by the base to produce the value. You can multiply a number by its base simply by shifting the point to the right and adding a trailing zero if required. A negative exponent represents the number of divisions by the base required to produce that number, in other words, the number of times the point must be shifted to the left with leading zeros inserted if necessary. One standard way to express numbers in this form is to adjust them so that exactly one non-zero digit is placed to the left of the point, as in 5.035×10^3. We say that a number in this format is **normalized**.

Single Precision Format

To express a number in BASIC's single-precision format you begin by normalizing it in base 2. We'll work with the number 1234567, or 12D687H. In base 2, this is $10010110101101010000111B \times 2^0$. Normalized, this would be $1.0010110101101010000111B \times 2^{20}$. Formatting a single-precision number starts with putting this form into three bytes low order first, and then putting the exponent in the fourth byte. There are not enough digits to fill three bytes but we want to align the number so that the point comes after the high-order digit. We fill in with trailing zeros. So far, then, our four bytes look like this:

0011	1000	1011	0100	1.001	0110	0001	0100
3	8	D	2	9	6	1	4
low		middle		high			exp

(The point is assumed; it's not actually stored in the number.) Three more steps are required before the single-precision format is complete:

1. Add 129 (81H) to the exponent.

2. The high-order digit is always 1, so there's no need to store the 1; we'll just assume it. Remove the 1.

3. Use the high-order bit position for a sign bit. If the number is positive, put 0 in the bit; if negative, 1. Note that only the sign bit is involved. In single-precision format, negative numbers are not in two's complement notation.

Now our number looks like this:

0011	1000	1011	0100	0001	0110	1001	0101
3	8	D	2	1	6	9	5
low		middle		high			exp

And, that is indeed how it will be stored in single precision format.

If you want to work out another example for yourself, try a negative number; -1234 should end up as 00 40 9A 8BH. Remember, you're not using the two's complement; convert 1234 and then put 1 in the sign bit.

From Single Precision To Binary

In dealing with single-precision integers, the real issue is how to convert them to binary—especially how to do it in a MASM program. We'll use 38D21695H as an example, knowing that it ought to come out 12D687H (1234567). Here's how our number looks when we read it into our MASM program:

0011	1000	1011	0100	0001	0110	1001	0101
3	8	D	2	1	6	9	5

First of all, let's reverse the steps that ended the last section. We'll start by subtracting 129 (81H) from the exponent and replacing the sign bit by 1. (Don't lose track of the sign, though; you'll need to know it later.) Here's how our number looks now:

```
0011    1000    1011    0100    1.001    0110    0001    0100
  3       8       D       2       9        6       1       4
     low             middle           high              exp
```

We included the assumed point for convenience; it's not in the byte as stored. We could quit now, just converting the three-byte number to two's complement if it's negative, but you will find it much easier to use the number in arithmetic or conversions if you get rid of the assumed point and fractional places.

First, we'll save the exponent in another field and zero-fill the fourth byte so we can use all four bytes for our number. Then, let's consider what the new exponent will be when we get rid of the fractional places.

The number now has 23 fractional places—all but one of the 24 digits. To end up with no fractional places, you must shift the point 23 places to the right, subtracting 1 from the exponent for each place. In our example, the original exponent is 20, so after the shift it will be -3. This means that our number would need to be divided by 2 three times to produce the original value with an exponent of zero or to express it in a form that does not include an exponent.

Since the point is assumed, the number undergoes no actual change. How do you know, then, if an exponent belongs to a normalized or non-normalized number? You know because you control the program. Either leave all of your converted numbers with 23 fractional places or without fractional places.

What does it mean if you end up with a positive exponent? Suppose your original exponent was 25. After subtracting 23 your new exponent is 2. The number must be multiplied by 2^2 to arrive at its value with no exponent.

It's often desirable to go ahead and divide or multiply as indicated by the exponent. Here is where you use the shift instructions. To divide by 2, shift each bit to the right (SHR) and adjust the exponent; to multiply by 2, shift each bit to the left (SHL) and adjust the exponent. If you can get to a zero exponent this way, fine. Make sure, though, that you don't shift out significant bits. Don't do a right shift if the low-order bit is 1. In a left shift, the high-order bit must be reserved for a sign, so don't shift if the next-to-high-order bit is 1. After all of the manipulation is done, convert the number to two's complement if the original sign bit was 1.

```
CONVERT_SP        MACRO  BIN,SINGLE,EXP
                  LOCAL  NEXT_LEFT,RIGHT_SHIFT,NEXT_RIGHT
                  LOCAL  CONT1,END_RIGHT,STORE_NUMBER,CONT2
                  PUSH   AX
                  PUSH   CX
                  PUSH   DX
                  XOR    CX,CX            ;ZERO CX
                  XOR    DX,DX            ;   AND DX
                  MOV    CL,SINGLE+3      ;  CX WILL HOLD EXP
                  MOV    AL,SINGLE        ;MOVE SP NUMBER TO DX:AX
                  MOV    AH,SINGLE+1
                  MOV    DL,SINGLE+2
                  OR     DL,80H           ;HIGH-ORDER DIGIT IS 1
                  SUB    CX,152           ;ADJUST EXP (-129-23)
                  JS     RIGHT_SHIFT      ;IF NEG EXP SHIFT RIGHT
NEXT_LEFT:
                  TEST   DH,40H           ;IF BIT 6 SET STOP SHIFT
                  JNZ    STORE_NUMBER
                  SHL    DX,1             ;OTHERWISE SHIFT DX
                  SHL    AX,1             ;   THEN AX
                  ADC    DL,0             ;   PUT SHIFTED BIT INTO DL
                  LOOP   NEXT_LEFT        ;DEC EXP AND REPEAT
                  JMP    STORE_NUMBER     ;QUIT WHEN EXP 0
RIGHT_SHIFT:
                  NEG    CX               ;CHANGE EXP TO POSITIVE
NEXT_RIGHT:
                  TEST   AL,1H            ;IF BIT 1 SET STOP SHIFT
                  JNZ    END_RIGHT
                  SHR    AX,1             ;ELSE SHIFT AX
                  SHR    DX,1             ;   AND DX
                  JNC    CONT1            ;IF SHIFTED BIT SIGNIFICANT
                  OR     AH,80H           ;   PUT IT IN HIGH BIT OF AX
CONT1:
                  LOOP   NEXT_RIGHT       ;DEC EXP AND REPEAT
                  JMP    STORE_NUMBER     ;QUIT WHEN EXP = 0
END_RIGHT:                               ;IF QUIT BEFORE EXP=0
                  NEG    CX               ;   REMAINING EXP IS NEG
STORE_NUMBER:
                  MOV    EXP,CX           ;SAVE THE NEW EXPONENT
                  TEST   SINGLE+2,80H     ;IF ORIGINAL NUMBER NEGATIVE
                  JZ     CONT2
                  NOT    DX               ;   CONVERT TO TWOS COMPLEMENT
                  NOT    AX
                  ADD    AX,1
                  ADC    DX,0
CONT2:
                  MOV    BIN,AL           ;NOW SAVE NEW BINARY NUMBER
                  MOV    BIN+1,AH
                  MOV    BIN+2,DL
                  MOV    BIN+3,DH
                  POP    DX
                  POP    CX
                  POP    AX
                  ENDM
```

Figure 15.1 Single Precision to Binary

Figure 15.1 contains a macro that converts a BASIC single-precision integer to a four-byte binary number with a separate exponent. To use the macro, specify the locations of the destination (the binary number), the source (the single-precision number), and the new exponent. The macro converts each number to a form with an exponent as close to zero as it can get without losing digits. All the conversion is done in the AX and DX registers, with DX holding the high-order digits and AX the low-order. The exponent is in CX. After all of the rest of the conversion is done, the macro looks back at the source's sign bit to decide whether to put the final result in two's complement form.

Double Precision Format

Double-precision numbers also use the exponent and mantissa form with base 2. They have eight bytes instead of four because the original decimal number can go as high as 17 digits, while single-precision can go only to 7 digits. The last byte is the exponent (plus 129). The other seven bytes contain the mantissa in normalized form, with a sign bit replaced by the 1 before the point and stored low-order first. In the normalized form, there will be 55 fractional places instead of the 23 in a single-precision format. If you want to convert double-precision numbers you should be able to code a macro based on the single precision one. Instead of trying to work in four registers at once, however, you may prefer to convert the original number to binary "in place". If you do that, make sure to keep track of whether the original was positive or negative; the sign bit won't be available when you are through with the conversion.

16

Using Assembler Subroutines in BASIC Programs

Assembler language programs can be used as subroutines in BASIC programs either with CALL or as a USR function. In an appendix of the BASIC manual, you will find a great deal of information about how to set up and use such subroutines. In this chapter, I will go over an example of one method of loading and calling a MASM subroutine from a BASIC program. Once you are comfortable with this procedure you should be able to learn to use the other methods from the BASIC manual.

The MASM Subroutine

Figure 16.1 contains a new version of the typing program developed in earlier chapters. We will use this program as an example of a MASM subroutine. Notice that there is no stack segment. Most subroutines use the calling program's stack. Since there's no stack, there's no SS parameter in ASSUME. ES is not needed in ASSUME either since the subroutine doesn't include any of the string operations that require ES. (If our program had no data, and therefore no data segment, we wouldn't have a DS parameter either.)

```
          PAGE,132
;
KEYBOARD          EQU      0
CRT               EQU      1
PRINTER           EQU      4
;
PROG_DATA         SEGMENT  'DATA'
TYPE_BUFFER       DB 130 DUP('  ')
PROG_DATA         ENDS
;
PROG_CODE         SEGMENT  'CODE'
MAIN_PROG         PROC     FAR
                  ASSUME   CS:PROG_CODE,DS:PROG_DATA
                  PUSH     AX
                  PUSH     BX
                  PUSH     CX
                  PUSH     DX
                  PUSH     DS
                  MOV      AX,PROG_DATA          ;INITIALIZE DS
                  MOV      DS,AX
                  STI
INPUT_STRING:
                  MOV      BX,KEYBOARD
                  MOV      AH,3FH
                  MOV      CX,130
                  LEA      DX,TYPE_BUFFER
                  INT      21H
OUTPUT_STRING:
                  MOV      CX,AX
                  MOV      BX,PRINTER
                  MOV      AH,40H
                  INT      21H
END_PROG:
                  POP      DS
                  POP      DX
                  POP      CX
                  POP      BX
                  POP      AX
                  RET
;
MAIN_PROG         ENDP
PROG_CODE         ENDS
                  END
```

Figure 16.1 TYPESUB.ASM

Unlike most MASM programs, this one doesn't start by putting the return address on the stack; the BASIC CALL takes care of that. The subroutine must, however, PUSH and POP any segment register that it changes, except CS. In this case, that's only DS; the subroutine's data-segment address is loaded into DS. If you don't preserve these registers, you will have trouble when you return to the calling program. You must also make sure that SP has not changed. The other registers and the flags don't need to be saved and restored.

Preparing the Subroutine

The subroutine is coded and assembled like any other program. Our source-code file is TYPESUB.ASM, so we assemble it like this:

```
MASM  TYPESUB;
```

Next, we link the subroutine using the /H option, like this:

```
LINK TYPESUB/H;
```

The /H option tells the linker to mark the EXE file so that the program will be loaded as high in memory as possible.

Saving a Memory Image

Now we use DEBUG to find out where the subroutine will be loaded and to save a version of the object code that can be loaded from a BASIC program.
    First, load BASIC under DEBUG, like this:

```
DEBUG BASIC.COM
```

When you see the DEBUG prompt (-), type R to get a display of the registers. Write down the values in CS, IP, SS, and SP. You'll need to know them later. When I did this, CS and SS both contained 0907; IP, 0100; and SP, FFFE.
    Now load your program's EXE file and display it's original registers. The sequence of instructions looks like this:

```
-N    TYPESUB.EXE
-L
-R
```

This time just copy the values from CS, IP, and CX. CS is where the code segment begins, IP is the offset of the first instruction within the segment (usually 0), and CX shows the size of the loaded program in bytes. In our

DEBUG session, CS was 3F94; IP, 0; and CX, B2. Notice that the whole subroutine was 0B2H, or 178 bytes; and 130 of that was for our input buffer.

Now we need to run BASIC (still under DEBUG) so we can BSAVE our subroutine. First, we have to restore BASIC's SS and SP registers and set CS and IP to point to the beginning of BASIC. To do these things, we need to change CS, IP, SS, and SP to the values they had when we first loaded BASIC. To change a register in DEBUG, use the R command with the name of the register. DEBUG will display the current value and then prompt you with a semi-colon for a new value. Here's how it went when I did it:

```
-R   CS
CS   3F94
:0907
-R   SS
SS   3F94
:0907
-R   IP
IP   0000
:0100
-R   SP
SP   0000
:FFFE
```

Now everything's set; G (for GO) will start BASIC running. At the BASIC prompt (OK), use DEF SEG to point to the subroutine's CS, like this:

```
DEF   SEG = &H3F94
```

Next, use BSAVE to copy to a disk file an image of the subroutine as it currently is in memory. You specify the disk file name and the subroutine's beginning offset and size. You recorded those last two values from IP and CX when the subroutine was loaded. In my example, BSAVE went like this:

```
BSAVE "TYPESUB.BIN",0,&H00B2
```

The memory image file usually has the extension .BIN as in this example.

Calling the Subroutine

Now you can write or finish writing your BASIC program. You can go ahead and do that while BASIC is loaded under DEBUG or you can quit DEBUG and restart BASIC. Your program may already almost have been finished, but the CALL routine can't be coded until the memory image file has been created.

Here's how the CALL routine goes:

■ First, use DEF SEG to point to the subroutine's CS address.

■ Then, use BLOAD to load the memory image file. You must specify the file name and the beginning offset (usually 0) that you found in IP when the subroutine was loaded.

■ Third, assign that same offset to a numeric variable.

■ Fourth, call the variable. Control will be transferred to the offset represented by the variable within the segment pointed to by DEF SEG.

In our example, the CALL routine goes like this:

```
1000   DEF SEG = &H3F94
1100   BLOAD "TYPESUB.BIN",0
1200   SUBR = 0
1300   CALL SUBR
```

To use TYPESUB a second time, you should be able to just repeat the CALL as long as you have not executed another DEF SEG, loaded another subroutine, or changed the value of SUBR.

Computer Exercise

Enter TYPESUB.ASM from Figure 16.1. Then, assemble and link the subroutine (use the /H option when linking) and use DEBUG to create the memory image file.

```
5 PRINT "START FROM BASIC"
10 DEF SEG=&H3F94
15 BLOAD "TYPESUB.BIN",0
16 FOR N%=1 TO 3
17 DEF SEG=&H3F94
20 SUBR=0
30 CALL SUBR
35 NEXT N%
40 PRINT "BACK TO BASICS":END
```

Figure 16.2 TESTSUB.BAS

Figure 16.2 shows the BASIC program we used to test TYPESUB. Use a similar program and run your own tests.

Using Arguments

TYPESUB doesn't use any variables from the calling BASIC program, but many subroutines do need to get input from or place results in BASIC variables. The CALL statement can include a list of variables, known as arguments or parameters, which are used by the called subroutine. The BASIC manual explains the use of these arguments, but I will mention a few points that you should keep in mind.

The argument list names the variables to be used by the subroutine. What is actually passed is the offset of each of the variables. These offsets are pushed on the stack in the order in which the variables appear in the list. CALL pushes two more items on the list also: CS and IP for the return to BASIC. When your subroutine starts, then, the last argument's address is the third item on the stack—it starts at SP + 4. You will need to use BP to access these arguments; so, your program should start by PUSHing BP and then copying SP to BP. Now, the last argument's address is at BP + 6, the next-to-last at BP + 8, and so on. To copy the offset of the third argument into DI, then, you could use this instruction:

```
MOV    DI , 10[BP]
```

Notice that you can't POP these addresses. POP always takes the top item on the stack. You would have to POP the return address before you got to the arguments and you shouldn't touch that.

When you access data with these offsets, remember that they point to locations in BASIC's data segment. If your program has changed DS, you must use BASIC's DS to address the arguments; it should be sitting in your stack as the second item your program PUSHed.

Before you return to BASIC, all of the items PUSHed by the subroutine should be POPped so that, immediately before the return, SP points to the saved return address. RET will use that address and remove it from the stack, but the argument offsets are still sitting there. RET must adjust SP to skip around these so that it is pointing to the item that was top-of-the-stack before CALL began. To do this, simply code RET as RET n where n represents the number of stack bytes to skip—two times the number of arguments. If your subroutine uses four arguments it should start like this:

```
PUSH    BP
MOV     BP,SP    ; BP+6 points to last argument
PUSH    DS       ; If subroutine has a data seg
. . .
```

and end like this:

```
POP     DS       ; if DS was PUSHed
POP     BP
RET     8        ; two for each argument passed
```

One more thing: if possible all arguments should be integers. As you learned in Chapter 15, BASIC integers are simply one-word binary numbers that can be handled easily in a MASM routine. Single- and double-precision take too much special handling in MASM. Strings also make trouble; the address passed for a string points to a special field that describes the string, not to the string itself. If you must pass string variables read the explanations in the BASIC manual appendix carefully.

A

Data Formats and Representation

This appendix presents a quick review of the binary number system, the use of signed binary numbers and two's complement notation, hexadecimal notation, binary-coded decimals, and ASCII code.

Decimal, Binary, and Hexadecimal

In daily life most of us use decimal numbers. Decimal numbers are made up of combinations of the 10 decimal digits (0, 1, 2, 3, 4, 5, 6, 7, 8, and 9) with each digit position representing a power of 10; we say that decimal numbers use **base 10**. The position to the left of the decimal point, actual or implied, represents 10^0. Moving to the left, each position represents a higher power of 10; moving to the right, a lower power. 327.025, then, represents $(3 \times 10^2) + (2 \times 10^1) + (7 \times 10^0) + (0 \times 10^{-1}) + (2 \times 10^{-2}) + (5 \times 10^{-3})$.

Computers use binary numbers. Binary numbers use base 2. There are two possible binary digits (0 and 1) and each position in a binary number represents a power of 2. The position to the left of the binary point, actual or implied, represents 2^0. Moving to the left, each position represents a higher power of 2; moving to the right, a lower power. (Remember that $2^{-1} = 1/2$, or .5; $2^{-2} = 1/4$, or .25; $2^{-3} = 1/8$, or .125; and so on.) In this book, as in MASM source code, binary numbers are indicated by "B" following the

---

number. 1001.101B, then, represents $(1 \times 2^3) + (0 \times 2^2) + (0 \times 2^1) + (1 \times 2^0) + (1 \times 2^{-1}) + (0 \times 2^{-2})$, or 9.625 $(8 + 0 + 0 + 1 + .5 + .125)$. The binary representation of 327.025 is 101000111.01B.

Each position in a binary number is referred to as a **bit** (for Binary digIT) or a **bit position**. Each bit can have a value of 0 or 1. Most computers work with groups of eight bits; such a group is called a **byte**. Computers also operate with **words**. In the IBM PC and its family, a word is 16 bits, or two bytes. Sometimes, it is also convenient to deal with four bits at a time; a 4-bit group is a **half-byte** or a **nibble**. In this book, I usually write binary numbers as half-bytes, bytes, or words. When we write 5 in binary form, then, we will write 0101B or 0000 0101B, not 101B.

The hexadecimal number system uses base 16. It has 16 possible digits (0, 1, 2, 3, 4, 5, 6, 7, 8, 9, A, B, C, D, E, and F), and each digit position represents a power of 16. "H" is used to indicate a hexadecimal number, as in 123H (291). For clarity, a hexadecimal number must always start with a digit from 0 through 9. 0BAH is a number equivalent to 186, while BAH is something Scrooge said before he reformed.

A distinct relationship exists between the binary and the hexadecimal system, based on the fact that $2^4 = 16$. Any hexadecimal digit can be represented by four binary digits. To convert a hexadecimal number to binary, you just need to replace each hexadecimal digit by its four-bit binary equivalent. To convert binary to hexadecimal, separate the binary number into groups of four bits (starting from the binary point) and convert each bit to its hexadecimal equivalent. Here's an example:

```
1001   0011   1111   0110B
  9      3      F      6H
```

It's much easier for humans to read and write hexadecimal numbers than the strings of 0s and 1s needed for binary. In most source code, displays, and discussions we use the hexadecimal equivalents of the binary numbers that the computer uses. Don't forget, though, that the computer uses only binary.

High- and Low-Order

We often refer to a number's rightmost digit position (the one that's the least power of the base) as the **low-order digit** and its leftmost digit position as the **high-order digit**. In 327.025, 5 is the low-order digit and 3 is the high-order digit. In 1001.101B, both the high- and low-order digits are 1. We extend this concept to refer to the high- or low-order nibble of a byte, the high- or low-order byte of a word, and so on. In the one-word number 0000

1111 1111 0000B, for example, the high-order byte is 0000 1111B, the low-order byte is 1111 0000B, the high-order bit of the low-order byte is 1, and the low-order bit of the low-order byte is 0.

Binary Addition

There's no need to go very deeply into binary arithmetic since by and large the computer takes care of such computations. But, to follow the rest of this discussion, you must know the facts of binary addition. These are very simple. There are only three basic facts.

```
0  +  0  =  0
1  +  0  =  1
1  +  1  =  10
```

Notice that when you add 1 and 1, you generate a **carry** that must be added into the next digit's sum. Here are two examples of multi-bit addition; you should be able to figure them out with no trouble.

```
      1111  0101                      0011  1011
  +   1011  1010                  +   0111  0100
    1 0110  1111                      1011  1111
```

Signed Binary Numbers

When we need to indicate that a decimal number is negative, we generally use a negative sign (−) before or after the number. A number without a sign is assumed to be positive, but if we want to emphasize this we can use a positive sign (+) before or after the number.

We can indicate signs in binary numbers by using similar techniques, but for the computer it's more efficient if the sign is part of the number. This can be done by reserving the high-order bit to indicate the sign; it is referred to as the **sign bit**. The rest of the number contains the absolute value, or magnitude. A one-byte signed number has a high-order sign bit and seven bits that contain the absolute value. A one-word signed number has a high-order sign bit and fifteen bits that contain the absolute value.

A negative number doesn't just have a negative sign, however; most computers, including the IBM PC, use **two's complement notation** for negative binary numbers. To form the two's complement of a binary number, change each digit to its opposite and then add 1 to the result. For example: to form the two's complement of 36H (0011 0110B), change each bit; the result is 0C9H (1100 1001B). Now add 1; the result is 0CAH (1100 1010B). Using signed numbers, then, 36H is 54 and 0CAH is − 54. By the way, if **x** is the two's complement of **y**, then **y** is the two's complement of **x**. Work out the two's complement of 0CAH; you'll find that it's 36H.

Ranges

A one-byte number can range from 0H to 0FFH. If the number is unsigned, this is a range of 0 to 255. If the number is signed, this is a range of − 128 (80H) to +127 (7FH).

A one-word number can range from 0H to 0FFFFH. If the number is unsigned, this is a range of 0 to 65535. If the number is signed, this is a range of − 32768 (8000H) to 32767 (7FFFH).

Binary Coded Decimals

It's often more convenient for us to work with decimal digits even though the computer uses only binary numbers. A special format called **binary coded decimal**, or **BCD**, has been devised for this purpose. It's based on the fact that the decimal digits (0 through 9) can be represented by the same 4-bit binary numbers used to represent the first 10 hexadecimal digits. To translate a decimal number into BCD format, just translate each digit into its 4-bit binary code. The number 123450, for example, in BCD format would be 0001 000 0011 0100 0101 0000B, or 123450H. To change a number written in BCD format back to decimal, translate each 4-bit group into its equivalent decimal digit. Notice that when numbers are written in BCD they can never contain the half-byte values 1010B, 1011B, 1100B, 1101B, 1110B, or 1111B. How can you tell whether the string of bits 1001 0001B (91H) is a binary number equivalent to 145 or a BCD representation of 91? It could be either one; you can't tell by looking at it. If the string is a value in a program you must know whether it was intended to be binary or BCD.

Packed and Unpacked Decimals

BCD numbers are used in two forms. So far we have looked at the **packed decimal** form. Packed decimals represent one decimal digit per half-byte, two per byte. **Unpacked decimals** have only one decimal digit per byte; the high-order half-byte is always zero. The packed decimal representation of 35, then, is 00110101B (35H), while the unpacked representation is 0000 0011 0000 0101B (0305H).

BCD Arithmetic

Arithmetic with BCD numbers, either packed or unpacked, is based on binary arithmetic. The answers, however, must be adjusted for any BCD digit position where the result is 10 or more. For example, let's add 35 and 26 in BCD format:

```
      0011 0101B   (35H)
  +   0010 0110B   (26H)
      0101 1011B   (5BH)
```

This answer, 5BH, would be right if we were adding binary or hexadecimal numbers; but it is wrong when you're adding decimal digits. The answer should be 61. An adjustment must be made to allow for the fact that BCD digits can only be 0 through 9. MASM provides adjustments for arithmetic operations with unpacked decimals, as well as for addition and subtraction with packed decimals.

The ASCII Character Code

Another way that data is represented in the IBM PC is in ASCII character code. Each character is represented by a one-byte value. Standard ASCII code uses only seven bits per character, so it can represent only 128 characters. But IBM uses a full eight bits per character, thus allowing an additional 128 characters to be part of the ASCII code set.

The values from 0 to 31 are generally used for control characters. Some of these, such as 10 for line feed, 12 for form feed, and 13 for carriage return, are generally accepted and recognized by most peripheral devices such as CRTs and printers. Values from 32 through 126 are part of the standard ASCII set. This includes 32 (20H) as the code for a space, 48 (30H) through 54 (39H) for the decimal digits, 65 (41H) through 90 (5AH) for the uppercase letters, and 98 (61H) through 122 (7AH) for the lowercase letters. The remaining values in this range are used for special characters. The rest of IBM's ASCII set, values 127 through 256, represent special typefonts and graphics characters.

When ASCII characters are included in programs or discussions, they usually are enclosed in single or double quotation marks.

Numbers in ASCII

Almost all data is input or output as ASCII characters. When you press a key on the keyboard, it is the ASCII code value for that key that is passed to the computer. When you display characters on the CRT or print them on a printer, the computer sends numbers to the output device, which interprets the numbers as ASCII code and displays or prints the corresponding characters.

What happens when you input a number such as 35 in response to a prompt? The ASCII code that is received is 3335H. This is *not* 35 in binary, in packed decimal, or in unpacked-decimal format. In order to use this input as a number, your program must usually convert the input to one of the formats that it can work with. The closest format is unpacked decimal; all that is necessary to convert an ASCII digit to an unpacked-decimal digit is to change the high-order half-byte from 3 to 0. That's the main reason for using unpacked decimals in your program. In the same way, numbers to be displayed or printed must usually be converted from another format to ASCII; the easiest conversion is from unpacked decimals.

B

The Macro Assembler Instruction Set

This appendix lists the Macro Assembler instructions grouped by functions and subfunctions. For each instruction, a very brief description of its purpose is given. An asterisk (*) marks instructions not discussed in this book. Use this appendix when you know what you want to do, but aren't sure what instruction(s) are available to do it. For a detailed description of an instruction's purpose, format, and operands, look the instruction up in the MASM manual.

Copying or Transferring Data

String Moves

LODS/LODSB/LODSW	* Load AL or AX from a string
STOS/STOSB/STOSW	Store from AL or AX to string
MOVS/MOVSB/MOVSW	Copy a string

I/O

IN   * Get one byte from an input port
OUT   * Send one byte to an output port

Stack Manipulation

PUSH   Push one word on top of stack
POP   Pop one word from top of stack
PUSHF   * Push flag register on top of stack
POPF   * Pop flag register from top of stack

Miscellaneous Data Transfers

MOV   Copy one byte or one word
XCHG   * Exchange values of operands
XLAT   * Place byte looked up in table into AL
LAHF   * Copy SF, ZF, AF, PF, and CF to AH
SAHF   * Copy from AH to SF, ZF, AF, PF, and CF
LEA   Loads computed EA into register
LDS   * Loads segment number into DS
LES   * Loads segment number into ES

Comparing or Testing Data

CMP   Compare bytes or words
TEST   Logical AND bit comparison
CMPS/CMPSB/CMPSW   Compare strings
SCAS/SCASB/SCASW   Search string for accumulator match

Changing Data

Arithmetic

ADD   Add without carry
ADC   Add with carry
SUB   Subtract without borrow
SBB   Subtract with borrow
MUL   Multiply unsigned numbers
IMUL   Muliplty signed numbers
DIV   Divide unsigned number
IDIV   Divide signed number

DEC	Subtract 1
INC	Add 1
NEG	Subtract from 0 (form two's complement)

Adjust Data

AAA	Adjust unpacked decimal after addition
AAS	Adjust unpacked decimal after subtraction
AAM	Adjust unpacked decimal after multiplication
AAD	Adjust unpacked decimal before division
DAA	Adjust packed decimal after addition
DAS	Adjust packed decimal after subtraction
CBW	Extend sign of AL through AH
CWD	Extend sign of AX through DX

Logical Bit Changes

AND	Logical AND (1 AND 1 = 1; $\times$ AND 0 = 0)
NOT	Logical NOT (Change each bit)
OR	Logical OR (1 OR $\times$ = 1; 0 OR 0 = 0)
XOR	Logical XOR (1 XOR 0 = 1; all others = 0)

Move Bits Within Field

RCL	Rotate left through CF
RCR	Rotate right through CF
ROL	Rotate left without CF
ROR	Rotate right without CF
SAR	Shift right retaining high-order bit
SHR	Shift right replacing high-order with 0
SAL/SHL	Shift left replacing low-order with 0

Change Flag Value

CLC	Clear CF
STC	Set CF
CMC	* Change CF (If CF = 0, CF = 1 and vice versa)
CLD	Clear DF
STD	Set DF
CLI	Clear IF
STI	Set IF

Control Program Flow

Unconditional Transfer of Control

JMP   Transfer control to target
CALL   Transfer control to procedure
RET   Return from procedure
INT   Transfer control to interrupt routine
INTO   * Transfer to interrupt on overflow
IRET   * Return from interrupt

Repetition with Counter in CX

LOOP   Transfer control if CX not 0
LOOPE/LOOPZ   Transfer control if CX not 0 and ZF set
LOOPNE/LOOPNZ   Transfer control if CX not 0 and ZF clear
REP   Repeat string operation if CX not 0
REPE/REPZ   Repeat string operation if CX not 0 and ZF set
REPNE/REPNZ   Repeat string operation if CX not 0 and ZF clear

Conditional Transfers

Note: op1 and op2 refer to operands in previous flag-setting instructions such as arithmetic, comparison, or logical instructions.

JA/JNBE   Transfer if unsigned op2 > op1
JB/JNAE   Transfer if unsigned op2 < op1
JAE/JNB   Transfer if unsigned op2 not < op1
JBE/JNA   Transfer if unsigned op2 not > op1
JG/JNLE   Transfer if signed op2 > op1
JL/JNGE   Transfer if signed op2 < op1
JGE/JNL   Transfer if signed op2 not < op1
JLE/JNG   Transfer if signed op2 not > op1
JE/JZ   Transfer if op2 = op1 (ZF set)
JNE/JNZ   Transfer if op2 not = op1 (ZF clear)
JC   Transfer if CF set
JNC   Transfer if CF clear
JO   Transfer if OF set

JNO		Transfer if OF clear
JS		Transfer if SF set
JNS		Transfer if SF clear
JP/JPE	★	Transfer if PF set
JNP/JPO	★	Transfer if PF clear
JCXZ	★	Transfer if CX = 0

Miscellaneous Instructions

ESC	★	Send instruction to another processor
HLT	★	Wait for external interrupt
WAIT	★	Wait for TEST signal from external processor
LOCK	★	Lock access to resources shared by co-processor
NOP	★	No operation

Index